Studies of the New Testament and Its World

EDITED BY JOHN RICHES

NAG HAMMADI AND THE GOSPEL TRADITION

Nag Hammadi
and
The Gospel Tradition

Synoptic Tradition
in the
Nag Hammadi Library

by
C. M. TUCKETT

edited by
JOHN RICHES

T. & T. CLARK
59 GEORGE STREET
EDINBURGH

Typeset by Print Origination Liverpool,
printed by Billing & Sons Ltd, Worcester,
bound by Hunter & Foulis Ltd, Edinburgh

for

T. & T. CLARK LTD
EDINBURGH

First printed 1986

British Library Cataloguing in Publication Data
Tuckett, C.M.
Nag Hammadi and the Gospel tradition: synoptic tradition in the Nag Hammadi Library.—(Studies of the New Testament and its world)
1. Jesus Christ—Biography—Sources
I. Title II. Riches, John III. Series
232 BT303

ISBN 0-567-09364-6

CONTENTS

PREFACE

The Nag Hammadi texts have generated an ever-increasing volume of secondary literature. The process of producing critical editions of the individual texts is gradually getting under way, and I have endeavoured to note all those that have been available to me. Unfortunately I have been unable to consult some of the most recent volumes produced in the BCNH Textes series. It is hoped that readers will make allowance for this in making use of the present study.

I wish to thank all those who have assisted in the production of this book. Professor R. McL. Wilson kindly read the entire work in typescript and made a number of helpful suggestions for improving it. I gratefully acknowledge his generous assistance, though the responsibility for the defects of the present work is mine alone. I am very grateful to John Riches for accepting my work into the present series and for all his assistance in the production process. Finally, my wife has been a continual source of support and encouragement during the whole period of research and writing.

Manchester
December 1983

Christopher Tuckett

ACKNOWLEDGEMENTS

I have re-used material published in earlier articles in *VigChr* 36 (1982) and in *JThS* 35 (1984). I am very grateful to the editors of these journals for permission to do this. All quotations of the English translations of the Nag Hammadi texts are taken from J.M. Robinson (ed.), *The Nag Hammadi Library in English,* Leiden 1977, unless otherwise stated. They are reproduced here by kind permission of the publishers, E.J. Brill, Leiden.

I. INTRODUCTION

Nobody writes in a vacuum. Every literary text presupposes various traditions. The use of language itself is limited by sets of conventions concerning the meaning and use of words and phrases. This is not to deny the possibility of innovation, linguistic or otherwise; but very often the force of the innovation is created precisely because of the tradition or convention which it seeks to modify. Behind every writer there are many different influences: these include linguistic traditions concerning the meaning of the language used, social traditions reflecting the social structures within which the writer works, and, in the case of a religious text, religious traditions presupposed by the author.

A writer's use of his tradition can be illuminating in different ways. Identification of the ideological tradition presupposed by a writer may help in the interpretation of his text. (An illustration of this is the very different interpretations which might be given to the term 'son of God', depending on the religious tradition which is presupposed.) Further, if one can identify a writer's tradition with some accuracy, one may be able to see how that writer modifies the source material he uses; this may then give further insight into what the author is trying to say. (This is often the method used in redaction-critical studies of the synoptic gospels: if Mark's gospel is taken to be the source of Matthew and Luke, the changes which the latter two evangelists make to their source may tell us something about their interests and concerns.) On the other hand, if the tradition in question is developing or changing, one might be able to identify the point in that development at which the author is writing. If one also has a detailed knowledge of the tradition in its various forms, this may reveal something of the situation of the author; alternatively, if one knows a great deal about the author, one may be able to make deductions about the changing state of the tradition. Usually one is a position mid-way between these two extremes, or one may be equally ignorant of both the author and the fluctuating state of his tradition. However, a study of a writer's use of tradition may be helpful in providing a sort of 'grid' of reference which may then be useful in determining something about the author, or his tradition, or perhaps both.

All these concerns are relevant when studying the texts of the Nag Hammadi Library. The heterodox nature of these texts is widely recognised. The precise reasons for their being collected together remain unknown,[1] and the texts probably have widely differing origins. The texts are almost certainly translations into Coptic from another language (probably Greek) and they come from various religious backgrounds. Identification of the religious background of each text is clearly an important factor in the interpretation of the text. Further, this background will be determined by the actual traditions which the text presupposes and uses. A text will be adjudged to be Christian if it shows knowledge and use of Christian traditions; a complete absence of reference to Christian

[1] Cf. the varying views of Säve-Södebergh, 'Holy Scriptures or Apologetic Documentations? The "Sitz im Leben" of the Nag Hammadi Library', *NHS* 7, Leiden 1975, 3-14 (the library was collected for heresiological purposes); F. Wisse, 'Gnosticism and Early Monasticism in Egypt', *Gnosis*, Göttingen 1978, 431-440; also C.W. Hedrick, 'Gnostic Proclivities in the Greek Life of Pachomius and the Sitz im Leben of the Nag Hammadi Library', *NT* 22 (1980) 78-94 (the texts could have been used positively in the nascent monastic movement).

tradition in a text will probably lead to the conclusion that that text is non-Christian.[2]

One of the ways in which several of the Nag Hammadi texts claim continuity with the Christian tradition is by identifying the revealer/saviour figure with the person of Jesus. Whether this identification is a necessary feature in the texts concerned, or whether it represents a secondary attempt to Christianise something that is basically non-Christian, is a problem which will be left on one side here. However, the fact is that in many of these texts several sayings and longer discourses are placed on the lips of Jesus. The question then arises of whether these sayings and discourses bear any relationship to the sayings of Jesus as known from 'orthodox' traditions, in particular from the canonical gospels. It is certainly the case that ever since the discovery of the Nag Hammadi Library in 1945, the Gospel of Thomas has attracted enormous interest in this respect, and a great deal of study has been undertaken to try to determine the relationship between Thomas and the tradition of the sayings of Jesus in the synoptic gospels.[3] However, relatively little attention has been paid to the similar question of the relationship between the tradition of the sayings of Jesus in the canonical gospels and the other texts in the Nag Hammadi Library. The purpose of this study is to offer a

[2] Though it does not, of course, necessarily follow that the author himself was non-Christian.

[3] For bibliographical details on the Gospel of Thomas (and indeed on all the Nag Hammadi texts), see D.M. Scholer, *Nag Hammadi Bibliography 1948-1969*, *NHS* 1, Leiden 1971, esp. 136-65, and the updating of this bibliography published in *NT* annually since 1971. On the specific question of the relationship between Thomas and the synoptics, one may note the full-length monograph of W. Schrage, *Das Verhältnis des Thomas-Evangeliums zur synoptischen Tradition und zu den koptischen Evangelienübersetzungen*, *BZNW* 29, Berlin 1964, as well as numerous other articles and sections of wider studies.

discussion of these texts[4] with this question in mind. Further, although the nature of the Gospel of Thomas as a collection of sayings of Jesus has invited comparison with the sayings of Jesus in the canonical gospels, it seems an unnecessary limitation to restrict discussion to a comparison involving sayings material only. Other texts in the Nag Hammadi Library refer to the life of Jesus in a more comprehensive way and do not restrict themselves to his sayings: e.g. there are allusions to his birth, his baptism, his miracles, his crucifixion etc. It thus seems appropriate to extend the range of comparison within the canonical gospels to cover all kinds of tradition, i.e. not just explicit sayings of Jesus. However, in view of the enormous discussion on this issue which the Gospel of Thomas has provoked, that gospel will not be considered in detail here. (Such a study of Thomas deserves a full monograph in its own right.) Further, attention here will be restricted to the use of synoptic tradition in these texts. (The use of Johannine tradition also deserves a full-length monograph.)[5]

The results of such a study will clearly be relevant in the interpretation of the Nag Hammadi texts themselves. It may be revealing to see how important the identification of the redeemer/saviour figure with Jesus really was for Gnostic writers. Did this identification simply extend to ascribing the name 'Jesus' to the revealer figure? Or was it

---

[4] I have also included the Gospel of Mary for discussion here. This gospel is found in the Berlin Codex BG 8502. The fact that the two texts which follow in the codex also appear within the Nag Hammadi Library (i.e. the Apocryphon of John and the Sophia of Jesus Christ) indicates that the texts of the codex may be closely related to some of the Nag Hammadi texts. This is supported by the clearly Gnostic nature of the Gospel of Mary.

[5] The work of E.H. Pagels, *The Johannine Gospel in Gnostic Exegesis, SBLMS* 17, Abingdon – New York 1973, covers some, but not all, of the Nag Hammadi texts.

important to make this figure recognisable as the Jesus of more 'orthodox' Christian circles at a deeper level than the common name? In some circumstances it might have been desirable to show that a Gnostic Jesus was indeed the same Jesus as in 'orthodox' faith, by constructing lines of continuity between what was said and done by the Gnostic Jesus and what was said and done by Jesus in the canonical gospels. It is possible that study of the links between the Nag Hammadi texts and the synoptic gospels may throw light on this question. Further, if one can identify the form of the synoptic tradition which is at times presupposed, then one may be able to apply redaction-critical techniques in looking at the modifications and adaptations which a writer makes to that tradition. These may then provide important aids for a better understanding of the text in question.

Another area in which this study may be able to make a contribution is the problem of the relationship between the newly discovered Nag Hammadi Library and the accounts of Gnostic teachings and sects which we have in the Church Fathers. It is becoming increasingly clear that, however accurate some of the heresiologists may have been in their reporting, it is extremely difficult to make any neat correlation between the individual tractates of the Nag Hammadi Library and the various sects described by the Church Fathers; indeed it is unclear how far one should think in terms of well-defined sects within Gnosticism at all[5a] The use of synoptic tradition by the

---

[5a] See especially F. Wisse, 'The Nag Hammadi Library and the Heresiologists', *VigChr* 25 (1971) 205-223, and the continuing debate concerning the attempt to identify a particular form of Gnosticism as 'Sethian': see the discussions in B. Layton (ed.), *The Rediscovery of Gnosticism II. Sethian Gnosticism*, Leiden 1981, with references to earlier literature, especially the essays of F. Wisse, 'Stalking those elusive Sethians', 563-576, and H.M. Schenke, 'The Phenomenon and Significance of Gnostic Sethianism', 580-616.

Nag Hammadi texts may be relevant in this discussion. Frequent reference is made by writers such as Irenaeus, Hippolytus and Tertullian to the fact that Gnostic teachers made great use of canonical gospel traditions.[5b] A correlation, or lack of correlation, between what is said by the Church Fathers on this issue and what is found in the Nag Hammadi texts will then be a small, but important, piece of evidence to contribute to the general problem of the heresiologists' accounts of the Gnostics.

In the general remarks made initially concerning a writer's use of his tradition, I argued that such a study may be useful in learning not only about the writer but also about his tradition. This is also true in the specific case of the use of synoptic tradition in the Nag Hammadi texts: such a study may contribute to our knowledge of the development of the synoptic tradition, or indeed to our knowledge of the sayings of Jesus in general. Much of the excitement associated with the Gospel of Thomas has been due to the contribution which it is believed that Thomas might make in this area. There is, for example, the possibility that Thomas may preserve genuine sayings of Jesus which would otherwise have been unknown.[6] Similarly it is no less possible that genuine sayings of Jesus may be preserved in the other Nag Hammadi texts.[7] There is also the possibility that the Gospel of Thomas may represent a tradition of the sayings of Jesus which is

---

[5b] For a recent attempt to find connections between the subjects of two different patristic reports, partly on the basis of their similar NT exegesis, see J. Frickel, 'Naassener oder Valentinianer?' *NHS* 17, Leiden 1981, 95-119.

[6] One saying which is often regarded as authentic is saying 82: 'He who is near me is near the fire; he who is far from me is far from the Kingdom': cf. J. Jeremias, *Unknown Sayings of Jesus*, London 1957, 54f.; N. Perrin, *Rediscovering the Teaching of Jesus*, London 1967, 67f.

[7] Cf. H. Koester, 'Apocryphal and Canonical Gospels', *HThR* 73 (1980) 105-130; see too the section below on ApocJas and the article of Hedrick ('Kingdom Sayings') discussed there.

independent of the canonical gospels.[8] For the study of the pre-Easter Jesus, this theory is extremely important. If Thomas is independent of the canonical gospels, then in the sayings where Thomas and the canonical gospels have parallel versions, one has an additional independent source for the same saying, and consequently more evidence for use in rediscovering the words of Jesus himself.

Such considerations are relevant not only to studies of the historical Jesus. *If* Thomas and the synoptic gospels are independent of each other and yet have parallel versions of various sayings, then there must be some link between Thomas or Thomas' tradition and the tradition behind the synoptic gospels. If Thomas is not dependent on the final versions of the synoptic gospels, his tradition must have diverged somewhere along the line from the synoptic evangelists' traditions. It might be that this point of divergence was at Jesus himself, so that there is no relationship at all between the synoptic line of tradition and that leading to the Gospel of Thomas (i.e. diagrammatically

Jesus
synoptic gospels — Thomas).

On the other hand the point of divergence may have been post-Easter at a later stage in the development of the synoptic tradition, but one which is nevertheless pre-redactional (diagrammatically

Jesus
|
synoptic gospels — Thomas).

This would mean that there might be some relationship

[8] This is, of course, a much debated issue. One should also note that the dependence/independence of Thomas in relation to the synoptic gospels is not necessarily a matter of mutually exclusive alternatives. Thomas may be dependent on the synoptic gospels at some points, but may represent earlier/independent traditions at others: see R. McL. Wilson's review of Schrage, *Verhältnis*, *VigChr* 20 (1966) 118-124.

between the Gospel of Thomas and one or more of the sources used by the synoptic evangelists. Some have claimed that this is indeed the case, and would see an early stage in the development of the sayings source Q (believed to have been a major source used by Matthew and Luke) reflected in the Gospel of Thomas.[9]

The preceding paragraph assumes that the Gospel of Thomas is independent of the synoptic gospels in their final form. Whether this assumption is justified is not a problem which can be dealt with fully here. However, the general possibility of the use of pre-synoptic traditions is relevant here. The discovery of the Nag Hammadi texts has given a glimpse of Christians in different situations using traditions about Jesus at a period for which our evidence of such activity is limited.[10] It may be that these texts reveal knowledge of independent traditions of the sayings of Jesus. In addition, some texts may reveal knowledge of pre-synoptic traditions, i.e. traditions which were also used by the synoptic evangelists.[11] In particular there is the possibility that the sayings source Q (if it ever existed as a unified source) was used for some of these texts. The fact that there is no evidence for the existence of Q outside Matthew and Luke has always been considered a problem for the theory of the existence of such a source.[12] However, J.M. Robinson has pointed

[9] See H. Koester, 'One Jesus and Four Primitive Gospels', in *Trajectories through Early Christianity*, Philadelphia 1971, esp. 186.

[10] The dating of the Nag Hammadi texts is notoriously uncertain, but some (at least in their original form) probably stem from the 2nd century; some *may* be 1st century. (The present Coptic translations are much later, i.e. mid 4th century or later.)

[11] See Koester's theories with regard to ApocJas and DialSav, discussed below.

[12] See, for example, A Farrer, 'On Dispensing with Q' in *Studies in the Gospels*, Oxford 1955, 58: 'To postulate Q is to postulate the unevidenced and the unique'. With regard to the theory that Q was an issue in the debate between Paul and the Corinthian Community in 1 Corinthians see my '1 Corinthians and Q', *JBL* 102 (1983) 607-619, where I have argued that this theory is not convincing.

to possible gnosticising tendencies in the genre of Q (not that Q need be gnostic, but simply that a source like Q could be read in a gnosticising way). He has suggested that perhaps Q could only be tolerated by 'orthodox' Christianity by being incorporated into a gospel of the type of Matthew and Luke with a passion narrative.[13] A corollary of this (which Robinson himself does not explicitly draw) is that Gnostic Christians might have been more ready to tolerate Q on its own. Robinson's essay thus provides a stimulus to look at the use of synoptic tradition by Gnostic Christians and to see if they might in fact have had Q available as a source and have used it positively. If this could be established it would be very important for synoptic studies, not only with regard to the synoptic problem but also with regard to the growing interest in Q for its own sake.

This was in fact the initial consideration which led to the undertaking of the present study. As will be seen, the results are largely negative: no firm evidence for the use of pre-synoptic sources (Q or otherwise) is found in these texts. Practically all the tractates appear to presuppose the synoptic gospels in their present final form. Nevertheless such results in themselves are not without their significance. The fact that one particular gospel was used by a writer shows that that gospel was available to him in the situation in which he was writing. This may then help to determine the date and provenance of the writer concerned; alternatively it may help in extending our knowledge of the times and places at which particular gospels were known and used. Arguments of this nature can, of course, very quickly become dangerously circular. The fact is that we know very little for certain about when

[13] 'Logoi Sophon: On the Gattung of Q', in *Trajectories through Early Christianity*, Philadelphia 1971, 71-113, esp. 112f.

or where any of the Nag Hammadi texts was originally written. Equally we know very little about the influence of individual gospels in different communities in the first two Christian centuries beyond the fact that Matthew's gospel was very popular.[14] Nevertheless the results of the present study may help in assessing the possible *Sitz im Leben* of each of the Nag Hammadi texts, as well as enabling us to see the influence of the synoptic gospels.

One problem which the present study may help to illuminate is that of the development of the New Testament canon. However, a great deal of caution is necessary here. An allusion to a synoptic gospel, or indeed to any New Testament document, shows that that document is known to the writer. It does not necessarily imply anything about the nature of the authority ascribed to the document by the writer.[15] Nevertheless one may be able to make some progress in this respect. On some occasions, interpretations are given of NT passages and these are often quite involved with extensive allegorisation (cf. GTr's allegorising of the parable of the lost sheep, or 2LogSeth's allegorisation of the Matthaean passion narrative). In these cases one may be justified in seeing these texts as having greater authority for those using them. In general one does not bother to allegorise a text which one knows but does not regard as important. The fact that an author takes the trouble to provide an interpretation of a text suggests that the text in question is

---

[14] Cf. the work of E. Massaux, *Influence de l'Évangile de saint Matthieu sur la littérature chrétienne avant saint Irénée*, Louvain 1950, who seeks to provide some sort of global picture; but one must admit that at times he is forced to make rather sweeping generalisations in view of the lack of evidence.

[15] Cf. the justified criticisms made by H. von Campenhausen, *The Formation of the Christian Bible*, London 1972, 140f. of the extravagant claims made about the state of the canon assumed by GTr (cf. van Unnik and others, cited below, p.57)

one whose correct interpretation is considered to be important and which therefore implicitly has a certain amount of authority for the person referring to it.[16] However, the precise nature of that authority is never spelt out in the Nag Hammadi texts. There is also no indication at all that authoritative NT texts are qualitatively distinguished from other texts. Indeed the whole basis of much Gnostic teaching is the claim to be able to supplement existing authorities by special revelations which have been given to the chosen few.[17] It is thus inherently unlikely that the Nag Hammadi texts would witness to the setting of limits round a collection of texts to be regarded as 'canonical' in some sense. All they can show is the possible existence of some texts which were to become, or perhaps were already for some, part of a NT canon.

A final problem to which the present study may be relevant is that of the text of the NT. If one can determine the precise textual form of a synoptic tradition known to a later author one may be able to identify this form as that of a specific textual tradition. It would clearly provide a very neat set of results if one particular Nag Hammadi text consistently presupposed, say, Western readings of the NT text.[18] In fact the allusions to synoptic material are frequently too allusive for one to be able to make such a precise comparison. One must also bear in mind the possibility that when the texts were translated into Coptic, any Biblical allusions may have been assimilated to the form of the NT text known to the translator.

---

[16] See F.F. Bruce, 'Some Thoughts on the Beginning of the New Testament Canon', *BJRL* 65 (1983) 37-60, esp. 47f.

[17] See P. Perkins, 'Johannine Tradition in *Ap.Jas.* (NHC I,2)', *JBL* 101 (1982) 403-414, for a good discussion of this in relation to ApocJas.

[18] Cf. A.K. Helmbold, *The Nag Hammadi Gnostic Texts and the Bible*, Grand Rapids 1967, 91f., who mentions briefly some possible corollaries of this.

Further, some variant readings in the later textual tradition may have originated in deliberate variations of the text by Gnostic writers.[19] Nevertheless this is an additional form of evidence which may help to illuminate the *Sitz im Leben* of the Nag Hammadi texts and also the history of the development of the NT text.

In this study I have assumed the standard two-document hypothesis as the solution to the synoptic problem.[20] I have assumed that Mark's gospel was the source of Matthew and Luke, and hence where Matthew and Luke change their Markan source these changes can usually be identified as redactional; I have also assumed the existence of a common tradition available to Matthew and Luke only, and I have called this Q; however, I have not made any assumptions about the unity of this Q material, nor about whether 'Q' was ever in the form of a single document. The main methodological principle used has been that an allusion to the redactional work of an evangelist presupposes the existence of that evangelist's finished gospel. Further, although such an allusion might on its own be due to the use of a post-synoptic harmony of more than one gospel, I have not assumed this possibility unless there is positive evidence in favour of it: thus an allusion to, for example, MtR has been taken as an indication of the *use* of Matthew's finished gospel unless there is further evidence to the contrary.[21]

[19] For example, the D reading at Mt 9.15, perhaps paralleled in GPh 72.20f. and 82.17 (see p. 78 below), has been sometimes regarded as due to Gnostic influence: cf. A Jülicher, *Die Gleichnisreden Jesus*, Tübingen 1899, *II*, 180f., cited by R. McL. Wilson, 'The New Testament in the Nag Hammadi Gospel of Philip', *NTS* 9 (1963) 291-294.

[20] I have tried to defend this hypothesis against at least one important modern rival in my *The Revival of the Griesbach Hypothesis*, Cambridge 1983.

[21] For a very similar methodology, cf Schrage, *Verhältnis*, 4ff.; H.K. McArthur, 'The Gospel according to Thomas', in *New Testament Sidelights*, Hartford 1960, 43-77. Note however the warning of Wilson (cf. n. 8 above) on this.

II. SYNOPTIC TRADITION IN THE NAG HAMMADI TEXTS

The heterodox nature of the Nag Hammadi texts clearly invites some classification into groups or classes of similar texts. With whatever definition of the term 'Gnostic' one works, some texts are clearly Gnostic (e.g. the Sophia of Jesus Christ) whilst others are clearly not (e.g. the Teachings of Silvanus). However, as has already been noted, there is great difficulty in trying to subdivide the Gnostic texts into separate groups corresponding to different Gnostic sects. Further, it is debatable whether some texts should be classified as 'Gnostic' (cf. the discussion below on AuthTeach). It is not the purpose of this study to make decisions on these issues, though the results established may help in such discussions. What is of more direct concern here is whether a text is Christian or non-Christian, rather than whether it is Gnostic or not. With this in mind one may be able to give a very rough division of the texts into three categories: (a) non-Christian texts, (b) Christian texts where the Christian elements are peripheral and are probably secondary additions,[22] and (c) Christian texts where Christian elements are more deeply embedded.[23] This is the order in which the texts will be treated here with some attempt

---

[22] It should, however, be noted that the fact that a text has only a small amount of Christian material does not necessarily imply that that material has been added later to the rest of the text. In a number of different studies, Wilson has raised the possibility that some texts may have undergone a process of de-Christianisation, so that the Christian elements remaining would be the vestiges of an earlier form of tradition, rather than secondary additions to a non-Christian *Vorlage*.

[23] A very similar division of the texts is given by M. Krause, 'Zur Bedeutung des gnostisch-hermetischen Handschriftenfunds von Nag Hammadi', *NHS* 6, Leiden 1975, 65-89, esp. 79ff. and 'Die Texte von Nag Hammadi', *Gnosis* Göttingen 1978, 216-243; also A. Böhlig, 'Zur Frage nach den Typen des Gnostizismus und seines Schriftums', in *Ex Orbe Religionum. I*, Leiden 1972, 395ff. though with small differences in the assignment of individual texts.

made to collect like texts within each larger group, if only for the purposes of convenience.

Several texts are widely recognised as showing no clear Christian influence at all (and hence no synoptic allusion). These include the three Hermetic discourses in Codex VI, *The Discourse on the Eighth and the Ninth* (VI.6), the *Prayer* (VI.7) and *Asclepius* (VI.8).[24] Further, it is probable that one can include in this category the version of Plato's *Republic* which also appears in Codex VI.[25] Other texts which should probably be included within the broad category of those which exhibit virtually no direct Christian influence are the *Letter of Eugnostos* (III.3 and V.1),[26] *The Thunder* (VI.2),[27] *The Three Steles of Seth* (VII.5),[28] *Zostrianos* (VIII.1),[29] *Norea* (IX.2),[30] *Marsanes* (X.1),[31] and *Allogenes* (XI.3).[32] Thus in any search for specifically synoptic tradition these texts can be discounted. Other texts may also be excluded from the

---

[24] Critical editions ot these can be found in D.M. Parrott (ed.), *Nag Hammadi Codices V,2-5 and VI with Papyrus Berolinensis 8502, 1 and 4*, *NHS* 11, Leiden 1979; also J.-P. Mahé, *Hermes en Haute Égypte*, *BCNH* Textes 3 and 7, Quebec 1978 and 1982.

[25] It is, however, perhaps worth noting that M. Krause and P. Labib, *Gnostische und hermetische Schriften aus Codex II und Codex VI*, *ADAI.K* 2, Glückstadt 1971, who published their texts prior to the identification of this particular text as a (very poor) translation of Plato (cf. H.M. Schenke, 'Zur Facsimile-Ausgabe der Nag-Hammadi-Schriften-Codex VI', *OLZ* 69 (1974) 229-243, cols. 236-241) gave as a parallel to the Coptic text's 'Good is he who has been done injustice completely' (48.20f.) the story of the passion of Jesus. The Coptic version here is clearly a misrepresentation of Plato's original Greek (cf. J. Brashler in Parrott (ed.) *Codices V and VI*, 328f.); but it is not impossible that some of the alleged 'blunders' in the translation may be due to 'interpretations' of the text by a Christian translator. However this must remain no more than a conjecture. Schenke, op. cit., col. 239 is rather less complimentary about the work of the Coptic translator!

[26] This is widely regarded as a non-Christian text: cf. M. Krause, 'Das literarische Verhältnis des Eugnostosbriefes zur Sophia Jesu Christi', *Mullus*, *JAC.E* 1, Münster 1964, 215-223; J.-É. Ménard, 'Normative Self-Definition in Gnosticism', in *Jewish and Christian Self-Definition Vol. 1*. London 1980, 134-150. Parrott, in his introduction to the text (*NHLE*, 206) says that the text 'is without apparent Christian influence'. R. McL. Wilson, *Gnosis and the New*

present discussion in that, although they are clearly Christian texts, the links which they have with the Christian tradition are not with the synoptic tradition of the canonical gospels. In this category one can place the *Prayer of Paul* (I.1) and the *Apocalypse of Paul* (V.1).

Some of the Nag Hammadi texts can contribute little

Testament, Oxford 1968, 115f., notes some possible Christian elements in the text, e.g. the reference to 'King of kings' (78.2., cf. Rev 17.14; 19.16), 'gods and archangels and angels for service' (77.20ff., cf. Heb 1.14); but these are mostly standard phrases and do not seem to be distinctive enough to warrant the claim that they are echoing NT language. The only synoptic reference noted by Wilson is the phrase 'the Kingdom of the Son of Man' (81.12f.), a phrase which also occurs in GMary 9.9f. and the latter text is almost certainly based on Mt 24.15 (see p. 38 below). However the 'Son of Man' is the son of the primal androgynous Man, and has no relationship to the phrase 'Son of Man' in the canonical gospels. The common language is probably purely coincidental.

27 Cf. MacRae's introduction to the text in *NHLE*, 271: 'It presents no distinctively Jewish, Christian or Gnostic themes'. Similarly H.G. Bethge, '"Nebront"—Die zweite Schrift aus Nag-Hammadi-Codex VI', *ThLZ* 98 (1973) 99; G. Quispel, 'Jewish Gnosis and Mandaean Gnosticism: Some Reflections on the Writing *Brontè*', *NHS* 7, Leiden 1975, 82-122 says: 'There is nothing explicitly or perhaps even implicitly Christian in this text' (82).

28 Cf. J.M. Robinson, Introduction to *NHLE*, 8; Böhlig, 'Typen des Gnostizismus', 398.

29 The general non-Christian character of the work is widely accepted: cf. J.H. Sieber, 'An Introduction to the Tractate Zostrianos from Nag Hammadi', *NT* 15 (1973) 223-240 who refers to 'the complete absence of Christian references in the work . . . we clearly have in *Zos* an example of non-Christian gnosticism' (239). Similarly Krause, 'Bedeutung', 81. However, one should note the possibility of some secondary Christian glosses to the text: e.g. in the report of the Berliner Arbeitskreis, this is suggested as the explanation of the text at 48.26-9 ('He was there again, he who suffers although he is unable to suffer') and 131.14f. ('The gentle Father has sent you the Saviour'): see K.W. Tröger (ed.), *Gnosis und Neues Testament*, Berlin 1973, 66. The warning in 131.2 ('Do not baptize yourselves with death') may also show awareness of 'orthodox' Christian baptism: cf. P. Perkins, *The Gnostic Dialogue*, New York 1980, 90.

30 Cf. Pearson, *Nag Hammadi Codices IX and X*, *NHS* 15, Leiden 1981, 91: 'There is no evidence at all of a direct Christian influence upon the tractate.' Also Tröger, (ed.) *Gnosis und Neues Testament*, 69.

31 Cf. Pearson, ibid., 244: the tractate 'shows positively no Christian elements or influence'.

32 Cf. Krause, 'Bedeutung', 81. For the close association between 3StSeth, Zost and Allog, see J.M. Robinson, 'The Three Steles of Seth and the Gnostics of Plotinus', in *Proceedings*, Stockholm 1977, 132-142.

here because they are so fragmentary in nature. The so-called *Fragments* (XII.3) are too poorly preserved to furnish any evidence for the present purposes. Wisse observes that 'the reference to "my Father" (Frag.1B 1.20) suggests that the speaker may be Jesus',[33] but beyond that the extant text is so meagre that one can say nothing. The same applies in the case of the tractate called *Hypsiphrone* (XI.4). Turner says that 'the fragmentary state of the tractate prevents a clear understanding of the nature and contents of the discourse'.[34] One cannot even say if the text is Christian or not, let alone whether there are allusions to synoptic material here.

Also very poorly preserved, and contributing little to the present discussion, is the version of the *Sentences of Sextus* found in the Nag Hammadi Library (XII.2). This is generally assumed to be a Christian work.[35] Although it is not a gnostic composition, its general ascetic tone would have made its contents congenial to those for whom many of the Nag Hammadi texts were written. The poor state of preservation of Codex XII means that only the sentences numbered 157-180 and 307-397 survive in this Coptic translation. Very few clearly Christian echoes are to be found in the sentences which survive here,[36] and there is thus no firm evidence on which to base any theories about the state of the NT (or synoptic) tradition presupposed by the text. Of those preserved here, the sentence which is closest to the synoptic tradition is

---

[33] *NHLE*, 460.

[34] *NHLE*, 453.

[35] Cf. H. Chadwick, *The Sentences of Sextus*, Cambridge 1957, 138.ff.; also R.A. Edwards and R.A. Wild, *The Sentences of Sextus, SBLTT* 22, Chico 1981, 1.

[36] For links between the Sentences in general and the NT, see G. Delling, 'Zur Hellenisierung des Christentums in den "Sprüchen des Sextus"', in *Studien, TU* 77, Berlin 1961, 208-241, esp. 219ff.

probably no.336: 'It is better to serve others than to make others serve you' (cf. Mk 9.35; 10.44 and pars.).[37] Perhaps too no.316 ('where your thought is, there is your goodness') may show dependence on the development of the saying in Mt 6.21 where καρδία is replaced by νοῦς.[38] But other sentences which show greater affinity with the synoptic tradition are not preserved here. In the Sentences as a whole, parallels with synoptic tradition reflect the use of Matthew's gospel,[39] and there is nothing in the present Coptic text which would appear to disturb that general pattern.[40]

There are some texts whose possible contribution to the present study is more debatable, and which arguably show more links with the synoptic tradition. One such text is the *Paraphrase of Shem* (VII.1). Many have regarded this as a non-Christian text, perhaps providing evidence of a non-Christian 'redeemer myth'.[41] However, this is not universally accepted. For example, K.M. Fischer sees the description of the Saviour in 36.2ff. as presupposing that of the Christian gnostic redeemer (though this is a somewhat circular argument);[42] he also

[37] Delling, op.cit., 232.

[38] See below, p.40f, for a full discussion of this saying in relation to G. Mary. Delling, op. cit., 231, says that the saying 'wird nur verständlich als Versuch, Mt 6, 21 in griechisches Sprachdenken zu übersetzen'.

[39] Delling, ibid., 237f.

[40] The Coptic version was, of course, unavailable to Delling at the time of the writing of his article. A collation of the readings of the Coptic version against the Greek witnesses is provided by Edwards and Wild, op.cit.

[41] Cf. F. Wisse, 'The Redeemer Figure in the Paraphrase of Shem', *NT* 12 (1970) 130-140; G.W. MacRae, 'Nag Hammadi and the New Testament', *Gnosis*, Göttingen 1978, 154; the text is also regarded as non-Christian by Krause, 'Bedeutung', 81.

[42] 'Die Paraphrase des Seem', *NHS* 6, Leiden 1975, 266. In fact the same passage, taken by Fischer as evidence of Christian influence, is cited by MacRae (ibid.) as evidence for the existence of a non-Christian redeemer myth subsequently used by Christians to interpret the Christ event.

refers to the stress on 'faith' (rather than 'knowledge', cf. 30.2ff.) and claims 'das ist ohne christlichen Einfluss nicht denkbar'.[43]

There are also some striking references to baptism in this text. 37.19ff. ('O Shem, they are deceived by manifold demons, thinking that through baptism with the uncleanness of water, that which is dark, feeble, idle and disturbing, he will take away the sins') looks very much as if it is directed against 'orthodox' Christian claims about water baptism.[44] Sevrin also finds allusions to the synoptic account of the baptism of Jesus by John the Baptist earlier in the text, in 30.23-25 ('the demon will also appear upon the river to baptize with an imperfect baptism') and 32.5f. ('then I shall come from the demon down to the water').[45] Sevrin points out that the reference to the baptism being 'imperfect' suggests a contrast with a 'perfect' baptism, yet elsewhere in ParShem any 'baptism' is seen in wholly negative terms. Hence the reference here may be due to a prior tradition as in Mk 1.7f. and pars, where John's baptism is contrasted with Jesus'. Further, the note in 32.5f. may suggest that the Saviour is not in charge of the situation, and as this would not fit the overall outlook of the text, it may reflect the use of a source here. Thus ParShem seems to presuppose the synoptic account of the baptism of Jesus by John. Sevrin seeks to go further and claims that the synoptic account which is closest to ParShem is that in Mark: 31.5f. (the

---

43 Fischer, ibid.

44 See J.M. Sevrin, 'A propos de la Paraphrase de Sem', *Muséon* 88 (1975) 92ff.

45 Ibid, 90f. Cf. too Tröger, *Gnosis und Neues Testament*, 58f.; K. Koschorke, *Die Polemik der Gnostiker gegen das kirchliche Christentum*, *NHS* 12, Leiden 1978, 146. However, for Wisse, the polemic is better seen as directed against Jewish baptismal sects; the references to 'baptism' and 'water', when referred to the Saviour, are purely metaphorical. That may be so, but the language could still derive ultimately from Christian vocabulary about baptism.

Saviour came 'from the demon') may be paralleled with Mk 1.9 (Jesus was baptised ὑπὸ Ἰωάννου), and the other differences in wording could be explained on the basis of a rewriting of the Markan text. Thus although Sevrin admits that 'il n'y trouve . . . aucune référence explicite au Nouveau Testament et au christianisme',[46] he concludes his discussion by saying:

> Le récit du baptême de Jésus n'est certes pas utilisé pour lui-même, mais fournit simplement des éléments à l'expression d'un mythe; cela n'empêche pas que ce récit est très probablement supposé, soit par notre texte, soit par une source qu'il retravaille; certains éléments pourraient même suggérer une utilisation du texte de Marc.[47]

Sevrin is generally persuasive in arguing that the present text does presuppose an account of Jesus' baptism by John. However, one must also acknowledge that the references to the synoptic tradition are extremely indirect,[48] and hence it is precarious to make very precise comparisons between this Coptic text and the Greek text of the synoptic gospels to try to determine which gospel tradition is presupposed. Although Mk 1.9 does contain the words ὑπὸ Ἰωάννου, all the gospels assume that Jesus was baptised by John, and hence any of the gospels (or their underlying sources) could have provided the basis

---

[46] Op.cit., 85.

[47] Op.cit., 91.

[48] It is not even certain that the text is presupposing a specifically *synoptic* account of Jesus' baptism at all. After the Saviour's descent to the water it is said: 'whirlpools of water and flames of fire will rise up against me' (32.7-9); this may reflect other traditions of Jesus' baptism: cf. Justin, *Dialogue* 88.3 for the reference to 'fire'; also the *Preaching of Paul* cited by Ps.-Cyprian, *De Rebapt.*, 17 (cf. Sevrin op.cit., 91, n.128); perhaps too one can compare the reference to a great light at Jesus' baptism in the Gospel of the Ebionites (Epiphanius, *Pan.* 30.13.7, cited in E. Hennecke, *NT Apocrypha I*, London 1963, 157).

for ParShem's language here. Sevrin's other arguments concern the differences between ParShem and the Markan text: they could therefore just as easily be applied to explaining the differences between ParShem and any of the other gospel accounts. Thus whilst Sevrin's analysis is persuasive with regard to his general claim that a narrative of Jesus' baptism by John is presupposed, his further claim, to see precisely the Markan account reflected here, is probably unjustified. All one can probably say is that, although ParShem presupposes Christian tradition, its use of it is too indirect for one to be able to specify its source more precisely.

Another text which has provoked great interest as to whether it is Christian or non-Christian is the *Apocalypse of Adam* (V.5).[49] The importance of this text in relation to the possible evidence which it might provide for the existence of a non-Christian redeemer myth is well-known. Its non-Christian nature is usually asserted by appealing to the absence of Christian motifs. However,

---

[49] The text is taken as non-Christian by G. MacRae in his introduction to the text in *NHLE*, 152: 'The most notable feature of this work is the absence of any explicit evidence of clear borrowings from the Christian tradition.'; cf. too his article 'The Coptic Gnostic Apocalypse of Adam'. *HeyJ* 6 (1965) 27-35. In an early edition of the text, Böhlig even claimed that 'die Schrift stammt aus vorchristlicher Gnosis (though 'vorchristlich' here means 'prior to the contact with Christianity', rather than 'prior to the existence of Christianity'). See A. Böhlig and P. Labib, *Koptisch-gnostische Apokalypsen aus Codex V von Nag Hammadi im koptischen Museum zu Alt-Kairo*, Halle-Wittenberg 1963, 95; Wilson, *Gnosis and the New Testament*, 135, admits that 'this document shows at most only slight traces of Christian influence', though he believes that the overall narrative about the Illuminator is 'too closely tailored to the figure of Jesus to be entirely independent' (136); cf. too H.M. Schenke, in his review of Böhlig's edition, in *OLZ* 61 (1966) cols. 31-34. A full bibliography on the question is given by F.T. Fallon, *The Enthronement of Sabaoth*, *NHS* 10, Leiden 1978, 69f., to which must now be added G.M. Shellrude, 'The Apocalypse of Adam: Evidence for a Christian Gnostic Provenance', *NHS* 17, Leiden 1981, 82-91.

there are some features in the text which, if one knew already that the text were Christian, would be regarded as clear echoes of Christian traditions. With regard to synoptic traditions, there is the reference in 76.15 to 'fruit-bearing trees' (applied to the saved remnant of the seed of Noah). This is reminiscent of Mt 7.16, a text which was used by other Christian Gnostic writers.[50] Similarly, the text at 77.1f. says that the Illuminator 'will perform signs and wonders'. This is not a quotation of a specific synoptic text but it could be a good summary of Jesus' activity in the synoptic gospels (and is very similar in this respect to Acts 2.22).[51] Clearly the argument here can become circular. The Christian allusions in this text, if they exist, are at best remote. Nevertheless, the occurrence of the reference to Gnostic Christians as fruit-bearing trees (or an equivalent phrase using the same imagery) elsewhere in Christian Gnostic literature may be an additional factor to be borne in mind when deciding whether the reference here is due to an allusion to the synoptic tradition or whether the common imagery is coincidental.[52]

The second major group of texts in the Nag Hammadi Library comprises those which are clearly Christian in their present form, but where the Christian elements which they contain are fairly easily detachable from their

---

[50] Cf. p. 152 below.

[51] Both examples are noted by MacRae, 'Coptic Gnostic Apocalypse of Adam', 32, and Shellrude, op.cit., 83, arguing to different conclusions.

[52] One should also note the difficulty of finding parallels to the use of the imagery of a 'tree' and its 'fruits'. S. Schulz, *Q—Die Spruchquelle der Evangelisten*, Zürich 1972, 319, n.459, comments: 'Zwar ist das Bildwort vom Baum und seiner Frucht im Spätjudentum ohne Analogie' (though the image of 'fruit' alone is common). However, Sir 27.6 is not far removed.

contexts. It is thus debatable whether they are originally Christian compositions, or whether they represent the Christianising of a non-Christian *Vorlage*. One may consider here the *Gospel of the Egyptians* (III.2, IV.2). In their edition of the text, Böhlig and Wisse say that the tractate 'can at best only be called marginally Christian'.[53] Whether or not the document is fundamentally a Christian composition is debatable.[54] However, none of the possible allusions to the Christian tradition which have been noted clearly involve the use of explicitly synoptic tradition.[55] There are some references to the person of Jesus and his crucifixion.[56] But the allusions are at best extremely remote and there is nothing which is clearly identifiable as an allusion to the tradition which appears in the synoptic gospels as such.

Another text about which differing opinions have been expressed as to its relationship to Christian tradition is the *Trimorphic Protennoia* from Codex XIII. For NT

---

[53] A. Böhlig and F. Wisse, *Nag Hammadi Codices III, 2 and IV,2: The Gospel of the Egyptians, NHS* 4, Leiden 1975, 21.

[54] It is regarded as Christian by Krause, 'Bedeuting', 84; also R.McL. Wilson, 'The Gospel of the Egyptians', *StPatr* 14, *TU* 117, Berlin 1976, 243-250. On the other hand, C.W. Hedrick, 'Christian Motifs in the *Gospel of the Egyptians*', *NT* 23 (1981) 242-260, argues that the Christian elements are probably secondary additions to a non-Christian *Vorlage* and are easily detachable from their contexts. The most Christian part of the text is probably the colophon.

[55] One exception might be the text at 66.7f. ('these will by no means taste death'). Böhlig and Wisse see an allusion to Jn 8.52 here, though the phrase also occurs in Mk 9.1 and pars. However, the phrase is a common one in Jewish and Christian writings: cf. Perrin, *Rediscovering*, 19; also B.D. Chilton, '"Not to Taste Death". A Jewish, Christian and Gnostic Usage', in *Studia Biblica 1978 II.*, Sheffield 1980, 29-36, who traces a change in meaning of the phrase from Jewish to Gnostic sources (though his sole evidence in the latter context is GTh). The existence of the phrase thus by no means demands an allusion to synoptic (or Johannine) tradition to explain its presence here. (Cf. also Hedrick, op.cit., 257)

[56] See 64.1-4; 65.18, where there may well be an echo of Col 2.14: cf. Wilson, op.cit., 246. Hedrick, op.cit., 258, is more doubtful.

studies, the most interesting feature of this text is its links with the prologue of John's gospel, together with the question whether it may illuminate the background of the prologue.[57] According to some, the text is fundamentally non-Christian with a thin Christian veneer. Thus G. Schenke says:

> Eindeutig 'christlich' ist nur ein einziger Satz am Ende der dritten Rede (50,12-15) und der Umstand, dass der blosse Christusname dem göttlichen Autogenes beigefügt oder unterschoben wird (38,22; 39,6f.; 49,8).[58]

Others have been more positive about this text's relationship to Christianity. For example, in her two published editions of the text, Y. Janssens has noted a number of parallels with the NT.[59] In his brief essay on the text, Wilson tentatively takes up these references as indicating a Christian background to the text, and raises the possibility of the text having been secondarily de-Christianised.[60]

There are only two specifically synoptic parallels noted by Janssens. The apocalyptic section in 43.4ff. uses several motifs common to apocalyptic literature in

---

[57] Cf. C. Colpe, 'Heidnische, jüdische und christliche Überlieferung in den Schriften aus Nag Hammadi. III', *JAC* 17 (1974) 109-125, esp. 122-24, J.M. Robinson, 'Gnosticism and the New Testament', in *Gnosis*, Göttingen 1978, 128ff.; ibid., 'Sethians and Johannine Thought. The Trimorphic Protennoia and the Prologue of the Gospel of John', in *Sethian Gnosticism*, Leiden 1981, 643-662; C.A. Evans, 'On the Prologue of John and the *Trimorphic Protennoia*', *NTS* 27 (1981) 395-401.

[58] G. Schenke, '"Die dreigestaltige Protennoia"—Eine gnostische Offenbarungsrede in koptischer Sprache aus dem Fund von Nag Hammadi', *ThLZ* 99 (1974) 731-746, esp. 733. Similarly Colpe and Robinson as in the preceding note.

[59] 'Le Codex XIII de Nag Hammadi', *Muséon*, 87 (1974) 341-413, and *La Protennoia Trimorphe*, *BCNH* Textes 4, Quebec 1978, though she nowhere appears to discuss the nature of the relationship involved.

[60] R. McL. Wilson, 'The Trimorphic Protennoia', *NHS* 8, Leiden 1977, 50-54. Wilson's suggestions are treated as a firm theory by Robinson which he in turn rejects: see his 'Sethians and Johannine Thought' and the discussion recorded there, where Wilson clarifies his position.

general (e.g. cosmic upheavals, great anguish similar to birth pangs);[61] but at 44.33f. the phrase ⲧⲥⲩⲧⲉⲗⲉⲓⲁ ⲙⲡⲁⲓⲱⲛ, is used. As Janssens says, this is the same expression as in Mt 24.3 (συντέλεια τοῦ αἰῶνος)[62] The significance of the parallel is however doubtful. It is true that the phrase is confined to Matthew among the synoptic gospels, and seems quite characteristic of the first gospel (cf. Mt 13.39, 40, 49; 24.3; 28.20). However it can hardly be said to be only explicable in another text on the basis of knowledge of Matthew's gospel. The use of the phrase is one example (among many) of Matthew's use of standard Jewish terminology.[63] There is thus nothing here to demand a theory that the author of TriProt is using terminology which is specifically Christian.[64] The other synoptic parallel noted by Janssens concerns the text at 44.16 ('the times are cut short and the days have shortened'). This is reminiscent again of the synoptic apocalypse (cf. Mt 24.22/Mk 13.20).[65] At first sight this might appear to be a closer link, since there are not many parallels to the synoptic phrase,[66] yet there are some.[67] In any case the context seems to imply that the 'shortening' refers to the

---

61 Cf. Is 13.8; Hos 13.13; Mt 24.7f.; Jn 16.21.

62 *La Protennoia Trimorphe*, 73.

63 Cf. W.C. Allen, *A Critical and Exegetical Commentary on the Gospel according to St Matthew*, Edinburgh 1907 153; A.H. NcNeile, *The Gospel according to St. Matthew*, London 1915, 201, says that the phrase 'is thoroughly Jewish, occurring in different forms in the Apocalypses'. Cf. too G. Delling, art. συντέλεια, *ThWNT* 8, 66.

64 Janssens herself refers to similar terminology elsewhere in the Nag Hammadi texts: cf. ApocJohn (CG II 31.2; CG IV 48.2); GEg 61.3; 62.21.

65 Noted by Janssens, ibid., 75.

66 V. Taylor, *The Gospel according to St. Mark*, London 1952,512,cites Dan 12.7; 1 En 80.2; 4 Ezra 4.26; 2 Bar 20.1; Barn 4.3. But only 1 Enoch and Barnabas use the actual verb 'shorten', and in 1 Enoch it refers to the shortening of the year so that the normal agricultural growth processes will be impossible (rather than to the shortening of the time before the end). ApocAbr 29.13 may be a closer parallel.

67 Cf. the ApocAbr passage just mentioned.

length of each day so that darkness prevails, rather than to the number of days remaining before the End.[68] It is thus doubtful if there is any echo of synoptic tradition here: rather, it is simply a case of TriProt using current terminology and imagery.

There is thus nothing in TriProt to suggest that the author was acquainted with synoptic tradition, even indirectly. Alleged links with that tradition turn out to be illusory.

A text which is clearly Christian in its present form, but where the Christian elements may again represent secondary additions to a non-Christian *Vorlage*, is the *Apocryphon of John* (II.1, III.1, IV.1, BG 8502.2). The situation here is complicated by the fact that we have four versions of the text,[69] and these show some disagreements with each other. Such Christian elements as exist are not numerous. Wilson says: 'Extensive and direct quotations (of the NT) are conspicuous by their absence, and even such allusions as have been detected must be considered doubtful'.[70] In its present form the discourse is given by the risen Jesus and is set in the context of a dialogue with John. Many have regarded this dialogue setting as secondary,[71] and it is here that the closest links with the NT in general, and the synoptic tradition in particular, occur. In his edition of the Berlin text, Till cites only four

[68] The use of the imagery is thus closer to that of 1 En 80.2.

[69] Editions of the Coptic text of the three Nag Hammadi versions may be found in M. Krause–P. Labib, *Die drei Versionen des Apokryphon des Johannes im koptischen Museum zu Alt-Kairo*, *ADAI.K* 1, Wiesbaden 1962, and of the Berlin text in W.C. Till, *Die gnostischen Schriften des koptischen Papyrus Berolinensis 8502*, *TU* 60, Berlin 1955.

[70] *Gnosis and the New Testament*, 105.

[71] E.g. H. Koester, 'Dialog und Spruchüberlieferung in den gnostischen Texten von Nag Hammadi', *EvTh* 39 (1979) 535.

parallels with the NT, of which the only synoptic one occurs in the introductory scene, viz. CG II 2.12f.; BG 21.18f.: 'I am the one who is with you for ever', which is reminiscent of Mt 28.20.[72] In his edition of the Codex II text, S. Giversen cites this parallel; he also sees a synoptic parallel to the words of Jesus in 2.10f. ('John why do you doubt (διστάζειν) and why are you afraid?)' in Mt 14 31[73] Whilst the use of διστάζειν in both contexts is striking,[74] a more probable source for the words used here is the note in Matthew's resurrection scene that 'some doubted (ἐδίστασαν)'.[75] Thus it is most likely that the author of ApocJohn built up the introductory scene from the material of Matthew's resurrection appearance scene,[76] Thus ApocJohn is probably presupposing Matthew's gospel.[76a]

Other synoptic allusions are harder to find. One may be found in the passage referring to the fate of apostates from the true faith, where it is said (following the *NHLE* translation of the Codex II text) 'they will be kept for the

---

[72] Till, *Papyrus Berolinensis 8502*, p.8. Wilson, *Gnosis and the New Testament*, 106, calls this example 'the strongest claimant' to be considered as a NT allusion in the text.

[73] S. Giversen, *Apocryphon Johannis*, Copenhagen 1963, 156.

[74] One should, however, be wary of assuming that a Greek loan word in a Coptic text necessarily implies the presence of the same Greek word in the original. διστάζειν occurs in the Codex IV version (3.2f.) but not in the Berlin text at this point. However, the latter version (ετβε ογ εκο ν2ητ cναγ) uses what is probably the standard Coptic equivalent (cf. W.C. Crum, *A Coptic Dictionary*, Oxford 1939, 714b, and Mt 14.31 boh). διστάζειν is used in the sahidic version at Mt 14.31 and 28.17. The relevant part of the text is missing from the Codex III version.

[75] R.M. Grant, *Gnosticism. An Anthology*, London 1961, 70, gives Mt 28.17 as the parallel here.

[76] Janssens, 'L'Apocryphon de Jean', *Muséon* 83 (1970) 161f.; Perkins, *Gnostic Dialogue*, 55.

[76a] Mt 28.16-20 is widely recognised as being heavily influenced by MtR. See G. Strecker, *Gerechtigkeit*, 208ff.; Barth in G. Bornkamm, G. Barth, H.J. Held, *Tradition and Interpretation in Matthew*, 131ff., and others.

day on which those who have blasphemed the spirit will be tortured' (27.27-29). This seems to be reminiscent of the synoptic saying about blasphemy against the Holy Spirit (Mt 12.31/Mk 3.29/Lk 12.10), and this allusion seems to be stronger in the Codex III and BG versions of the text which both refer to the 'holy spirit'.[77] The Coptic ϫⲉ ⲟⲩⲁ (used in all four versions) is regularly used as a translation of the Greek *βλασφήμειν* so that it may well be that a synoptic allusion is indeed present.[78] Even if this is the case, the text still permits no decision about which form of synoptic tradition is presupposed here. The saying about blasphemy against the Holy Spirit is a Markan (and conceivably also Q) saying which occurs in all three synoptic gospels. Hence one cannot say on the basis of this evidence alone which gospel (or source) is presupposed by ApocJohn here. The opening scene shows clear dependence on the gospel of Matthew; this later allusion could perfectly well have been derived from Matthew's gospel as well, though one cannot by the very nature of the case prove this.

In conclusion, ApocJohn (at least in its final form) shows knowledge of Matthew's gospel, and the evidence of the text is at least consistent with the theory that it is Matthew's gospel alone which provides all the synoptic tradition alluded to in this text.

---

[77] The parallel is noted by Krause in his translation of the BG text in Foerster (ed.), *Gnosis*, Oxford 1972, 119; also Grant, op.cit., 84; Giversen, op.cit., 268, calls it 'a clear allusion to Matthew 12,31'.

[78] Hence the Christianising process (if such it is) has gone a little deeper than merely providing the setting for the discourse. It is, however, striking that the allusion is clearer in the two shorter recensions of the text. In general, the longer recensions are often considered to be more 'Christianised', in that the functions of various revelatory figures are there concentrated on to the person of Christ: see S. Arai, 'Zur Christologie des Apokryphons des Johannes', *NTS* 15 (1969) 302-318; Perkins, op.cit., 91f.

The *Hypostasis of the Archons* (II.4) is another text exhibiting only marginal Christian influence.[79] The opening of the text includes a citation of Eph 6.12 and at the end there is a clear allusion to Jn 14.26 (96.35: 'the Spirit of Truth which the Father has sent').[80] The most probable example of a synoptic allusion in the body of the text is the note in 88.2f. about the archons 'not understanding the force (δύναμις) of God', which may be a reminiscence of the words of Jesus in Mk 12.24/Mt 22.29.[81] Bullard notes no biblical parallel here, but he does suggest that that the use of the noun 'God' here is unusual and he ascribes the phrase to a Christian gnostic redactor (who he believes is combining two prior sources to produce the present text).[82] The fact that the language is not unrelated to synoptic tradition may add some support to Bullard's theory, and the latter in turn may equally add some weight to the view that synoptic language is indeed echoed here. However one cannot be any more precise about which form of synoptic tradition is closest to the text, since Mark and Matthew are almost identical here.

Other synoptic allusions are difficult to establish with any degree of certainty. The appearance of the angel to Norea who asks about the angel's identity (93.8–11) is similar in general terms to the encounter between

---

[79] For editions and translations of the text, see P. Nagel, *Das Wesen der Archonten aus Codex II der gnostischen Bibliothek von Nag Hammadi*, Halle 1970; R.A. Bullard, *The Hypostasis of the Archons*, *PTS* 10, Berlin 1970; B. Layton, 'The Hypostasis of the Archons', *HThR* 67 (1974) 351-425, and 69 (1976) 31-101; also M. Tardieu, *Trois Mythes Gnostiques. Adam, Éros, et les animaux d'Egypte dans un écrit de Nag Hammadi* (II.5), Paris 1974, who includes a translation of this text.

[80] Cf. Wilson, *Gnosis and the New Testament*, 125, who also says that in between these two, 'there appear to be no obvious Christian elements'.

[81] Cf. Nagel, op.cit., 34; Layton, *HThR* 69, 38; Tardieu, op.cit., 285.

[82] Bullard, op.cit., 65.

Zachariah and Gabriel in Lk 1.19;[83] however, the scene has other parallels (cf. Gen 32.39; Jud 13.17; cf. also Tob 12.15) and it seems unnecessary to see any direct synoptic influence here. Again, the description of the angel's clothing in 93.14f. ('his appearance is like fine gold and his raiment is like snow') exhibits some parallelism with Mt 28.3;[84] but again the language is not unique to the Matthaean account,[85] and there seems little justification for assuming an allusion to the synoptic narrative.

One further possible synoptic allusion may be present in the text at 87.10f. Layton's translation in the *NHLE* volume ('by starting from the invisible world the visible world was invented') is fairly free: a more literal translation would be that of Bullard 'for out of the hidden have been found the revealed'.[86] Tardieu suggests a parallel in the synoptic saying Mk 4.22 and pars, as well as referring to GTh 5, 6, 83, 108 (which in turn probably bear some relationship to the synoptic saying) as well as GPh 57.24-26 and ThomCont 138.24-30.[87] The synoptic saying is explicitly cited in OrigWorld (see below) and the close relationship between these two texts may suggest that the saying is echoed here. Nevertheless if it is echoed, it is used here in a very indirect way, and Bullard prefers to think of the phrase as 'evidently a proverb handed down in the Gnostic tradition.'[88]

---

[83] The parallel is pointed out by Nagel, op.cit., 52; Layton, op.cit., 43; Tardieu, op.cit., 290.

[84] Cf. Nagel, op.cit., 54; Tardieu, op.cit., 291, compares Mt 17.2 as well but this is less close.

[85] For the 'snow' imagery, cf. Dan 7.9; Rev 1.14; ApocAbr 11; 1 En 14.20; 106.2; Hermas, *Sim*, 8.2.3; for the 'gold' imagery, cf. Dan 10.5; Rev 1.13.

[86] Bullard, op.cit., 23; Similarly Tardieu, op.cit., 284, and Nagel, op.cit., 33. The Coptic is ⲉⲃⲟⲗ ϩⲛ ⲛⲉⲑⲏⲧ ⲁⲩϩⲓⲉ ⲁⲛⲉⲧⲟⲩⲟⲛϩ ⲉⲃⲟⲗ Layton himself admits that his translation is a free one (*HThR* 69, 48).

[87] Tardieu, ibid.

[88] Bullard, op.cit., 55.

This text thus gives at best indirect allusions to the synoptic tradition, and there is not enough evidence to determine the form of the synoptic tradition which is presupposed (if indeed it is at all) by the author.

Similar results emerge from the closely related tractate which follows HypArch in Codex II, *On the Origin of the World* (II.5). There is however one explicit citation of synoptic tradition in 125.17f., where the 'Logos' is quoted as saying 'There is nothing hidden which will not appear, and what was unknown will be known'. The reference here to 'being known' suggests that the Q version of the saying (Mt 10.26/Lk 12.2) is in mind, rather than the Markan one (Mk 4. 22; Lk 8.17 represents a conflation of the two forms). However it is impossible to say whether it is Q or Matthew or Luke or another post-synoptic source which is presupposed here.

Some have claimed that there is a clear synoptic allusion in the reference to the 'blessed little guileless spirits' and 'the angel who appears before them' and who 'stands in front of the Father' (124.10-23, cf. Mt 18.10).[89] However, the idea of guardian angels is well-established in the NT period and there seems insufficient reason for seeing a synoptic allusion here. Tardieu refers to a number of synoptic parallels throughout his translation of this text. But nearly all of them involve at best a loose parallel in content but little verbal agreement, and in most cases the synoptic passage in question is simply reflecting standard ideas for which there are numerous non-

[89] A. Böhlig & P. Labib, *Die koptisch-gnostisch Schrift ohne Titel aus Codex II von Nag Hammadi*, Berlin 1962, 33, 100. Tardieu, op.cit., 331, also compares Mt 5.8 but this does not seem so close. (On 44 n.186 he implies that the allusion is to Mt 5.3). On 72 n.163 he notes that Mt 18.10 and 5.8 are connected in *ExcTheod* 11.1—but there it is a case of an explicit citation.

synoptic parallels. For example, the description of the woes in 126.10ff. ('The sun will darken and the moon will lose its light. The stars of heaven will disregard their course and a great thunder will come out of a great power . . . ') has parallels with the synoptic apocalypse (cf. Mt 24.29) but both texts are clearly reflecting typical apocalyptic imagery.[90] Perhaps a stronger case can be made for seeing some influence of the synoptic tradition in the reference to the three baptisms in 122.14-16: 'the first is spiritual, the second is a fire, the third is water'.[91] This does appear to be reminiscent of the Q account of John the Baptist's preaching of a coming baptism with spirit and fire which will supersede his own water baptism (Mt 3.11/Lk 3.16), though this prophecy is given an individual interpretation in that the future baptism is apparently further subdivided.

There is thus little that is explicitly Christian here,[92] and very little to determine which form of synoptic tradition was presupposed by the author/redactor who produced the final text. The clearest synoptic echoes are of Q material, though the allusions involved are too meagre for one to be able to say whether it is Q, rather than Matthew's or Luke's gospel, which is presupposed here.

It is almost universally agreed that the *Sophia of Jesus Christ* (III,4 and BG 8502,3) represents the Christianising of a non-Christian *Vorlage*. In this case we have the *Vorlage* itself, for SJC is a re-working by a Christian editor of the non-Christian letter of Eugnostos.[93] SJC

---

[90] Tardieu himself gives numerous parallels here (op.cit., 338).

[91] Tardieu, op.cit., 328.

[92] The Christian elements are regarded as secondary according to Tröger (ed.), *Gnosis und Neues Testament*, 36.

[93] See the essays of Krause and Ménard, mentioned above (n.26) on Eug.

adds to the monologue of Eug various questions posed by the Christian disciples of Jesus to create a dialogue between Jesus and the disciples (though the fact that the questions fit so badly, so that frequently a question is unrelated to the 'answer' which follows, shows that the dialogue structure is secondary). SJC clearly shows some knowledge of synoptic tradition, though in fact the greater part of the extra material added by SJC to Eug is not self-evidently Christian apart from the identification of the speakers in the dialogue as well-known Christian figures.[94] The names of the speakers do not reveal very much: the disciples named are Philip, Matthew, Thomas, Mariamme and Bartholomew, nearly all of whom appear elsewhere in the Nag Hammadi texts.[95]

The opening scene is richest in its allusions to synoptic tradition. At 90.15ff. (77.12ff.)[96] the text provides a setting for the discourse as a resurrection appearance of Jesus to the 'twelve disciples and seven women' on a mountain in Galilee. It is likely that the model for this scene is the resurrection appearance tradition in Mt 28.16-20. The fact that this tradition is known to the author is probably confirmed by a later addition made in SJC to Eug at 101.13f., which talks of the redeemer 'who is with you until the end of the poverty of the robbers', probably echoing Mt 28.20. 91.18ff. (79.7f.) appears to refer to the transfiguration tradition[97] (though in such

---

94 The largest addition in SJC is an explicit account of the fall of Sophia (114.13ff.) to explain the deficiency of the woman; Eug omitted this episode, apparently assuming it as well-known: cf. Ménard, 'Normative Self-Definition', 139f.

95 Philip appears in GPh and EpPetPhil; Matthew in GTh, DialSav; Thomas in GTh, ThomCont; Mariamme in DialSav; Bartholomew does not appear elsewhere in the Nag Hammadi texts; however, all five appear in the Pistis Sophia.

96 The first reference is to the Codex III version; the bracketed reference refers to the BG version.

97 Cf. Wilson, *Gnosis and the New Testament*, 114.

general terms that one cannot identify the form of the tradition presupposed with any more precision). The scene is located 'on the mountain called "of the Olives" in Galilee' (91.20). To what extent this shows knowledge of the synoptic tradition is not clear. The Mount of Olives is mentioned by the synoptic evangelists (cf. Mk 11.1; 13.3; 14.26 and pars.; Lk 19.37; 21.37; Acts 1.12), though only the Acts 1 passage is remotely relevant here. Acts 1 suggests an appearance of the *risen* Jesus on the Mount of Olives. It is possible that in fact the writer is referring to an earlier *resurrection* appearance on the Mount of Olives, rather than to the transfiguration story; alternatively, it is just possible that the transfiguration story is being interpreted as a resurrection appearance (though whether this is a pre-synoptic or post-synoptic feature is impossible to say).[98] In any case it may be that SJC is here presupposing Luke's resurrection tradition as well as Matthew's. This possibility may receive some support from the words of the Saviour which follow: 'Peace to you. My peace I give you'. This may reflect knowledge of Lk 24.36. However, this verse is paralleled in Jn 20.19 and is also, notoriously, a 'Western non-interpolation'; further, the second half of the greeting is close to the wording of Jn 14.27 with no Lukan parallel, so that it may be that all the language here is inspired by John's gospel rather than Luke's. The following words of the Saviour

[98] Such an interpenetration of the two traditions may be reflected in 2 Pet 1.16f.: see J.M. Robinson, 'Jesus from Easter to Valentinus (or to the Apostles' Creed)', *JBL* 101 (1982) 5-37, 8f. There is of course great debate as to whether the transfiguration story was originally an account of a resurrection appearance. Cf. the differing views of C.H. Dodd, 'The Appearances of the Risen Christ: An Essay in Form-Criticism of the Gospels', in *Studies in the Gospels*, Oxford, 1955, 9-35, and R.H. Stein, 'Is the Transfiguration a misplaced Resurrection Account?', *JBL* 95 (1976) 79-96. on the one hand, and C.E. Carlston, 'Transfiguration and Resurrection', *JBL* 80 (1961) 233-240, and Robinson, ibid., 9f., on the other.

('What are you thinking about? Why are you perplexed? What are you searching for?' 92.1-4 (79.13-18)) may also reflect Luke's gospel, viz. Lk 24.38,[99] though again such questions recur elsewhere in the NT. Probably the most one can say is that a consistent picture emerges if one postulates dependence of SJC on the Lukan account, but one must admit that there is nothing which positively demands such a theory.

Further synoptic allusions may be found elsewhere. Four times SJC adds to Eug by repeating the stereotyped formula 'He who has ears to hear let him hear' (97.21f.; 98.21f.; 105.9-11; 107.19f. (89.4f.; 90.13f.; 100.10-12; 107.18-108.1), and this is probably intended to echo texts such as Mk 4.9 and pars., Mt 11.15 etc.[100] However, it is clearly impossible to say precisely which form of synoptic tradition is presupposed here. The saying has evidently become a stock phrase pointing to a deeper interpretation of an obscure saying.[101] On another four occasions SJC refers to the 'robbers', apparently as those who imprison the soul in this corporeal existence (cf. 101.15; 107.16; BG 121.3, 10). This *may* be an allusion to a specific interpretation of the parable of the Good Samaritan, where the action of the robbers is interpreted as that of imprisoning the soul in the world. The parable was widely known and used in the early church, and appears to have been popular in Gnostic circles.[102] Further, this particular

---

[99] So Till, *Papyrus Berolinensis 8502*, 199.

[100] Cf. Till, ad locc.; Wilson, op.cit., 114.

[101] Cf. J.M. Robinson, 'Gnosticism and the New Testament', 135f.

[102] Cf. W. Monselewski, *Der barmherzige Samariter. Eine auslegungsgeschichtliche Untersuchung zu Lukas 10,25-37*, *BGBE* 51, Tübingen, 1967, esp. 49. He argues that Gnostic interpretations of the parable were current very early, and that interpretation by the 'orthodox' fathers can be seen as an attempt to counter Gnostic exegesis. However, Monselewski does not note the Nag Hammadi evidence in his otherwise exhaustive survey of interpretations of the parable, as his work appeared before much of this evidence was published.

interpretation of the action of the robbers appears to have been characteristic of Gnostic exegesis.[103] However, one must also admit that if an allusion to the parable is intended here, it is very indirect. A further synoptic allusion is probably present in 119.4-8 ('I have given you authority over all things as sons of light so that you might tread upon their power with your feet'). The language is similar to Lk 10.19 and may be derived from there but it is not identical.

At 93.16-19 (82.9f.) the author of SJC rewrites his source in Eug to read 'Whatever is fitting for you to know, and those who are worthy of knowledge, will be given them'. The grammar here seems somewhat disrupted but there may be an echo of the synoptic saying Mt 13.11 and pars., though it is fairly remote. Finally, in 94.9-13 (83.13-15) SJC qualifies Eug's claim that the supreme being is known to no sovereignty, authority or creature except himself, by adding 'and anyone to whom he wills to make revelation through him who is from the First Light'. This looks very much like a re-writing of the Q saying Mt 11.27/Lk 10.22, though the parallel is not close enough for one to be able to say precisely which version is presupposed.

In conclusion, the author of SJC seems to know both Matthew's and Luke's gospels and uses the traditions as found in these gospels to Christianise his basic source of Eug.

Finally in the category of texts which may represent a secondary Christianising of non-Christian source material, one should probably include the *Gospel of*

[103] Ibid., 22ff.

Mary from BG 8502.[104] The NT echoes in this text are spread very unevenly, and this fact, along with other considerations, has led to the belief that there may originally have been two separate sections of source material which were subsequently combined by a Christian redactor.[105]

Whatever the precise prehistory of the text, there is a very striking cluster of synoptic allusions at 8.14-22: '(14) Peace be with you. Receive (15) my peace to yourselves. Beware that no one (16) lead you astray, saying (17) "Lo here!" or "Lo (18) there!" For the Son of Man (19) is within you. Follow (20) after him. Those who seek him will (21) find him. Go then and preach (22) the gospel of the Kingdom.' This seems to be a deliberate attempt to supply material known to be authentically Christian. 8.14f. recalls Lk 24.36 (perhaps also Jn 20.19) and Jn 14.27, though the standard Semitic peace greeting cannot of itself prove very much.[106] 8.15f. recalls Mt 24.5/Mk 13.5. 8.17f. is perhaps closest to Luke's version of this saying (Lk 17.23) since the parallels in Matthew and Mark both add ὁ Χριστός (Mt 24.23; Mk 13.21); further, Matthew's version has a repeated ὧδε rather than ὧδε and ἐκεῖ.[107] If one can rely on the Coptic version here as

[104] Editions of the text can be found in Till, *Papyrus Berolinensis 8502*, and in Parrott (ed.) *Codices V and VI*, 453-471. The NT allusions are discussed by R. McL. Wilson, 'The New Testament in the Gnostic Gospel of Mary', *NTS* 3 (1957) 236-243.

[105] Cf. Till, op.cit., 26; Wilson, op.cit., 238.

[106] Cf. the similar problems with the very similar text in SJC 91.21-23 discussed above (p. 33).

[107] Wilson, op.cit., 241, says that there is variation in the textual tradition of Luke here, with B reading ὧδε repeated. This does not agree with the note in the critical apparatus of the Nestle-Aland text, according to which B reads ἐκεῖ. . .ὧδε. . .ὧδε.ἐκεῖ is read by a large number of MSS, including A D W Θ old lat and most later MSS. If translated strictly, the Coptic text here ⲙⲡⲉⲓ̈ⲥⲁ. . . ⲙⲡⲉⲉⲓ̈ⲙⲁ might suggest that the version from which this derived read ἐκεῖ. . .ὧδε (cf. Crum's *Dictionary*, 154b, 313a), although Till translates '"Sieht hier" oder "Sieht da"'. However, it is dubious if one can place too much weight on such tiny details of a text in translation.

accurately reflecting differences in the original Greek,[108] then this implies knowledge of Luke's (or perhaps Mark's) text. 8.18f. looks very much like a revised version of Lk 17.21, with 'Son of Man' replacing 'Kingdom of God', a change which may have received some impetus from the fact that the following verses in Lk 17 talk of the coming of the 'Son of Man'. This would also support the view that it is the Lukan, rather than the Markan, version of the saying in Mk 13.21 / Lk 17.23 which is reflected in GMary 8.17f. just considered.[109] The saying about seeking and finding (8.20f.) seems to be very closely related to the Q saying in Mt 7.7 / Lk 11.9, though again with a Christological twist whereby the Saviour himself becomes the object of the seeking. This saying was widely used by the Gnostics,[110] and the presence of the saying here within a cluster of synoptic allusions makes it reasonable to suppose that the author deliberately intended to allude to this gospel saying. However, Matthew and Luke are identical here, so that it is impossible to say whether GMary is dependent on Matthew or Luke or a prior source.

The final allusion in this catena is the charge 'go and preach the gospel of the kingdom' (8.21f.). Till here refers to Mt 4.23; 9.35,[111] presumably because of the phrase 'gospel of the kingdom'. Wilson disagrees and,

---

[108] The existence of a Greek *Vorlage* to the present Coptic text is rendered even more probable by the existence of an early (3rd century) Greek papyrus fragment of the gospel: see C.H. Roberts, *Catalogue of the Greek and Latin Papyri in the John Rylands Library of Manchester III,* Manchester 1938 18-23.

[109] Cf. also below, p.128, on 2LogSeth 65.20.

[110] Cf. B. Gärtner, *The Theology of the Gospel of Thomas*, London 1961, 258ff.; J-É. Ménard, *L'Évangile selon Thomas*, *NHS* 5, Leiden 1975, 193; H. Koester, 'Gnostic Writings as Witnesses for the Development of the Sayings Tradition', in *The School of Valentinus*, Leiden 1980, 238-240. See too the extended discussion by Tertullian *De Praescr.* 8-13 and 43.

[111] Op.cit., 65.

presumably on the basis of the 'go and preach' phrase, refers to Mk 16.15.[112] But it seems doubtful whether one should give so much weight to the 'go and' element. A far more likely source is Mt 24.15 which also contains the phrase 'gospel of the kingdom'. For a little later in GMary, the disciples echo the Saviour's command and imply that they have been told to go to the Gentiles: 'How shall we go to the Gentiles and preach the gospel of the kingdom of the Son of Man?' (9.8-10). Only Mt 24.15 of the possible NT texts explicitly refers to the Gentiles ('This gospel of the kingdom must be preached . . . as a testimony to all the Gentiles'). Moreover, this text in Matthew is due to MtR of Mark, and hence GMary presupposes Matthew's finished gospel rather than Matthew's source here. If this is the case, then four of the five synoptic allusions here derive from the apocalyptic discourses of the synoptic gospels. Further, GMary appears to presuppose Matthew's redactional work and also Luke's (probably redactional) arrangement of his material in Lk 17. It looks very much as if the author here knew these discourses in their present synoptic form (or at least Matthew and Luke) and wove together various sayings to form the present cluster of allusions.

Other synoptic allusions in GMary are rare, and it is less certain if any deliberate allusion is intended. Wilson refers to the words 'He who has ears to hear, let him hear' in 7.8f. and 8.10f. (cf. Mt 11.15 and similar texts in the synoptics).[113] However, as already noted, the saying had become something of a stock phrase,[114] and this probably makes it precarious to conclude too much about GMary's

---

[112] Op.cit., 243.

[113] Op.cit., 240.

[114] Cf. p. 34 above and the discussion on the four occurrences of this in SJC.

dependence on the synoptic tradition. It may be significant that GMary at one point quotes a variant of this aphorism in the form 'He who understands, let him understand', which may link with a similar version in some Western MSS at Mk 4.9.[115] Since this variant appears to occur nowhere else in the synoptic tradition, this might show knowledge of the Western text of Mark by the author of GMary here. However, the proverbial nature of the saying necessitates caution here.[116]

The second part of the document tells of the journey of the soul who converses with five great powers. During the conversation with the third power, ignorance, the latter says 'Do not judge', to which the soul replies 'Why do you judge me, although I have not judged?' (15.16-18). Some have suggested that this alludes to Mt 7.1f./Lk 6.37.[117] However, this is by no means certain. The words 'Do not judge' are here placed on the lips of the hostile power. Further, the words of the soul's reply appear to have been proverbial and not peculiarly Christian.[118] It is thus doubtful if there is any conscious allusion to the synoptic tradition. Similarly, the saying in 17.4f. ('From this time on I will attain to the rest') *may* allude to Mt 11.29;[119] but

---

[115] Wilson, op.cit., 241.

[116] See too Wilson's cautious remarks (241, n.3): 'The words might be only a literary variation of the earlier part of the verse. Nor do we know whether these words stood in the Greek original or are due to expansion by the Coptic translator.' It must also be borne in mind that the relationships between texts like GMary and variant readings in the canonical gospels are not necessarily one-way only: see n.19 above.

[117] Wilson, op.cit., 243.

[118] See Allen, *Matthew*, 66; also D. Zeller, *Die weisheitlichen Mahnsprüche bei den Synoptikern, FzB* 17, Würzburg 1977, 115f. On the other hand, the saying was known and used as a saying of Jesus very early, possibly independent of the synoptic tradition: see H. Koester, *Synoptische Überlieferung bei den apostolischen Vätern, TU* 65, Berlin 1957. 12-16, commenting on the use of a similar saying in 1 Clem 13.2.

[119] Cf. Wilson, op.cit., 238.

the 'rest' motif recurs frequently elsewhere in Gnostic circles and in primitive Christianity,[120] and its occurrence here needs no NT text to explain it.

The final saying to be considered here occurs in 10.15f.: 'Where the mind is, there is the treasure.'[121] Quispel refers to similar versions of this saying in Clement of Alexandria (*Strom.* VII. 12.77; *Q.D.S.* 17; cf. *Strom.* IV. 6.33), Macarius (*Hom.* 43.3) and above all Justin (*Apol.* 1.15.16). He argues that the variant forms of what appear to be synoptic allusions in Justin, which frequently agree with 'quotations' in the Pseudo-Clementine Homilies and Recognitions, are due to common dependence on an independent gospel, the Gospel of the Hebrews.[122] However, the recent studies of Bellinzoni and Kline have suggested that these variant forms are more probably due to use of a post-synoptic harmony of the present gospels, rather than to dependence on an independent gospel.[123] In this case, the widespread occurrence of this form of the saying suggests a common tradition, but Bellinzoni

---

[120] See Gärtner, *Thomas*, 265ff.; P. Vielhauer, 'Ἀνάπαυσις' in *Apophoreta*, *BZNW* 30, Berlin 1964, 281-299; M.L. Peel, *The Epistle to Rheginos*, London 1969, 54, 142f.

[121] For this translation, see G. Quispel. 'Das Hebräerevangelium im gnostischen Evangelium nach Maria; *VigChr* 11 (1957) 139. Till allows 'treasure' as a possible rendering, but prefers 'your face' (πε-ϩο for π-εϩο). Quispel's argument has evidently been accepted by MacRae and Wilson in their translation of the text, in *NHLE* and in Parrott (ed.) *Codices V and VI.*

[122] Quispel, op. cit., 139-141. The same version of the logion is also alluded to in Auth Teach 28.23-7 (see p. 49 below) and probably Sentences of Sextus 316 (see p. 17 above).

[123] A. Bellinzoni, *The Sayings of Jesus in the Writings of Justin Martyr, Nt.S 17*, Leiden 1967; L.L. Kline, *The Sayings of Jesus in the Pseudo-Clementine Homilies, SBLDS* 14, Missoula 1975. But see too the discussion of G. Strecker, 'Eine Evangelienhamonie bei Justin und Pseudoklemens?', *NTS* 24 (1978) 297-316, who argues that it is probably wrong to look for a single literary explanation of all these agreements: one must take into account that citations were often very free, and one must also not ignore the possible existence of oral tradition.

argues that its ultimate source is Mt 6.21 (or Lk 12.34).[124] It is possible that the change from 'heart' to 'mind' was due to an attempt to use more philosophical, and less Jewish, terminology;[125] also the inversion of the order of the phrases produces a significant alteration in meaning: the 'place' which is valued is no longer defined to be where 'treasure' is, but where *νοῦς* is. This looks to be a secondary development of the original saying. If this is so, then GMary gives a developed form of the logion, and this may mean that it is only indirectly dependent on the synoptic tradition at this point.[126]

If one accepts Till's and Wilson's division of the text into two parts, then it would appear that each section within itself makes only passing reference to the synoptic tradition, using either stock phrases (7.8f; 8.10f.), or sayings which reveal secondary development from their synoptic form (10.15f.). These sections are not using in any direct way a stratum of the synoptic tradition which can be readily identified. The situation seems to be quite different in 8.14-22 (perhaps the work of a later redactor), where the author appears to be deliberately alluding to synoptic sayings. Moreover, the forms of these sayings suggests that the author was acquainted with the finished gospels of Matthew and Luke, and that he formed this section from texts which were mostly taken from the apocalyptic discourses. It was clearly very important for

---

[124] Op. cit., 92, 98.

[125] So E. Massaux, 'Le texte du sermon sur la Montagne utilisé par Saint Justin', *EThL* 28 (1952) 437f.; cf. too Delling's comment, cited above (n 38). Massaux attributes the change to Justin himself, but it is hard to see GMary as dependent on Justin's work.

[126] I would thus agree with Quispel that there is not necessarily any direct use of synoptic tradition here. Whether the source for the saying is the Gospel of the Hebrews is, however, uncertain. There is nothing to indicate that this form of the saying is not a development of the synoptic saying, though when this development first took place is not clear.

the compiler of this section of GMary that the speaker be plainly identifiable as Jesus in a way that was apparently not the case for the rest of the text.

One may now turn to the rest of the Nag Hammadi corpus and to texts which are more fundamentally Christian. As has already been noted, the Nag Hammadi texts are not all Gnostic. One such non-Gnostic text is the *Teachings of Silvanus* (VII, 4). This is a Christian-Wisdom text, teaching a non-docetic Chistology and a non-gnostic soteriology. Its 'orthodox' nature is such that a section of it was later appropriated and attributed to St. Anthony.[127] There are very clear theological affinities linking this text with the Wisdom literature[128] and with Alexandrian Christianity.[129] For the present purposes, however, its primary interest is the link with the synoptic tradition. It is perhaps surprising that despite the great stress here on Christ as a teacher (cf. for example 91.1; 110.18) and on exhortations to 'keep the holy commands of Jesus Christ' (cf. 91.25f.), there is no explicit quotation of anything which claims to be Jesus' teaching. The author chooses to write his treatise as coming from the lips of Silvanus (presumably Paul's companion is in mind) rather than Jesus. Nevertheless, it is clear that at times synoptic tradition is echoed. In the case of this text it is even more difficult to know when that tradition is clearly in mind. For when the links are with the teachings of Jesus in the gospels which in their turn show links with

[127] Cf. W.-P. Funk, '"Die Lehren des Silvanus"—Die vierte Schrift aus Nag-Hammadi-Codex VII' *ThLZ* 100 (1975) 7-23.

[128] Cf. W.R. Schoedel, 'Jewish Wisdom and the Formation of the Christian Ascetic', in *Aspects of Wisdom*, Notre Dame-London 1975, 169-199.

[129] See especially J. Zandee, *"The Teachings of Silvanus" and Clement of Alexandria: A New Document of Alexandrian Theology*, Leiden 1977.

Jewish Wisdom teachings, one cannot be sure whether TeachSilv is presupposing the gospel tradition or the Wisdom tradition underlying it.

Some passages, however, clearly refer to the gospel tradition and to the life of Jesus. In 109.15-20 there is an allegorical interpretation of the cleansing of the temple: 'Let him enter the temple which is within you so that he may cast out all the merchants. Let him dwell in the temple which is within you, and may you become for him a priest and a Levite, entering in purity.'[130] However, one cannot really say which synoptic version is presupposed here, as the reference is very general. Jesus' life and death are referred to in 104.12f., where it is said that the incarnation (here described under the image of a *descensus ad infernos*)[131] took place so that Jesus 'might die for you as a ransom for your sin'. This appears to reflect Mt 20.28/Mk 10.45 (or perhaps 1 Tim 2.6). *If* synoptic tradition is in the writer's mind, one can only say that it cannot be Luke's gospel here.

In the actual teaching that is given in the text, there are numerous echoes of the NT,[132] though one cannot be certain how much is coincidental. The saying in 88.20-22 ('do not become a guide on behalf of your blind ignorance') echoes Mt 15.14,[133] but sayings about 'blind guides' are proverbial[134] so that one cannot be certain that it is the gospel tradition which has supplied the thought here. Just prior to this is the exhortation 'Accept the light for your eyes and cast the darkness from you. Live in

130 Cf. Schoedel, op. cit., 195; also M.L. Peel-J. Zandee, 'The Teachings of Silvanus from the Library of Nag Hammadi', *NT* 14 (1972) 294-311, esp. 301.
131 On these *descensus* passages, see M.L. Peel 'The "Decensus ad Infernos" in "The Teachings of Silvanus" (CG VII, 4)', *Numen* 26 (1979) 23-49.
132 Peel and Zandee, op. cit., 302f.
133 Ibid.
134 See W. Schrage, art. *Τυφλός*, *ThWNT* 8, 275.

Christ, and you will acquire a treasure in heaven' (88.13-17). Both parts of this exhortation are perhaps commonplaces, but it may be significant that two related sayings occur next to each other in Mt 6: Mt 6.22 has 'the lamp of your body is your eye', and 6.19-21 has the saying about laying up treasure in heaven. It may be, therefore, that the author of TeachSilv has put these two together on the basis of his source material; further, since the two sayings are separated in the Lukan parallels, and since Q's order is usually taken to be more faithfully preserved by Luke, the collocation of these two sayings in Mt 6 is probably due to MtR. Thus TeachSilv presupposes Matthew's redactional arrangement and hence Matthew's finished gospel.

A further allusion to synoptic material may be present in 95.7-11: 'It is fitting for you to be in agreement with the intelligence of these two: with the intelligence of the snake and the innocence of the dove'. This is clearly similar to Mt 10.16.[135] Further, the reference to 'innocence' is really extraneous to the context here (where the main concern is 'intelligence'); it thus looks as if the 'innocence of the dove' is a traditional feature for the writer, linked in his tradition with the 'intelligence of the snake' which is what he is really concerned with here (cf. line 6f.). Dependence on Mt 10.16 would fit the facts very well; the saying in Mt 10 has all the hallmarks of a piece of proverbial wisdom although it is difficult to parallel it exactly elsewhere.[136] It may well be, therefore, that TeachSilv reflects Mt 10.16 directly and there is nothing so far to suggest that the author is dependent on anything other than Matthew's finished gospel for his synoptic material.

---

[135] Peel and Zandee. op. cit., 302.

[136] The parallel always quoted in relation to Mt 10.16 is MidrCant ii.14: 'God saith of the Israelites, Towards me they are sincere as doves but towards the Gentiles they are prudent as serpents.'

It is said in 99.16-20 that Christ 'gives light to every place. This is also the way in which he speaks of our mind, as if it were a lamp which burns and lights up the place. Being in a part of the soul, it gives light to all the parts.' Peel and Zandee refer here to Lk 11.34-36, saying that the replacement of *οφθαλμός* with *νοῦς* is due to Stoic influence.[137] This latter claim about the difference in terminology may well be right, but there is little to distinguish Lk 11.34-36 from its Matthaean parallel in Mt 6.22f. in this respect. In fact the text here seems to conflate the saying about the mind/eye being a lamp (Mt 6.22f/Lk 11.34-36) and that of the lamp lighting up the whole 'place' (cf. Mt 5.15/Mk 4.21/Lk 8.16; 11.33). It may be significant that the two sayings come next to each other in Lk 11. On the other hand the lamp is said explicitly to 'light' the whole place where it is set only in Mt 5.15.[138] It may be therefore that TeachSilv has conflated Mt 5.15 with 6.22f/Lk 11.34f. There is thus no need to see dependence here on Luke and the text can be adequately explained on the basis of Matthew's gospel alone.

In 103.19-26, the text says 'those who walk in the broad way will go down at their end to the perdition of the mire. For the Underworld is open wide for the soul and the place of perdition is broad. Accept Christ the narrow way.' This appears to be inspired by Mt 7.13f.,[139] and indeed by the Matthaean form of the saying, since Luke's parallel (Lk 13.23f.) speaks only of entering through a narrow door. TeachSilv seems to be referring both to a door (probably implied in the note that 'the Underworld is open wide for the soul') and to a 'way'. This is thus again

---

[137] Op. cit., 302

[138] Although it must be admitted that this might be derived from Lk 11.36 (end) where it is said that the light lights 'you'.

[139] Peel and Zandee, op. cit., 302.

consistent with the view that TeachSilv presupposes Matthew's gospel. The text in 104.21-24 ('if you humble yourself, you will be greatly exalted. And if you exalt yourself, you will be exceedingly humbled') has parallels in the gospels in Mt 23.12; Lk 14.11; 18.14, although the sentiment can be paralleled in Judaism (cf. Prov 29.23; Ezek 21.26; LevR 1.5; Erub 13b).[140] One cannot be entirely sure that the gospel saying itself is echoed here; and even if it is there is nothing to decide between Matthew and Luke as the source of the allusion. Finally the text in 117.5-9 ('Open the door for yourself that you may know what is. Knock on yourself that the Word may open for you') and 117.19-22 ('That which you will open for yourself, you will open. That which you will knock upon for yourself, you will knock upon') looks as if it may reflect the 'knock and it shall be opened to you' saying in Mt 7.7/Lk 11.9.[141] Other possible synoptic allusions seem more remote.

In all, TeachSilv clearly seems to presuppose Matthew's gospel. Further, there is nothing here which would suggest that the author knew any other form of synoptic tradition: all the synoptic allusions can be satisfactorily explained on the basis of a knowledge of Matthew's gospel alone.[142] Such a conclusion may have repercussions about the dating of the text,[143] and may indicate a slightly earlier date than has been suggested in the past (though arguments from silence of this nature

140 Cf. J. Jeremias, *The Parables of Jesus*, London 1963, 107; I.H. Marshall, *The Gospel of Luke*, Exeter 1977, 583.

141 Schoedel, 'Jewish Wisdom', 195.

142 Thus contra Peel and Zandee who claim that TeachSilv knows Luke as well as Matthew.

143 The extensive use of NT traditions (including allegedly three gospels) is one of the factors used by Peel and Zandee in dating the document around 165 A.D. (op. cit., 310).

must probably be regarded as fairly weak).[144]

There are other texts in the Nag Hammadi library which may also not be Gnostic (though in most cases the issue is disputed). One such text is the *Authentic Teaching* (VI.3).[145] There have also been doubts expressed as to whether it is a Christian text or not.[146] However, it would seem that, at least in its present form, the text is Christian: for example, 'evangelists' (35.6) is a word which is scarcely ever attested outside Christian sources;[147] further, the sequence of thought in 33.21-26 ('if he is not silent as he asks, they will kill him by their cruelty, thinking they have done a good thing for themselves. Indeed they are sons of the devil!') appears to presuppose knowledge of the scene in Jn 8, where Jesus claims that the Jews' attempt to kill him shows that they are really sons of the devil.[148] It thus

[144] See the concluding remarks, p. 151 below.

[145] It is regarded as Gnostic by W.P. Funk, '"Authentikos Logos"-Die dritte Schrift aus Nag-Hammadi-Codex VI', *ThLZ* 98 (1973) 251-259; J.-É. Ménard, *L'Authentikos Logos BCNH* Textes 2, Quebec 1977 and 'Gnose paienne et gnose chrétienne: L'Authentikos Logos et L'Enseignements de Silvain de Nag Hammadi', in *Paganisme, Judaisme, Christianisme*, Paris 1978, 287-294; K. Koschorke, '"Suchen und Finden" in der Auseinandersetzung zwischen gnostischem und kirchlichem Christentum', *Wort und Dienst* 14 (1977) 51-65 (at least by implication: he sees the text as reflecting the opposition faced by Gnostic communities). It is regarded as not necessarily Gnostic by G. MacRae 'A Nag Hammadi Tractate on the Soul', in *Ex Orbe Religionum I*, Leiden 1972, 471-479; also R. van den Broek, 'The Authentikos Logos: A New Document of Christian Platonism', *VigChr* 33 (1979) 260-286. Editions and translations of the text are to be found in the works of Funk and Ménard mentioned above; also MacRae in Parrott (ed.) *Codices V und VI*, and Krause and Labib, *Codex II and Codex VI*.

[146] It is regarded as non-Christian by MacRae (at least in his earlier essay; in his later work he seems more prepared to recognise a few features of the text as Christian) and Ménard (cf. *Authentikos Logos*, 3). It is regarded as Christian by Funk, Koschorke, and van den Broek (see previous note for references).

[147] Cf. Koschorke, op.cit., 54f; G. Friedrich, art. εὐαγγελιστής *ThWNT* 2, 734f.

[148] Van den Broek, op.cit., 273; Koschorke, op.cit., 54, 57, suggests that Jn.16.2 may also be in mind.

seems reasonable to conclude that the document is in its present form Christian.[149]

The extent to which synoptic tradition is reflected here is debatable. One example of the use of synoptic tradition may be the comparison of the ignorant with the pagans: 'They are more wicked than the pagans . . . For even the pagans give charity, and they know that God who is in the heavens exists' (33.10ff.); similarly 34.12ff.: 'he is worse than a pagan, for the pagans know the way to go to their stone temple'. Van den Broek sees here a reflection of similar comparisons in the Sermon on the Mount, e.g. Mt 5.47/Lk 6.33.[150] He suggests that AuthTeach's 'give charity' is closer to the Lukan version's 'do good' than to the Matthaean 'greet'; however, this is by no means certain, and the reference to 'giving charity' is not easily derivable directly from either synoptic version. In fact 'pagans' occurs only in Mt 5.47 (Lk 6.33 has 'sinners') and this suggests that it is Matthew's version which is presupposed here. Luke's version is probably secondary in this respect,[151] so that one cannot tell from this alone whether it is Matthew's gospel or Matthew's source (presumably Q) which is presupposed. Nevertheless it may be significant that, immediately after this verse in the Matthaean context, there is Jesus' teaching about the proper way to give alms (Mt 6.2-4). It is possible that the reference to 'giving charity' in AuthTeach 33.27 may be inspired by this passage,[152] coming just after Mt 5.47 in

[149] This does not exclude the possibility that the Christian features are secondary additions to the text: cf. Tröger (ed.), *Gnosis und Neues Testament*, 49.

[150] Op. cit., 273.

[151] So H. Schürmann, *Das Lukasevangelium I*, *HThK* 3/1, Freiburg 1969, 353; Schulz, *Q*, 129f.; Marshall, *Luke*, 263.

[152] Krause and Labib, *Codex II und Codex VI*, 147, actually cite Mt 6.2 as a parallel at this point in the text.

Matthew's gospel. It would thus be a 'reminiscence'[153] of the source used. If so it indicates that AuthTeach here is presupposing a text in which Mt 5.47 and 6.2-4 are closely linked. This certainly cannot be Q, and is probably Matthew's finished gospel.

Synoptic tradition may also be reflected indirectly in 28.23-27: the soul 'runs upward into her treasure-house–the one in which her mind (νοῦς) is–and into her storehouse which is secure'. This appears to be an allusion to the variant of the synoptic saying Mt 6.21/Lk 12.34, with 'mind' replacing 'heart' and inverting the phrases so that the treasure is defined to be where the νοῦς is.[154] The same form of this saying is probably reflected in GMary 10.15f. In the discussion of GMary above, it was argued that this form of the saying represents a secondary development of the synoptic version;[155] thus AuthTeach here presupposes this developed form and this suggests that the dependence on the synoptic tradition is only indirect at this point. Nevertheless, the reference to the 'storehouse being secure' may imply that the synoptic context of the saying is assumed (cf. Mt 6.20f./Lk 12.33b).[156]

Other synoptic allusions are rather harder to establish. Koschorke notes the frequent references in the document to 'seeking', and he relates this to the writings of many of the church fathers which suggest that the gospel saying 'seek and you shall find' (Mt 7.7/Lk 11.9) was a favourite text for Gnostics. However, it is never explicitly stated that this gospel saying is itself in mind.[157] Indeed

[153] Cf. the important work of Schürmann in this respect, using reminiscences to tackle source-critical questions.
[154] Van den Broek, op. cit., 274f.
[155] See p. 40f. above.
[156] Van den Broek, op. cit.. 275.
[157] Nor indeed does Koschorke himself explicitly ever say so in his article; but the arrangement of his article suggests that this is the case.

references to 'finding' are much rarer: all that is referred to is a constant 'seeking', and such language seems too general to imply a definite allusion to the synoptic saying. A further synoptic allusion is seen by Koschorke in 24.31-33, which refers to the son as looking again 'for the way to double the things he has received'; this may be reminiscent of the parable of the talents/pounds (Mt 25.14ff./Lk 19.11ff.),[158] though again one must say that the language is very general. Finally, Koschorke compares the parable of the prodigal son (Lk 15.11ff.) with the language of the text at 23.12ff. ('when the spiritual soul was cast into the body, it became a brother to lust, and hatred, and envy, and a material soul') and 24.14ff. ('That one will fall into drinking much wine in debauchery. For wine is the debaucher. Therefore she does not remember her brothers and her father, for pleasure and sweet profits deceive her . . . .But, on the other hand, the gentle son inherits from his father with pleasure').[159] It is true that some of the themes of the parable are also present here (different children of the same father, inheritances, debauchery). However, some of this imagery is commonplace and, for example, the metaphor of intoxication to describe the lost condition of the soul was common in Gnosticism.[160] There is in fact virtually nothing here to suggest an allusion to the actual story part of the gospel parable. It would probably therefore be precarious to draw any firm conclusions in this context from such general parallels.

In the second part of his article, Koschorke refers to several patristic passages which claim to show how

---

158 Koschorke, op. cit., 54.

159 Ibid.

160 See H. Jonas, *The Gnostic Religion*, Boston 1958, 68ff.; cf. also Ménard, *Authentikos Logos*, 48.

Gnostics interpreted scriptural texts (OT and NT) in support of their own beliefs. He thus suggests:

> Als der Gegenstandsbereich, an dem sich solches Suchen vorzugsweise übte, erweisen sich für den gnostischen Christen primär jene Traditionen, die ihm mit seinem kirchlichen Gegner gemeinsam waren, in erster Linie also die *neutestamentlichen Schriften.*[161]

Whilst this might be justified as a general claim about some Gnostic works (e.g. ApPet), there is little in AuthTeach to justify this claim. The whole question of patristic reports about the Gnostics' use of scripture will be examined at the end of this study. But there is no evidence here that the author of AuthTeach is specifically seeking to find an esoteric interpretation of NT texts, or to oppose other interpretations of the NT put forward by his opponents. Whilst AuthTeach does give evidence of hostility between the group for whom it was written and outsiders,[162] there is nothing here to suggest that interpretation of the NT text was a point at issue. The synoptic tradition is reflected only in passing, and mostly in a form which suggests dependence on Matthew's gospel alone. Matthew's arrangement is presupposed at one point, and the other texts which do seem to be clearly echoed also appear in Matthew (though also in Luke). There is no need to see dependence on any other source to explain the extent of the synoptic tradition which is presupposed here.

Similar in some ways to AuthTeach is the tractate *The Exegesis on the Soul* (II.6). This text is unique amongst the Nag Hammadi texts in giving explicit biblical (and Homeric) quotations to back up its argument: indeed, ExegSoul is perhaps the closest to what one might have

---

[161] Op. cit., 62.

[162] Cf. the references to those who enquire about salvation being killed (33.22).

expected a Gnostic text to look like from the reports of the Church Fathers. Although it has been claimed that the quotations are secondary additions to an underlying, possibly non-Christian, source,[163] most scholars now take the opposite view and see the quotations as an integral part of the tractate.[164] The OT and Homeric quotations have already attracted detailed examination;[165] the NT quotations are less extensive and have not recieved the same amount of attention.

With regard to synoptic material, there is not very much to consider. However, in one short passage there is a group of citations from synoptic material. As part of the exhortation to the soul to repent and turn to the Father, the text quotes the words of 'the Saviour':

> The Saviour said
> 'Blessed are those who mourn, for it is they who will be pitied;
> blessed, those who are hungry, for it is they who will be filled.'
> Again he said
> 'If one does not hate his soul he cannot follow me.'
> For the beginning of salvation is repentance. Therefore,
> 'Before Christ's appearance came John, preaching the baptism of repentance' (135.16-24).

It is not absolutely certain whether the final clause is

---

163 See W.C. Robinson, 'The Exegesis on the Soul'; *NT* 12 (1970) 102-117; also Tröger (ed.), *Gnosis und Neues Testament*, 38f.

164 See R. McL. Wilson, 'Old Testament Exegesis in the Gnostic Exegesis on the Soul', *NHS* 6, Leiden 1975, 217-224; M. Krause, 'Die Sakramente in der *Exegese über die Seele*', *NHS* 7, Leiden 1975, 47-55, esp. 49; F. Wisse, 'On Exegeting "The Exegesis on the Soul"', *NHS* 7, Leiden 1975, 80; S. Arai, 'Simonianische Gnosis und die *Exegese über die Seele*', *NHS* 8, Leiden 1977, 185-203, esp. 196; J.M. Sevrin, 'La rédaction de l'exégèse de l'âme (Nag Hammadi II,6)', *Muséon* 92 (1979) 237-271.

165 P. Nagel, 'Die Septuaginta-Zitate in der koptisch-gnostischen "Exegese über die Seele" (Nag Hammadi Codex II)', *APF* 22-23 (1974) 249-269; A. Guillaumont, 'Une Citation de l'Apocryphe d'Ezéchiel dans l'Exégèse au sujet de l'âme', *NHS* 6, Leiden 1975, 35-39; M. Scopello, 'Les citations d'Homère dans le traité de l'Exégèse de l'Âme', *NHS* 8, Leiden 1977, 3-12, and 'Les "Testimonia" dans le traité de "l'exégèse de l'âme" (Nag Hammadi II, 6)', *RHR* 191 (1977) 159-171. Wilson, 'Old Testament Exegesis'.

intended to be an explicit citation, or simply the author's own summary of the events concerned. If it is the former, Acts 13.24 is probably closest in wording. This might imply knowledge of the Lukan writings. The latter theory seems to be confirmed by a consideration of the previous citation about 'hating one's soul'. The first half of this saying is very close to Lk 14.26a. In general terms Luke's form of this saying in terms of 'hating' is usually considered to be more original than Matthew's parallel (Mt 10.37) which speaks instead of 'he who loves . . . more than me'.[166] However, Luke's reference to 'one's own soul' is almost certainly due to LkR.[167] It is thus highly likely that ExegSoul here is presupposing Luke's finished gospel rather than Luke's prior source (in this case probably Q). The second half of the citation does not agree precisely with any canonical version. Lk 14.26 has 'cannot be my disciple'; Lk 14.27 has 'come after me' in a slightly different place in the saying, where Matthew's parallel (10.38) has 'follow'. There is also a related complex of sayings in Mk 8.34f. and pars., where references to 'saving one's soul' and 'following' occur in close proximity, though there is nothing here about 'hating' one's soul.[168] One can probably do no more than endorse Sevrin's comment that this citation is intended to be of Lk 14.26 'cité assez librement'.[169]

The double beatitude immediately preceding this citation has some interesting features. The first clause

---

166 T.W. Manson, *The Sayings of Jesus*, London 1949, 131; Schulz, *Q*, 446; Marshall, *Luke*, 592.

167 Schürmann, *Lukasevangelium*, 544; Schulz, *Q*, 447.

168 This seems an important factor in seeing the citation here as closer to the tradition reflected in Lk 14.26 rather than Lk 9.23 (as claimed by H.G. Bethge, 'Die Exegese über die Seele', *ThLZ* 101 (1976) 93-104 at col. 103; also Krause and Labib, *Codex II und Codex VI*, 83.)

169 Op.cit., 240

appears to combine Mt 5.4 and 7. It is possible that Mt 5.7 is due to MtR;[170] on this basis one could argue that ExegSoul presupposes Matthew's redactional work and hence Matthew's finished gospel. However, the motif of 'mercy'/'pity' is deeply embedded in the text,[171] and it could be that the reference here to 'pity' is due not to a conflation of Mt 5.4 and 5.7 but to a redactional change of Mt 5.4 alone by the author of the tractate.[172] Certainty is thus not possible.

The second beatitude also raises some problems. It might be considered significant that Mt 5.6 follows immediately after 5.4 in some (predominantly Western) MSS of Matthew.[173] On the other hand the two beatitudes must have been adjacent to each other in Q. There is thus the possibility that the author derived his material from Matthew's source Q rather than from Matthew.[174] This possibility may also be suggested by the fact that the reference to 'righteousness' in Mt 5.6, almost

---

[170] For all the beatitudes which appear in Matthew alone as due to MtR, see N. Walter, 'Die Bearbeitung der Seligpreisungen durch Matthäus', *StEv* 4, *TU* 102, Berlin 1968, 246-268, esp. 248f.; H. Frankemölle, 'Die Makarismen (Mt 5,1-12; Lk 6,20-23): Motive und Umfang der redaktionellen Komposition', *BZ* 15 (1971) 52-75, esp. 68-73; also my 'The Beatitudes: A Source-Critical Study', *NT* 25 (1983) 193-207, esp. 201.

[171] Krause, 'Sakramente' 50, referring to 129.32; 134.23; 135.18; 136.10.

[172] Though one could equally well argue that redactional concerns have led to the conflation of the two Matthaean verses.

[173] D 33 b f q vg sy^{c} bo Clem Orig.

[174] This would in turn entail the theory that the reference to 'pity' in the earlier beatitude is either redactional (which is possible: cf. above) or that Mt 5.7 is indeed cited here but that this verse was also part of Matthew's source, i.e. a Q^{mt} known to Matthew only. For this theory in relation to the beatitudes, see G. Strecker, 'Die Makarismen der Bergpredigt', *NTS* 17 (1971) 255-275; O.H. Steck, *Israel und das gewaltsame Geschick der Propheten*, Neukirchen-Vluyn 1967, 20-27. I have argued elsewhere (see my 'Beatitudes' article) that this is an unnecessary hypothesis to explain the synoptic evidence.

universally recognised as due to MtR,[175] is not present here. The citation is thus closer to the wording of Lk 6.21 which is often thought to preserve the Q wording more accurately. Further, whilst the first beatitude fits very well into the present context (an exhortation to repent by mourning so as to receive the divine pity), the note about hungering and being filled looks at first sight somewhat out of place.[176] It might be argued on this basis that the double beatitude reflects the writer's source.

All this is probably rather speculative. The reference to hungering may not be quite so out of place as appears at first sight. Scopello has shown that the OT and Homeric citations in the tractate can be paralleled with similar uses of the same, or related, texts by Alexandrian exegetes such as Clement, Origen and Didymus the Blind.[177] A comparison with Clement's citation of this beatitude is instructive. For whilst Clement usually cites the beatitude in its Matthaean form, referring to a hungering after righteousness,[178] on one occasion he omits the reference to righteousness and adds another interpretation:

> If then it is agreed among us that knowledge is the food of reason, 'blessed truly are they', according to the scripture, 'who hunger and thirst after truth, for they shall be filled with everlasting food'.[179]

---

[175] Cf. G. Strecker, *Der Weg der Gerechtigkeit*, *FRLANT* 82, Göttingen 1962 and many other recent studies on Matthew; though one should also note the recent work of B. Przybylski, *Righteousness in Matthew and his World of Thought*, *MSSNTS* 41, Cambridge 1980, who argues that the term may not have been so important for Matthew.

[176] Cf. Wisse, 'On Exegeting *The Exegesis on the Soul*' 76f., who is led to postulate a possible reference here to an otherwise unknown penitential discipline of self-denial within the writer's community.

[177] See the articles cited above (n.165).

[178] *Q.D.S.* 17.5; *Eclog.* 14.4; *Strom.* I.7.2; IV.25.2; IV.26.2;

[179] *Strom.* V.70.1.

The allusion is thus to knowledge as the food of reason. This interpretation also fits very well in the passage in ExegSoul. The fact that the soul is ignorant is alluded to elsewhere (cf. 131.16f.; 133.10ff.) and the immediately preceding passage refers twice to being 'empty'.[180] This too would correspond with the promise of the beatitude that the hungry soul will be 'filled'. It may be, therefore, that the author of the tractate shares the same exegetical tradition as Clement, interpreting the beatitude as a promise to those who are empty of knowledge and hungering for it. Thus the presence of this beatitude, together with its precise wording, *can* be explained as an integral part of the text's argument at this point and by no means requires a theory that it is simply the relic of a prior source. There is thus nothing impossible in the theory that ExegSoul is dependent on Matthew's gospel, conflating vv.4 and 7 (or redacting v.4 alone) and redacting v.6 (or using the Lukan version as from Lk 6.21) to produce the present text.[181]

One final possible allusion to synoptic tradition, apart from the explicit citations, may occur at the start of the tractate in 127.26f. In referring to the soul's fall into the corporeal world, the writer says 'she fell into the hands of many robbers'. This *may* be an allusion to Gnostic interpretation of the parable of the Good Samaritan, as already noted,[182] though the allusive nature of the reference means that one cannot be certain.

The dependence of our text on Lk 14.26 suggests that

---

180 135.10 'empty deception'; 135.11 'empty zeal'.

181 If the link with Clement's use of the beatitude is accepted, it may be noteworthy that Clement himself is clearly interpreting Matthew's version (cf. the reference to the thirsty). It is probably easier to assume that ExegSoul is also interpreting Matthew's version.

182 See p. 34 above.

the author knew at least Luke's gospel. There is in fact nothing to compel the belief that he knew any other form of the synoptic tradition: the versions of the beatitudes cited could be derived from Luke, though it may be easier to see dependence on Matthew's version here. Certainly there is no positive evidence for the use of pre-synoptic traditions. There is dependence on Luke, and probably Matthew as well, with a certain amount of freedom in citing and interpreting the texts chosen.

Amongst the texts which are more clearly Gnostic, some texts seem to be identifiable as belonging to Valentinian Gnosticism. Prime among these is the *Gospel of Truth* (I. 2).[183]

There are few who would question the fact that GTr alludes to many of the NT writings. The classic treatment of the subject is the essay of van Unnik, who came to the conclusion that

> the writer of the *Gospel of Truth* was acquainted with the Gospels, the Pauline epistles, Hebrews and Revelation, while there are traces of Acts, 1 John and 1 Peter . . . It appears that he used practically the same Books as constitute our present New Testament Canon.[184]

> Round about 140-150 a collection of writings was known at Rome and accepted as authoritative which was virtually identical with our New Testament.[185]

---

183 For editions and translations, see M. Malinine–H.-C. Puech–G. Quispel (eds.), *Evangelium Veritatis*, Zürich 1956; H.M. Schenke, *Die Herkunft des sogenannten Evangelium Veritatis*, Göttingen 1959; W.C. Till, 'Das Evangelium der Wahrheit', *ZNW* 50 (1959) 165-185; K. Grobel, *The Gospel of Truth*, New York 1960; J.-É. Ménard, *L'Évangile de Vérité, Rétroversion et Commentaire*, Paris 1962 and *L'Évangile de Vérité, NHS* 2, Leiden 1972. (References to Ménard are to the later work unless otherwise stated.).

184 'The "Gospel of Truth" and the New Testament', in *The Jung Codex*, London 1955, 81-129, on 122.

185 Ibid., 124. Van Unnik believed that the author of GTr was Valentinus himself (hence the date and place given).

This conclusion, at least with regard to GTr's use of NT gospel traditions, appears to have been widely accepted.[186] Indeed, this 'result' has become something of a 'canon' in that the developed nature of the NT canon postulated by van Unnik's theory has led some to doubt whether GTr can be dated as early as 150;[187] others have claimed that the evidence of GTr calls into question traditional theories about the development of the canon.[188] I leave aside here the question of the nature of the authority ascribed to the NT books.[189] The issue here is the question of which synoptic traditions are alluded to in GTr. The thesis of this section will be that all the allusions to the synoptic tradition in GTr can be explained as due to dependence on Matthew's gospel alone.

One of the clearest examples of an allusion to the synoptic tradition occurs in the saying about the lost sheep in 31.35ff.: 'He is the shepherd who left behind the ninety-nine sheep which were not lost. He went searching for the one which was lost. He rejoiced when he found it . . . ', followed by a discussion of the numbers concerned and the fact that they are connected with the left hand and

---

186 R. McL. Wilson, *The Gnostic Problem*, London 1958, 156: 'It (GTr) presupposes the Synoptics and the Fourth Gospel.' G. MacRae, art. 'Truth, Gospel of', *Interpreter's Dictionary of the Bible* (Supplementary Volume, 1976), 925b: 'There are clear allusions to all the gospels.' Cf. too Helmbold, *The Nag Hammadi Gnostic Texts and the Bible*, 43; C.I.K. Story, *The Nature of Truth in "The Gospel of Truth" and in the Writings of Justin Martyr*, *NT.S* 25, Leiden 1970, p. 50. (GTr alludes to all the gospels except Mark).

187 Cf. Wilson, *Gnosis and the New Testament*, 98; also his 'Valentinianism and the *Gospel of Truth*' in *The School of Valentinus*, Leiden 1980, 138,141.

188 So, for example, van Unnik, op.cit., 124; Helmbold, op.cit., 89; cf. too K.H. Schelke, 'Das Evangelium Veritatis als kanongeschichtliches Zeugnis', *BZ* 5 (1961) 90-91. GTr's apparent allusions to Hebrews and Revelation are considered very important in this context.

189 See p.10 above: knowledge and use of a document does not necessarily imply that the document has canonical status.

the right hand. Clearly the synoptic parable of the lost sheep (Mt 18.12-14/Lk 15.4-7) is in mind.[190] Further, most agree that it is Matthew's version, rather than Luke's, which is in mind.[191] It is uncertain which version is more original here,[192] so that one cannot conclude from this example alone that GTr derived its ideas from Matthew's gospel rather than Matthew's source. However, the example is perfectly consistent with the theory that GTr is dependent on Matthew's gospel.[193]

Further progress can be made by considering the passage which follows in GTr (32.18ff.). 'Even on the Sabbath, he labored for the sheep which he found fallen into the pit'. Although there is almost certainly an echo of Jn 5.17 here, there is clearly an allusion to Mt 12.11.[194] It

---

190 See van Unnik, op.cit., 112f.; Schenke, op.cit., 47; Grobel, op.cit., 129; Ménard, op.cit., 7, 149. The identification of Jesus with the shepherd probably derives from Jn 10: cf. Grobel, ibid.; Story, op.cit., 21.

191 Van Unnik and Ménard both refer to Matthew's use of πλανᾶν twice in Mt 18.12 as indicating this; but the Coptic word used here (ⲥⲱⲣⲙ) can be used for both Matthew's πλανᾶν (e.g. Mt 18.12 sah boh) and Luke's ἀπόλλυμι (e.g. Mt 10.6 sah boh): cf. Crum's *Dictionary*, 355. They also point to the references to 'little ones' (Mt 18.10) and 'the Father's will' (Mt 18.14) elsewhere in GTr (19.29, 37.21ff. respectively) as evidence of knowledge of the Matthaean context; but these are very remote, and in any case 37.21ff. probably alludes to Mt 10.29 (see below). Story's argument seems more cogent: 'The five Coptic words (four in the perfect, one in the temporal tense) of which the shepherd is the subject parallel exactly the verbal forms in Mt 18.12-14, including their order (ἀφήσει, πορευθείς, ζητεῖ, εὑρεῖν, χαίρει) The Lucan parallel has καταλείπει for ἀφήσει and omits the verb ζητεῖν' (op.cit., 21). The reference to 'searching', found only in Matthew, does seem to indicate that Matthew, not Luke, is in mind.

192 According to Schulz, *Q*, 387f., Luke is secondary in using ἀπόλλυμι and omitting ζητεῖν Cf. too Marshall, *Luke*, 601.

193 According to van Unnik, op.cit., 113, and Story, op.cit., 22, the 'left-hand-right-hand' imagery may derive from Mt 25.31ff., thus showing links between GTr and M material in Matthew. Whilst not impossible, this is certainly not necessary. The idea of 'left' as 'sinister' and 'right' as 'favourable' was very widespread. Cf. too the very close connections between this passage and Irenaeus' account of the theories of the Marcosians in *A.H.* I.16.2.

194 Van Unnik, op.cit., 113f.; Grobel, op.cit., 135; Ménard, op.cit., 7, 152.

is also clear that, although Mt 12.11 has a synoptic parallel in Lk 14.5, the reference here is to the Matthaean version of the saying, since only Matthew speaks of a 'sheep' falling into a pit.[195] Further, it is significant in this context that Matthew's reference to the 'sheep' is probably due to MtR.[196] Thus GTr here shows knowledge of MtR and hence presupposes Matthew's finished gospel, not just one of Matthew's sources.[197]

A similar situation occurs in 33.30f. and 33.38f.: 'So you, do the will of the Father', and 'For by the fruits does one take cognizance of the things that are yours.' The former echoes various Matthaean texts, e.g. 7.21; 12.50; 21.31. The latter also echoes NT language, notably Mt 7.16-20.[198] The close proximity of these two allusions in both GTr and Mt 7 suggests that Mt 7 is the source of the

---

[195] Lk 14.5 speaks of 'a son or an ox', with some MSS support for reading 'ox or ass' though the Western text does have 'sheep' here.

[196] *πρόβατον* is a favourite Matthaean word; also the reference to an animal in the saying seems to be secondary, since it was not considered legitimate to lift an animal out of a pit on the sabbath: see my *The Revival of the Griesbach Hypothesis*, *MSSNTS* 44, Cambridge 1983, p. 99.

[197] R. McL. Wilson, 'A Note on the Gospel of Truth' (33.8-9)', *NTS* 9 (1963) 295-298, has hinted that the saying about the animal in the pit may also be in mind a little later in GTr 33.8f. ('you are the understanding that is drawn forth/up'). He argues that the Coptic verb used in 33.9 ⲧⲱ̄ⲕⲙ may be the equivalent of the Greek *ἀποσπάω*, and he finds a parallel in the Marcosian formula cited in Irenaeus *A.H.* I.13.6. At the end of his note Wilson points out that *ἀποσπάω* is used in Luke's version of the saying about the animal/person in the pit (Lk 14.5), thus supporting Grobel's suggestion (op.cit., 141) that the saying about the sheep in the pit may still be in mind. However, in his reconstruction of the original Greek, Ménard gives *ἡ σύνεσις ἕλκουσα* at this point (see his 1962 commentary, 64; he still assumes the same in his 1972 work, 156), comparing GTr 34.12 and 36.28 for similar ideas. If this were the case, the language could be seen as more Johannine (cf. Jn 6.44; 12.32). It is thus uncertain whether there is a synoptic allusion here at all. Even if Wilson's argument about the uses of the verb here is accepted, the common use of *ἀποσπάω* here and in Lk 14 may be no more than coincidental. (In any case the two contexts in GTr are separated by 24 lines in the text.)

[198] Grobel, op.cit., 149.

language used in GTr.[199] Further, the form of the sayings in Mt 7.16, 20 is probably due to MtR.[200] Thus GTr again betrays knowledge of Matthew's redactional work, and thus of Matthew's finished gospel.

Another allusion to Matthew's gospel seems certain in 33.15f.: 'Do not return to what you have vomited to eat it. Do not be moths, do not be worms.' The second sentence here alludes to Mt 6.19f./Lk 12.33, both of which mention 'moths'.[201] Menard refers to Mk 9.48 also, presumably because of the reference to the 'worm'. But it is quite possible that this is part of the same allusion to Mt 6. 19, i.e. to *βρῶσις* since *βρῶσις* may have this meaning.[202] If this is the case, then there is no reference to Mk 9.48; also the allusion must be to Mt 6.19f. rather than Lk 12.33, since Luke's version does not mention *βρῶσις*. It may well be the case that Matthew's version is more original,[203] so that GTr does not necessarily show knowledge of MtR here. Nevertheless, this example fits the pattern of dependence on Matthew established so far. Whether there is a synoptic allusion in the first sentence quoted above is rather doubtful.[204] There is possibly some

---

[199] Schenke, op.cit., 49, and Ménard, op.cit., 158, refer to Mt 12.33/Lk 6.44 for GTr 33.38, but the link with 33.31 suggests otherwise.

[200] E. Schweizer, *The Good News according to Matthew*, London 1976, 187.

[201] Grobel, op.cit., 143f.; Ménard op.cit., 7, 156.

[202] Cf. RSV note; W. Pesch, 'Zur Exegese von Mt 6, 19-21 und Lk 12,33-34', *bib* 41 (1960) 356; also Bauer's *Lexicon*, 147b. Cf. Mal 3.11 LXX, where *βρῶσις*= אכל (locust, devourer). See too Grobel, op.cit., 145. Moths and worms are also associated in GTh 76.

[203] Cf. J. Schmid, *Matthäus und Lukas*, *BSt* 23.2-4, Freiburg 1930, 237; Pesch, op.cit., 358f.; Schulz, *Q*, 142.

[204] Grobel, op.cit., 140-2, has a quite different translation: 'Do not buy them back to submit to them', deriving ⲙⲡⲣⲥⲱⲧⲉ from ⲥⲱⲧⲉ (to buy back, redeem). He suggests that this alludes to Lk 12.33a and that the connection between the sentences is determined by the Lukan context, thus implying knowledge of Luke's gospel. However, ⲥⲱⲧⲉ is used at 38.2f., where the meaning must be 'return', either as a variation for ⲥⲱⲧ (so Malinine et al., op.cit., 58) or instead of ⲕⲱⲧⲉ (cf. Ménard's 1962 work, 74f.; also W.C. Till, 'Bemerkungen zur

reminiscence of the language of 2 Pet 2.22.[205] This in turn echoes Prov 26.11 so that one cannot deduce too much from this (e.g. about knowledge of 2 Peter by the author of GTr).

The remaining echoes of the synoptic tradition are less conclusive for the purposes of this study. There are several allusions which could derive from outside Matthew, but where Matthew could equally well be the source of the language used, since these are texts where Matthew and the other gospels are closely parallel. Thus the text at 17.3f. ('being discovery for those who search for him') may echo the language of the Q saying Mt 7.7/Lk 11.9.[206] Matthew and Luke are identical here, so the most one can say is that the language used could have derived from Matthew, though the saying appears to have been widespread in Gnostic circles.[207] 18.19f. ('out of oblivion he enlightened them, he showed them a way. And the way is the truth which he taught them') may allude to the synoptic saying in Mk 12.14 and pars.[208] If so, Mt 22.16 is closely parallel to Mk 12.14 so that there is nothing to suggest that the allusion is to Mark (or Luke) rather than Matthew. However, Jn 14.6 seems a much more likely source for the language used here.[209] The text at 19.22f. ('there came the wise men–in their own estimation–putting him to the test') seems to echo various synoptic passages (e.g. Mt 16.1; 19.3; 22.18, 35; Mk 8.11;

Erstausgabe des "Evangelium Veritatis"', *Or* 27 (1958) 280.) The idea of buying back, or redeeming, seems quite extraneous here, whereas the idea of 'return' makes good sense. It seems best therefore to accept the *NHLE* translation and see probably no synoptic allusion at all.

205 Till, 'Das Evangelium der Wahrheit', 179.

206 Van Unnik, op.cit., 115; Ménard, op.cit., 3, 78.

207 See n.110 above.

208 van Unnik, op.cit., 116; Ménard, op.cit., 4, 87.

209 Malinine et al., op.cit., 51; Grobel, op.cit., 51.

10.12; 12.18).[210] Again the source of the language could easily be Matthew's gospel, though Grobel's comment, that this is 'summarizing, not alluding to any specific scene of any gospel',[211] seems apt. The author of GTr continues to speak of these 'wise' men, saying that 'they were foolish. They hated him because they were not really wise. After all these, there came the little children also, those to whom the knowledge of the Father belongs.' It is very probable that the Q saying Mt 11.25/Lk 10.21 is in mind.[212] Once again it is impossible to distinguish between Matthew and Luke and so determine which is the source of the language used: it is another case where Matthew could have been the source. However, it is also possible that the language of Mt 18.2-6, 10 (the reference to *μικροί*) is also echoed.[213] If this is so, then it is significant that the stress on *μικροί* in Mt 18 is due to MtR (though the word is used in Mk 9.43).[214] Again GTr may show dependence on MtR.

The text at 20.11-14 ('Jesus was patient in accepting sufferings . . . since he knows that his death is life for many') may well echo Mk 10.45 and par.[215] Here again Mt 20.28 is identical with Mark, so Matthew's gospel is equally likely to be the source of the language used. The promise to the one who has knowledge, that 'he receives rest' (22.12), recalls Mt 11.29.[216] This is part of the M

[210] Malinine et al., op.cit., 52; Ménard, op.cit., 4, 93.
[211] Op.cit., 59.
[212] Malinine et al., op.cit., 52; van Unnik, op.cit., 117 and others.
[213] Cf. van Unnik, op.cit., 117; Schenke, op.cit., 36; Story, op.cit., 5.
[214] Cf. G.D. Kilpatrick, *The Origins of the Gospel according to St. Matthew*, Oxford 1946, 29; G. Barth, in G. Bornkamm, G. Barth & H.J. Held, *Tradition and Interpretation in Matthew*, London 1963, 121f.
[215] Malinine et al., op.cit., 53; van Unnik, op.cit., 112; Ménard, op.cit., 97, and others.
[216] Grobel, op.cit., 79.

material in Matthew, i.e. material peculiar to Matthew. However, the 'rest' motif was very widespread, and probably needs no NT text to explain its presence here.[216a] The reference in 24.23f. to 'the world, that in which he served' may again echo Mk 10.45,[217] though the language is very general and, as before, Mt 20.28 is an equally likely source. The text at 27.24f. says that 'the Father is perfect', which brings to mind Mt 5.48.[218] Matthew's language here is almost certainly redactional,[219] so that GTr may once again show knowledge of MtR.[220] 30.15f. ('blessed is he who has opened the eyes of the blind') may allude to various synoptic passages, but it is equally likely that Jn 9 is in mind.[221] 30.32 refers to 'the beloved Son' which could be an echo of texts like Mt 3.17; 17.5 and parallels.[222] Again this could be derived from Matthew's gospel (though not necessarily so).

The injunctions in 33.1-8 show some similarity with Mt 25.35-37,[223] though the details differ. One of the injunctions is to 'give repose to those who are weary', which may allude to Mt 11.28,[224] again showing a link between GTr and Matthew's M material. 33.19f. ('do not

---

216a See n.120 above

217 So Malinine et al., op.cit., 55 ('peut-être'); Ménard, op.cit., 121 ('un rapprochement lointain est possible').

218 Van Unnik, op.cit., 119; Ménard, op.cit., 6, 132.

219 Cf. Schmid, op.cit. 229f.; Strecker, *Gerechtigkeit*, 141; Schulz, *Q*, 130.

220 However, the idea of the 'perfect Father' is thoroughly at home in Valentinianism: Cf. Irenaeus, *A.H.* I.2.2 (cited by Ménard, op.cit., 132), so there is not necessarily any allusion here to Matthew's gospel.

221 Malinine et al., op.cit., 56; Schenke, op.cit., 45.

222 Van Unnik, op.cit., 120; Schenke, op.cit., 46; Ménard, op.cit., 6, 143. Cf. also the use of this term in TriTrac 87.8, and also in Valentinus frag. 6 (in Clement, *Strom*, VI. 52.4). One does not therefore necessarily need a synoptic text to explain the use of the term.

223 Noted by Grobel, op.cit., 141; Story, op.cit., 24.

224 Grobel, ibid.

become a dwelling place for the devil') may have been evoked by the Q saying Mt 12.43-45/Lk 11.24-26.[225] There is nothing to distinguish Matthew and Luke as the source of the allusions here. 37.21-24 says that 'nothing happens without him, nor does anything happen without the will of the Father.' This is clearly close to the language of Mt 10.29 (/Lk 12.6).[226] Matthew's ἄνευ phrasc hcrc is generally taken as more original than Luke's version, though the reference to God as 'Father' could be due to MtR.[227] However, 'Father' is also a favourite description of God for the author of GTr so one cannot place too much weight on this coincidence in usage. It *may* be that GTr echoes MtR, but this is not certain. In any case, nothing tells against the theory that GTr is using Matthew.[228] The text at 42.17f. ('they do not go down to Hades') is similar to the language of the Q saying Mt 11.23/Lk 10.15;[229] and 42.36f. ('will not suffer loss to his soul') recalls Mt 16.26 and pars.[230] In both cases Matthew's gospel could be the source of the language used (though the other gospels are closely parallel).

All the allusions discussed so far have been consistent with the theory that Matthew's gospel is the sole source for GTr's synoptic material. Further allusions to synoptic material have been noted by others, but very often the language does not seem distinctive enough to warrant the

225 Ménard, op.cit., 157.
226 Malinine et al., op.cit., 58; van Unnik, op.cit., 120f.; Ménard, op.cit., 175.
227 See Schulz, op.cit., 159; Marshall, *Luke*, 514.
228 Helmbold, *The Nag Hammadi Gnostic Texts and the Bible* 91, sees evidence here of use of a Western reading of Matthew ('without the will of your Father' is found in some old latin MSS, though not in D itself). However, both 'without him' and 'without the will of the Father' occur in the saying here, so one cannot place too much weight on this.
229 Malinine et al., op.cit., 60; van Unnik, op.cit., 121; Ménard. op.cit., 189.
230 Maline et al., op.cit., 60; van Unnik, op.cit., 121; Ménard, op.cit., 19.

theory that any allusion to the synoptic material exists.

The text of 18.14f. ('through the mercies of the Father') is not dissimilar to Lk 1.78;[231] but the language is not specifically Lukan,[232] so that one cannot deduce that the author of GTr knew Luke's gospel. At 19.19f. the author says that Jesus 'went into the midst of the schools and he spoke the word as a teacher'. Some have seen an allusion to Lk 2.46-49 here;[233] but again the language is very general and need only imply a knowledge of Jesus' teaching activity amongst the Jews, and not necessarily of the specific story in Lk 2.[234] The language of 20.15f. ('just as there lies hidden in a will, before it is opened . . . ') has reminded some of the covenant language of Mk 14.24 and pars.[235] Here again Matthew's gospel could just as well be the source since Mt 26.28 and Mk 14.24 are closely parallel; but it is much more likely that the author is simply using the analogy of an ordinary human will.[236] 30.27-31 says of Jesus: 'For when they had seen him and had heard him, he granted them to taste him and to smell him and to touch the beloved Son'. It is possible that Lk 24.36ff. is in mind,[237] but this is by no means certain. The

---

[231] Noted by Malinine et al., op.cit., 51; van Unnik, op.cit., 116; Ménard, op.cit., 4.

[232] The parallel in TLevi 4.4 is often noted in commentaries on Luke here.

[233] Malinine et al., op.cit., 52; Schenke, op.cit., 36; Ménard, op.cit., 4, 92. Reference is often made to a possible infancy gospel used by the Valentinians: cf. Irenaeus, *A.H.* I.20.1 (though the reference here seems to be to the Infancy Gospel of Thomas: cf. Hennecke I, 394). Cf. too the use of the Lk 2 story by Valentinians according to Irenaeus, *A.H.* I.20.2. However, the use made of the story is different.

[234] *If* the allusion in 19.21-23 (see above) were to the 'testing' references in Mt 22, the note here about Jesus' teaching activity could be referring to the whole complex Mt 21.23ff.

[235] Van Unnik, op.cit., 112; Ménard, op.cit., 5, 97.

[236] Cf. Grobel, op.cit., 63. In any case Heb 9.15 is as likely to be the source of the language used (as is said by Ménard).

[237] So van Unnik, op.cit., 120; Ménard op.cit., 6, 143.

language used, and ideas expressed, are also paralleled in Jn 20.19-27 and other texts such as Heb 6.4f.; 1 Pet 2.3; 1 Jn 1.1.[238] In view of the extensive use of the fourth gospel by the author of GTr, it is probably dangerous to try to see a use of Luke's gospel in this example. A similar situation arises in the case of 38.10f. which says of the Father and Jesus 'he begot him as a son'. Although it is possible that Lk 3.22 (quoting Ps 2.7) is the source of the language used here, [239] other passages may have been in mind: e.g. Heb 1.5; 5.5 also quotes Ps 2.7, and in the light of the apparent knowledge and use of Hebrews by the author of GTr,[240] it is just as likely that this is the source of the talk here of 'begetting the son' (if it is not Ps 2 itself). Other synoptic parallels which have been noted by others seem even more general or remote.[241]

The conclusion of this section is that the source of the synoptic material in GTr seems to be Matthew's gospel alone. There is no clear indication that GTr used Mark or Luke. All the clear synoptic allusions could have been derived from Matthew; some could only have been

---

238 Cf. Malinine et al., op.cit., 57; Schenke, op.cit., 46.

239 Cf. Ménard, op.cit., 179. Helmbold, op.cit., 91, sees this as further evidence for the use of the Western text by GTr (since, of course, the full version of Ps 2.7 only occurs in the Western text of Lk 3.22).

240 Cf. van Unnik, op.cit., 110, referring to the description of Jesus as 'merciful and faithful' in 20.10 (cf. Heb 2.17); also Helmbold, op.cit., 90.

241 Malinine et al., op.cit., 51, cite Lk 19.8f. as a parallel to the text at 18.28f. ('to those who ate it, it gave cause to become glad in the discovery'), but this seems extremely remote. Van Unnik, op.cit., 118, sees an echo of Lk 15.17 in the text at 22.18 ('having returned to himself'), but the language does not seem distinctive enough to be certain. The text at 33.24ff. ('for the unjust one is someone to treat ill rather than the just one . . . ') *may* echo Mt 12.34f./ Lk 6.45 (so Schenke, op.cit., 49; Ménard, op.cit., 7, 157f.) but the parallel is not certain. 36.35 says of the Father 'He is good', possibly alluding to Mk 10.18 (cf. Grobel, op.cit., 171), but again the language is very general and commonplace. 42.19f. ('nor have they envy nor groaning nor death within them') may allude to the language of Mt 12.50 (so Ménard, op.cit., 7, 189), but the parallel is again a very general one (e.g. there is no reference to 'gnashing teeth' in GTr).

derived from Matthew or his source; further, some reflect MtR and hence presuppose Matthew's finished gospel. It thus seems reasonable to conclude that the finished gospel of Matthew was the sole source for synoptic material used by the author of GTr.

Any further conclusions drawn from this must be extremely tentative. The absence of allusions to Mark and Luke does not necessarily imply that those two gospels were unknown, nor that they were known but considered less authoritative than Matthew. However, one could argue that this pattern of use of gospel material is consistent with an early date for GTr, i.e. prior to a time when the four-fold gospel canon was the accepted norm. An argument from silence of this nature is clearly highly precarious and cannot prove anything. Nevertheless, these considerations may serve as something of a counterbalance to arguments that an early date for GTr is precluded by the highly developed nature of the NT canon which it presupposes.[242]

Another Valentinian text is the *Treatise on Resurrection* (I. 4.)[243] This is clearly dependent on Christian tradition, and the author makes frequent use of the Pauline corpus. Synoptic tradition is presupposed at times, though it is not often used. One famous example is its use of the Transfiguration story to prove the reality of the resurrection: 'For if you remember reading in the

---

242 Cf. p. 58 and n. 187 above.

243 For texts and translations, see M. Malinine–H.-C. Puech–G. Quispel–W.C. Till–R. McL. Wilson–J. Zandee (eds.), *De Resurrectione (Epistula ad Rheginum), Codex Jung F.XXII*^{r} *–FXXV*^{v}, Zürich–Stuttgart 1963; Peel, *The Epistle to Rheginos*; R. Haardt '"Die Abhandlung über die Auferstehung" des Codex Jung aus der Bibliothek gnostischer koptischer Schriften von Nag Hammadi', *Kairos* 11 (1969) 1-5, and 12 (1970) 241-269; B. Layton, *The Gnostic Treatise on Resurrection from Nag Hammadi, Harvard Dissertations in Religion* 12, Missoula 1979.

Gospel that Elijah appeared and Moses with him, do not think the resurrection is an illusion.' (48.8-11). The question arises of which version is in mind. For many, the fact that Elijah is mentioned before Moses seems to be the decisive factor in seeing the allusion here as being to the Markan account (Mk 9.4).[244] However, this is by no means certain. The importance of the order is discounted by Layton: 'Nothing can be concluded as to which gospel text is used here: perhaps all three.'[245] The slightly unusual order *may* be significant,[246] though one cannot build too much on this.

Other synoptic references are not very numerous. The text in 44.8-10 ('many are lacking in faith in it (i.e. the resurrection) but there are few who find it') may reflect Mt 7.13f. (The reference to 'finding' is slightly unexpected: one might have expected something like 'there are few who have (this faith). This use of the verb 'find' may well then reflect the influence of source material.) Matthew's version here, especially his use of the verb 'to find', is probably more original than Luke's *καὶ οὐκ ἰσχύσουσιν* which is probably LkR.[247] Thus one can say that the reference to 'finding' clearly points to the Matthaean rather than the Lukan version, but one cannot

[244] Malinine et al., op.cit., xxx, 38; Peel, op.cit., 19; Haardt, op.cit., 264.

[245] Op.cit., 94. However, his suggestion that Elijah may have been put first by the author because Elijah is the one who will 'restore' all things (Mk 9.12 and pars., cf. Mal 3.23 LXX) and 'restoration' is an important theme in the text here (cf. 44.31) seems difficult. There is nothing explicit here about Elijah's function as a 'restorer'.

[246] Malinine et al., op.cit., 38, refer to other passages where the appearance of Moses and Elijah at the transfiguration is referred to in discussions of the resurrection (e.g. Terullian, *De res. mort.* 55.10; Origen, *In Ps.* I.5 (PG XII, 1096A); Methodius, *De Resurr.* I. 22-27 (PG XVIII, 317C-319B)), but in all of these, Moses is mentioned before Elijah.

[247] Cf. Schulz, *Q*, 310; A. Denaux, 'Der Spruch von den zwei Wegen im Rahmen des Epilogs der Bergpredigt (Mt 7, 13-14 par. Lk 13, 23-24). Tradition und Redaktion', in *Logia*, *BEThL* 59, Leuven 1982, 324.

say from this text alone whether it is Matthew's gospel or Matthew's source which is presupposed. The former possibility is rendered more likely by the next text to be considered. At 47.2f. the author encourages his reader(s) not to 'doubt' (διστάζειν) the resurrection, and the same Greek verb recurs in 47.36f. ('Let no one be given cause to doubt concerning this'). One may perhaps see here an echo of Matthew's resurrection account, especially Mt 28.17, where the appearance of the risen Jesus counters the disciples' 'doubts' (διστάζειν)[248] The fact that this verb is used redactionally at Mt 14.31 suggests that it is due to MtR here, and hence TreatRes presupposes Matthew's finished gospel at this point, not just Matthew's tradition.

Other alleged synoptic allusions are less certain. The text at 45.6-9 ('so as not to leave anything hidden, but to reveal all things openly') is not unlike Mk 4.22 and pars., Mt 10.26 and par.;[249] however, Peel points out that Pauline texts (e.g. 1 Cor 2.7; 4.5; Col 1.26; Eph 3.9) are equally close, so that 'while none of these passages are truly "echoed" in 45.5-9, the ideas they contain may have been a stimulus to our author'.[250] Other alleged synoptic allusions seem even more remote.[251]

---

[248] Cf. Peel, op.cit., 82, 87.

[249] Malinine et al., op.cit., 25; Peel, op.cit., 64f.

[250] Op.cit., 65.

[251] E.g. the identification of the Son of God with the Son of Man (44.21-23) is compared by Peel (op.cit., 61) with Mt 16.13, 16; Jn 5.25-7, but this is unnecessary. As in general 2nd century usage, the two terms have become simply synonymous with the divinity and humanity of Jesus (cf. Haardt, op.cit. 251). The contrast between wisdom and foolishness (46.28-32) has been compared with Mt 25.1-13 (cf. W.C. van Unnik, 'The Newly Discovered "Epistle to Rheginos" on the Resurrection', *JEH* 15 (1964) 141-167, on 166). But the contrast between wisdom and folly is extremely widespread in Jewish wisdom literature and elsewhere in the NT: cf. Peel, op.cit., 80, 151. The reference here seems far too general to be certain that any synoptic allusion is in mind. The text at 48.24f. ('The rich have become poor and the kings have been

The author thus clearly knows Matthew's finished gospel; one could argue that the reference to the transfiguration story implies knowledge of Mark's gospel as well but this is probably less certain.

A Valentinian text which yields little evidence for the present discussion is the very long *Tripartite Tractate.*[252] Very few clear synoptic echoes can be found and the author is generally content to expound the myth he wishes to present in his own words without direct allusion to the synoptic tradition. There are some very general references to the coming and suffering of the Saviour (cf. 114.31ff.), but very few clear echoes of synoptic language.

There are a few exceptions to this rule. One such may be the text at 116.10ff.: 'Others are from prayer so that they heal the sick, when they have been appointed to treat those who have fallen. These are the apostles and the evangelists.' The synoptic mission charge may be in mind,[253] but the allusion is too indirect to be more precise about which version is presupposed. At 118.23f., the writer says: 'Each of the three essential types is known by its fruit.' This echoes Mt 7.16 and is a text which is referred to in other Valentinian texts (e.g. GTr 33.31ff. and ValExp 36.32ff.).[254] It looks as if Mt 7.16 was a favourite Valentinian text.[255]

Other parallels are less striking. In 87.8 one of the titles

overthrown') has been compared with Lk 1.52f. (cf. Malinine et al., op.cit., 39). However, the reference is too general to be certain: Peel, op.cit., 91, notes a large number of possible Biblical parallels to the general idea; Layton, op.cit., 98, refers to several non-Biblical texts, and says that the examples given here are 'commonplace paradigmatic examples'.

[252] The editio princeps is R.Kasser–M. Malinine–H.-C. Puech –G. Quispel–J. Zandee–W. Vychichl–R. McL. Wilson (eds.), *Tractatus Tripartitus.* Bern Pars I 1973, Pars II 1975.

[253] Kasser et al., op.cit. II, 211; cf. Mt 10.8; Lk 9.2; 10.9.

[254] Kasser et al., op.cit. II, 214.

[255] Origen, *De Princ.* 1.8.2 explicitly says this (cited by Kasser, ibid.).

given to the Son is 'the Beloved', which has a parallel in Mk 1.11 and pars., though one cannot really tell if the source of the title here is the synoptic tradition itself.[256] The reference to the 'little ones' (89.9-20) may be inspired by Mt 18 but again one cannot be sure since the language is so general.[257] The reference to the pit which is called 'the Outer Darkness' (89.26) uses similar imagery and language to texts like Mt 8.12 etc.,[258] but one can hardly say more than this. 127.25ff. speaks of baptism 'which is the redemption into God, Father, Son and Holy Spirit'. This recalls the language of Mt 28.19, though it would clearly be dangerous to deduce direct dependence when contemporary liturgical practice is likely to have been just as influential.[259]

These seem to be almost the sum total of possible direct allusions to synoptic tradition in this text. Generally this author seems content to present his work on its own merits, and apparently sees no need to relate what he says about Christ to what the 'orthodox' might want to claim that Jesus had said or done.

Within the general category of Valentinian texts, a document which yields far more for the present discussion is the *Gospel of Philip* (II.3).[260] The problem of

---

[256] The term occurs in other Valentinian sources: cf. above p. 64 n.222. Cf. Kasser et al, op.cit., I, 358.

[257] The parallel is noted by U. Luz, 'Der dreiteilige Traktat von Nag Hammadi', *ThZ* 33 (1977) 386.

[258] Luz, ibid.

[259] Of course Mt 28.19 itself probably also reflects such practice.

[260] For texts and commentaries, see H.-M. Schenke, 'Das Evangelium nach Philippus', *ThLZ* 84 (1959) 1-26; R.McL. Wilson, *The Gospel of Philip*, London 1962; C.J. de Catanzaro, 'The Gospel according to Philip', *JThS* 13 (1962) 35-71; W.C. Till, *Das Evangelium nach Philippos*, *PTS* 2, Berlin 1963; J.-É. Ménard, *L'Évangile selon Philippe*, Paris 1967. The use of the NT in GPh is discussed in passing in the various commentaries, and in Wilson, 'New Testament in Philip'.

determining allusions to the NT in GPh is complex. Wilson writes: 'These echoes and allusions are fairly numerous, although not always easy to detect. In some cases, indeed, what appears to one scholar a clear and unmistakable echo may to another seem quite insignificant.'[261] However, a clear starting point seems to be provided by part of saying 123: 'That is why the word (*λόγος*) says "Already the axe is laid at the root of the trees"' (83.11-13). It is universally agreed that this is a quotation of the saying preserved in Mt 3.10/Lk 3.9.[262] Although it is not precisely clear to what *λόγος* refers, it does seem to be the case that the writer here is quoting the words of a prior source. Whether this source was Matthew's gospel, or Luke's, or Q, or a post-synoptic harmony, cannot be determined at this stage since Matthew and Luke are identical here. Nevertheless one can say that the author of GPh knows at least some of the synoptic tradition, and he feels it appropriate to use it in the form of a quotation.[263]

Further progress can be made by considering part of saying 89: 'For he (i.e. Christ) said "Thus we should fulfil all righteousness"' (72.34-73.1). Although there are some lacunae in the manuscript at this point, the reading of this part of the saying is not in doubt, and it seems clear that this is a quotation of Mt 3.15.[264] Its significance in the present discussion is that this verse in Matthew is almost universally recognised as due to MtR.[265] GPh thus shows knowledge of MtR and therefore of Matthew's finished

[261] 'New Testament in Philip', 291.

[262] Cf. Schenke, op.cit., 23; Wilson, *Philip*, 187; Catanzaro, op.cit., 66; Till, op.cit., 81; Ménard, op.cit., 241.

[263] What stage of 'canonicity' this implies is another matter.

[264] So Schenke, op.cit., 18; Wilson, op.cit., 153; Catanzaro, op.cit., 56; Till, op.cit., 79; Ménard, op.cit., 208.

[265] Cf. Strecker, *Gerechtigkeit*, 150; Schweizer, *Matthew*, 53.

gospel. In fact all the remaining allusions to the synoptic tradition are, with one major exception, consistent with the theory that GPh is dependent on Matthew's gospel alone for the material it shares with the synoptic tradition. Several of these allusions are not very clear, and I shall discuss them in an order of decreasing closeness to the synoptic tradition.

In saying 23, there is the comment: 'He who has received these (i.e. the flesh of Jesus which is the word, and the blood of Jesus which is the Holy Spirit) has food, and he has drink and clothing' (57.7-8).[266] This seems to be a clear reference to the Q sayings about cares (Mt 6.25ff./Lk 12.22ff.). However, it is only in Matthew's gospel that the three items of food, drink and clothing are explicitly mentioned together. In Mt 6.25 there is strong MSS support for the version which has Jesus tell the disciples not to worry about what they will eat, or what they will drink or how they will be clothed.[267] Luke's parallel here (Lk 12.22) mentions only food and clothing. In Mt 6.31 the three-fold form is textually certain, as the disciples are told not to worry and say 'What shall we eat, what shall we drink, or how shall we be clothed?' Luke's parallel at this point (Lk 12.29) says 'Do not seek what you shall eat, or what you shall drink, neither be of doubtful mind'. It is difficult to decide which version is more original here.[268] Nevertheless it is only Matthew's

---

[266] There is some uncertainty about the text here. The translation given assumes the emendation of ϩⲓ ϩⲃⲥⲱ for ϩⲓ ⲃⲥⲱ proposed by Till, op.cit., 75; Cf. Wilson, op.cit., 89; and A.K. Helmbold, 'Translation Problems in the Gospel of Philip', *NTS* 11 (1964) 91. Schenke, op.cit., 9, translates 'in fulness' instead of 'clothing', but Wilson says that he is 'unable to identify the final word in a form to produce this meaning.'

[267] However, the reference to drinking (ἢ τί πιήτε) is omitted by some MSS, notably ℵ f^{1}vg sy^{c} a b etc.

[268] E.g. Marshall, *Luke*, p 529, thinks that Matthew is more original here; Schmid, *Matthäus und Lukas*, 236, thinks Luke is more original. Schulz, *Q*, 151, is undecided.

version which explicitly refers to the triple problem of food, drink and clothing in a single saying (though this is implicit in the saying in Lk 12.22, 29). GPh thus has more affinities with Matthew's gospel than Luke's, so that this example is at least consistent with the theory that GPh is dependent on Matthew's gospel (though it cannot of itself give any stronger proof of this).

Saying 122 says of outsiders: 'Let them feed from the crumbs that fall from the table, like the dogs' (82.23-24). The imagery seems to be derived from the saying of the Syro-Phoenician woman to Jesus in Mt 15.27/ Mk 7.28. However, there are differences between Matthew and Mark at this point. Mk 7.28 reads: 'The dogs under the table eat of the children's crumbs'; Mt 15.27 reads: 'The dogs eat of the crumbs which fall from their masters' table'. The 'table' is linked with the dogs in Mark, but with the crumbs in Matthew; further, the crumbs are said to 'fall' only in Matthew's version. In each of these instances, GPh follows Matthew's version rather than Mark's. Further, Matthew's version here is due to his redaction of Mark.[269] Thus once again, GPh shows knowldge of MtR, and this strengthens the theory that the writer is dependent on Matthew's final gospel.[270]

Saying 69 includes the words: 'He said, "My Father who is in secret". He said, "Go into your chamber and shut the door behind you, and pray to your Father who is in secret"'. (68.9-13) That this is a quotation of Mt 6.6 is accepted by all.[271] Within Matthew's gospel, this is part of Matthew's M material. The ultimate origin of the

[269] Unless we are to assume two independent versions here (so B.H. Streeter, *The Four Gospels*, London 1924, 260), but this seems unnecessary.

[270] Only Catanzaro, op.cit., 65, refers explicitly here to Mt 15.27.

[271] Schenke, op.cit., 17; Wilson, op.cit., 133; Catanzaro, op.cit., 52; Till, op.cit., 78; Ménard, op.cit., 89.

tradition is uncertain, and it is not clearly redactional. Thus the presence of this saying in GPh cannot prove that the latter presupposes Matthew's gospel rather than Matthew's source here. However, given the dependence of GPh on MtR which we have already seen, the use of the saying here fits well with the theory that GPh is dependent on Matthew.

Further allusions which are consistent with this theory include Jesus' cry of dereliction, which is quoted in saying 72: 'My God, my God, why, O Lord, have you forsaken me?' (68.26f.). Clearly this cannot be derived from Luke's gospel; however, since Mk 15.34 and Mt 27.46 are almost identical in their versions of Jesus' cry, either could theoretically be the source of GPh (though there appears to be no support in the textual tradition for reading an extra 'O Lord' here in either Matthew or Mark). This example is at least consistent (though we can say no more) with the theory that GPh is dependent on Matthew.

The same applies to the reference to the veil of the temple. In saying 76 it is said that 'its veil was rent from top to bottom' (70.1-3); and in saying 125 there is an extended discussion, claiming that it is highly significant that the veil was torn not only at the top, nor only at the bottom, but from top to bottom (85.5-10). Once again, this excludes Luke's version as a possible source of the allusion, since Lk 23.45 lacks the phrase 'from top to bottom' which is so crucial for the writer of GPh. Mt 27.51 and Mk 15.38 both have the relevant phrase. In fact, Matthew and Mark are all but identical here, so that again, either could theoretically be the source of GPh, and this is once more consistent with the theory that GPh is dependent on Matthew.

The remaining synoptic allusions are much more indirect than those considered so far, though nearly all of them can be explained as being derived from Matthew. Saying 22 includes the words 'No one will hide a large valuable object in something large . . . ' (56.20-22). Some have cited Mt 13.45f. as a parallel.[272] If the parallel is accepted, it shows once again a link between GPh and M material, and would fit the theory that GPh is dependent on Matthew. However, the reference is very general, and the parallel is by no means certain. In saying 27 it is said that 'no one will be able to go into the king if he is naked' (58.15f.). Some connection with the parable of the man without the wedding garment (Mt 22.11-14) has been suggested.[273] This parable is peculiar to Matthew, and thus there might be another link between GPh and M material, though one must admit that the allusion (if such it is) is very indirect.

Saying 32 says: 'There were three who always walked with the Lord: Mary his mother, and her sister and Magdalene, the one who was called his companion' (59.6-10). There would appear to be some link with Mt 27.55f./Mk 15.40f. (perhaps also Jn 19.25),[274] but one cannot be more precise. Saying 48 says (presumably of the true Gnostic): 'When the pearl is cast down into the mud it does not become greatly despised' (62.17-19). A connection with the parable of the pearl of great price (Mt 13.45f.) has been suggested,[275] but Mt 7.6 may also be in mind.[276] No NT allusion may be intended at all, though such parallels as might exist are once again in Matthew's gospel alone.

---

272 Cf. Ménard, op.cit., 141; Catanzaro, op.cit., 40, refers to 'Mt 13.34', which must presumably be a misprint.
273 Wilson, op.cit., 93; Catanzaro, op.cit., 42; Ménard, op.cit., 147.
274 Wilson, op.cit., 97; Ménard, op.cit., 150f.
275 Catanzaro, op.cit., 46.
276 Ménard, op.cit., 164, gives a number of examples of the 'pearl' imagery being used to denote something of great value.

Saying 59 runs: 'If one goes down into the water and comes up without having received anything and says, "I am a Christian", he has borrowed the name at interest. But if he receives the Holy Spirit, he has the name as a gift. He who has received a gift does not give it back, but of him who has borrowed it at interest, payment is demanded.' (64.22-29). The first part of this saying may reflect Mt 3.16/Mk 1.10.[277] Possibly too the second half may reflect Mt 13.12.[278] However, the connection is not strong, and Mt 13.12 is closely parallel to Mk 4.24 and Lk 8.18. At the most one can say that. no other synoptic tradition is closer to GPh than Matthew's gospel.

Saying 87 may include a reference to 'the sons of the bridegroom' (72.20f.). The text is missing at the crucial point, and either 'bridegroom' or 'bridal-chamber' could have been the original reading. However, the phrase 'sons of the bridegroom' occurs again in saying 122 (82.17).[279] There may be a connection here with the D reading of Mt 9.15.[280] This variant is confined to Matthew's text. If there is a connection, it is once again with Matthew's gospel, with perhaps an indication of the textual tradition of Matthew involved. However, this evidence is not strong, and one should be wary of building too much on it.[281]

Saying 99 includes the words: 'For things are not imperishable, but sons are. Nothing will be able to receive imperishability if it does not first become a son'. (75.10-

---

277 Cf. Catanzaro, op.cit., 48.

278 Cf. Catanzaro, ibid.; Ménard, op.cit., 30.

279 Wilson, op.cit., 151f.; Ménard, op.cit., 206f.

280 Noted by R.M. Grant, 'The Mystery of Marriage in the Gospel of Philip', *VigChr* 15 (1961) 136.

281 It is possible that the variant is itself due to Gnostic influence, as was suggested long ago by Jülicher, *Gleichnisreden*, 180f., cited by Wilson, 'New Testament in Philip', 294. One must therefore allow for the possibility of *mutual* interaction between use of the gospel tradition and textual variants Cf. above p. 12.

14). It may be that the word for 'son' here should be taken as 'child', and that there is an allusion to the sayings in the synoptic gospels about receiving the kingdom as a child.[282] If this is so, it could be argued that GPh is closer to Matthew's version of the saying (Mt 18.3), where the child is explicitly an example to be imitated ('become like children'), than to Mark's version (Mk 10.15), where the point of comparison is rather more ambiguous ('receive the kingdom like a child').[283] The issue is by no means clear cut, but it should be noted again that Matthew's version is presumably due to his redaction of Mark. It may be, therefore, that this is another instance of a link between GPh and MtR.

Finally, saying 125 says that when the veil of the temple is rent, 'this house will be left desolate' (84.27f.). This appears to reflect the Q saying in Mt 23.38/Lk 13.35.[284] The text of this gospel saying is not certain, but there is strong MSS support for reading *ἔρημος* in Mt 23.38,[285] rather less for reading *ἔρημος* in Lk 13.35.[286] The textual difficulties make any conclusion uncertain, but it is not impossible that the language of GPh is derived from a text of Matthew's gospel.[287]

---

[282] Wilson, *Philip*, 161; Ménard, op.cit., 217.

[283] Is one to receive the kingdom as a child receives things, or is one to receive the kingdom as one receives a child?

[284] So Grant, op. cit., 136. Schenke notes no NT parallel here, and Ménard, op.cit., 243, expresses doubt about the existence of an allusion here; similarly Wilson, op.cit., 190f. However, a little later in the same saying GPh says that the Godhead will be 'under the wings' of the cross. This seems to reflect the imagery of the same gospel saying (Mt 23.37/Lk 13.34: a hen gathers her brood 'under her wings') and hence suggests that this gospel saying is indeed in mind.

[285] P^{77} ℵ C D W Θ f^{1} f^{13} lat $syr^{p,h}$ etc.

[286] D N Δ Θ H f^{13} etc. *ἔρημος* is printed in the 26th ed. of the Nestle-Aland Greek NT in the text of Mt 23.38 but not of Lk 13.35.

[287] It *may* be significant that ἔρημος is the reading of, amongst others, the Western text of Mt 23.38: cf. Helmbold, *The Nag Hammadi Gnostic Texts and the Bible*, 91, who sees this as an example of an allusion of GPh to the Western text of Matthew; but the reading is probably too widespread in texts of Matthew to justify such precision.

All the allusions considered so far have given positive support for, or are at least consistent with, the theory that GPh is dependent on Matthew's gospel alone. There is, however, one allusion which cannot possibly derive from Matthew. This is the reference in saying 111 to the parable of the Good Samaritan: 'The Samaritan gave nothing but wine and oil to the wounded man' (78.8f.), interpreted as referring to the 'ointment' of the true Gnostic. Whether this shows direct knowledge of Luke's gospel[288] is, however, uncertain. The parable of the Good Samaritan was widely known and used in the early church, and appears to have been popular in Gnostic circles.[289] The allusion indicates knowledge of the parable itself, but not necessarily of the whole gospel of Luke.

Other references to Luke's gospel have been alleged. For example, the start of saying 17: 'Some said "Mary conceived by the Holy Spirit"' (55.23f.) has been compared with Lk 1.35.[290] However, this very general reference to the Virgin birth could equally well be derived from Mt 1.18,20. The words in saying 95: 'It is because of the chrism that Christ has his name. For the Father anointed the Son' (74.15-18) may be an allusion to Lk 4.18, but other NT texts are equally close (e.g. 2 Cor 1.21f.), and Ménard points out how frequently Χριστός and χρίσμα are linked in Gnostic texts.[291]

The final example to be considered here occurs in saying 35: 'Without it (i.e. salt) no offering is acceptable' (59.30f.). Some have pointed to the D text of Mk 9.49 as providing a background here.[292] However, this reading in

---

[288] So Wilson, op.cit., 7: 'There is at least one distinct allusion to Luke'.
[289] see p. 34 above.
[290] Catanzaro, op.cit., 39; Ménard, op.cit., 30, 136.
[291] Ménard, op.cit., 213.
[292] Catanzaro, op.cit., 43.

Mark is itself an allusion to Lev. 2.13. Given the fact that GPh in general has a high regard for the OT,[293] it may well be that this saying in GPh is an OT, rather than a NT, allusion.[294]

The conclusion of this section is that, with the exception of the reference to the parable of the Good Samaritan, all the allusions to the synoptic tradition in GPh can be explained as deriving from Matthew's gospel.[295] GPh gives one saying as an explicit quotation, and the author clearly refers to MtR at least once and probably more often. Thus Matthew's gospel appears to be GPh's primary source of information for sayings of Jesus from the synoptic tradition.

The *Valentinian Exposition* (XI. 2) is somewhat fragmentary but there appear to be at least two clear echoes of synoptic tradition in it. The text at 36.32ff. says: 'The will of the Father is: always produce and bear fruit'. This may well be a reminiscence of Mt 7.16ff. where an exhortation about 'fruits' (7.16-20) is placed next to a reference to 'the will of the Father' (7.21). Although the note about 'bearing fruit' could show influence from elsewhere (e.g. Jn 15), it may be relevant to note that the two Matthaean passages are alluded to in close proximity in another Valentinian text, viz., GTr 33.31ff.[296] In Matthew, the references to God as 'Father' are probably

[293] Ménard, op.cit., 29f.

[294] Cf. Wilson, op.cit., 99.

[295] Thus supporting Wilson's general claim that 'of the four Gospels, the author's preference is clearly for Matthew and John' (op.cit., 7; also 'New Testament in Philip', 291), though Wilson does not undertake the detailed comparison offered here.

[296] See p. 60 above; also p. 71 above, on TriTrac 118.23f., and the note there about the popularity of Mt 7.16 among Valentinian Gnostics according to Origen.

due to MtR, so that the author of ValExp, if he is using the synoptic tradition, is probably presupposing Matthew's finished gospel. (On the other hand, the reference to 'the Father' in the text is by no means unusual, and thus does not require the synoptic text to explain its usage here.)

In the section of this text entitled 'On the Anointing', there is another clear synoptic allusion: 'It is fitting for thee at this time to send thy Son Jesus Christ and anoint us so that we might be able to trample upon the snakes and the heads of the scorpions and all the power of the Devil' (40.10-16). This seems to be a clear allusion to the material in Lk 10.19. The origin of the verse in Lk 10 is not certain,[297] but the very close relationship between the sayings (trample, snakes, scorpions, the power of the enemy/Devil) probably shows knowledge of Luke's gospel by the author of ValExp.

A further allusion may be found in the first section on Baptism. A somewhat fragmentary text says: 'The first baptism is the forgiveness of sins': this appears to be followed by an 'interpretation' which includes an allegorical exegesis of the names 'John' and 'Jordan' (cf. 41.15ff.). It looks as if some interpretation is being given of John the Baptist's practice of baptizing in the Jordan. Now John's baptism is related to the forgiveness of sins in Mk 1.4/Lk 3.3 but not in Matthew. However, certainty is not possible: it is not really clear whether the reference to the forgiveness of sins is due to an underlying text which is

---

[297] H. Schürmann, *Traditionsgeschichtliche Untersuchungen zu den synoptischen Evangelien*, Düsseldorf 1968, 146 n.37, argues for an origin in Q; so also Marshall, *Luke*, 427. On the other hand, P. Hoffmann, *Studien zur Theologie der Logienquelle*, *NTA* 8, Münster 1972, 252, argues that the verse fits so well with Luke's idea of mission that the verse may well be LkR in its final form, even though the individual motifs are traditional.

being interpreted, or whether it is the author's own interpretative addition to his source (which would then have simply spoken of John's baptism).

No other synoptic allusions appear to be identifiable in this tractate. Knowledge of Matthew's and Luke's gospel is thus probably implied, but the amount of relevant evidence is small.

In some of the Nag Hammadi texts, one of the disciples of Jesus plays a leading role in the narrative framework. Whether the identity of this disciple has any significance is uncertain, but it may be worthwhile to consider together texts in which one particular apostle is prominent. Thus for example, the common use of the figure of Thomas in the *Book of Thomas the Contender* (II, 7)[298] and in the Gospel of Thomas invites a comparison between the two documents. Yet it is perhaps surprising that these two texts are markedly different in the amount of synoptic material which they contain. For whilst the Gospel of Thomas is famous for its wealth of synoptic-type material, ThomCont appears to be almost totally lacking in such material.

ThomCont develops the motif of the ignorance of the disciples (e.g. 138.31-36), a motif which has some affinities with the picture of the disciples in Mark.[299] But there is no need to postulate a literary relationship here: the motif is extremely common in the Nag Hammadi texts, and it provides the situation necessary to provoke further esoteric teaching.[300] The saying in 140.41f.,

298 For editions and translations, see J.D. Turner, *The Book of Thomas the Contender*, *SBLDS* 23, Missoula 1975; D. Kirchner, 'Das Buch des Thomas. Die siebte Schrift aus Nag-Hammadi-Codex II', *ThLZ* 102 (1977) 794-804.

299 Cf. Mk 4.13, 41; 6.51f.; 7.17f.; 8.17-21. The parallel is noted by Turner, op.cit., 132f.

300 Cf. Robinson, 'Gnosticism and the New Testament', 133ff.

'Blessed is the wise man who (sought after the truth and) when he found it, he rested upon it for ever',[301] appears to allude to the synoptic saying of 'seeking and finding' (Mt 7.7/Lk 11.9); but, as has already been seen, the motifs of 'seeking/finding' and 'rest' were very widespread,[302] so that direct dependence on the synoptic tradition cannot be assumed. Rather, this looks more like the use of common themes, which may ultimately derive from the synoptic tradition, but whose ultimate origin has now been forgotten. At 144.2-6, ('Woe to you who dwell in error, heedless that the sun which judges and looks down upon the All will circle around all things so as to enslave the enemies') Turner suggests that Mt 5.45 may be in the background.[303] But the allusion is very remote, and certainly Mt 5.45 gives no idea of the sun's destructive powers.

Kirchner sees an allusion to Mt 10.28 in the words of Thomas in 140.38-40. He reconstructs and translates the texts as follows: 'Wappnet euch vor denen, die das Verderben für den Leib und die Seele nicht kennen'.[304] Even in this form, it is by no means clear that an allusion to Mt 10.28 is intended. (E.g. there is nothing of the contrast between killing the body alone as opposed to killing the body and the soul). Further, there are a number of lacunae in the text at this point, and Kirchner's text is a reconstructed one. Turner's translation here reads: 'Many are the things revealed to those who do not know that they will forfeit their soul' (which might suggest a very indirect

[301] For the text, see Turner, op.cit., 152f.

[302] Cf. above, p.37 n110 and p.40 n120. The two motifs are connected in GTh2 (in the Greek version of POxy 654) and in the Gospel of the Hebrews (cf. Clement *Strom.* II.9.45; V.14.96) with an additional reference to 'reigning' in each case. See too below on 145.10-14.

[303] Op.cit., 177.

[304] Op.cit., cols. 793, 799.

allusion to Mk 8.36). When there is so much uncertainty about the text, it is impossible to deduce very much about the nature of any alleged synoptic allusion.

The extended metaphor/parable of the sun, the weeds and the grapevine (144.20ff.) may owe something to biblical imagery. Turner suggests that there may be reflections of Mt 5.5 (inheritance of the land), 5.45 (the sun shining on both good and bad) and 13.30 (vine and weeds growing together). He says: 'It may be that the author was inspired by the discourses of the *Gospel of Matthew*, or another similar collection of such discourse material. But there is no single locus from which the metaphor of *Thomas the Contender* could have derived; rather we must accept its character as a *pastiche* of biblical motifs.'[305]

A much stronger case for a theory of direct use of the synoptic tradition by ThomCont can be made in the case of the two beatitudes on 145.3-8: 'Blessed are you who are reviled and not esteemed on account of the love their Lord has for them. Blessed are you who weep and are oppressed by those without hope, for you will be released from every bondage.' Turner points to the very close relationship which exists between the wording of the first part of each beatitude and that of Mt 5.11 and Lk 6.21 respectively.[306] If this is the case, it may also be significant that the reference to 'weeping' in Lk 6.21 is probably LkR.[307] This means that ThomCont shows knowledge of LkR, and thus presupposes Luke's finished gospel. Whether this is direct knowledge of the canonical beatitudes by ThomCont is, however, uncertain. Turner observes that it

---

305 Op.cit., 185f.

306 Op.cit., 188f.

307 See J. Dupont, *Les Béatitudes. I*, Paris 1969, 266-71; also my 'Beatitudes', 198.

is very strange that, if the author knew Mt 5.11, he should have omitted the phrase 'and they persecute you and say every evil thing against you, lying to you'.[308] (On the other hand, the conclusion of the second beatitude quoted here can easily be seen as the result of a change by the author of ThomCont, referring to the ascetic's release from the constraints of the body.)[309]

Finally, at the end of the document, 'Watch and pray' (145.8) recalls Mt 26.41/Mk 14.38 (Lk 22.46 has no 'watch').[310] 145.10-14 reads: 'As you pray, you will find rest, for you have left behind the sufferings and the disgrace. For when you come forth from the sufferings and passion of the body, you will receive rest from the Good One, and you will reign with the King.' Once again there is the collocation of 'finding' and 'rest', and the further connection between 'rest' and 'reigning' shows that one is within a pattern of motifs witnessed elsewhere in Christian tradition, and not necessarily directly dependent on the synoptic tradition.[311]

In summary, very few clear synoptic allusions can be

---

[308] Turner, op.cit., 189, says that these are 'notions which would have been very congenial to the intention of *Thomas the Contender*'.

[309] Ibid., 189f.

[310] Turner, op.cit., 190, also refers to Mk 13.33, but this has no 'pray'.

[311] Cf n.302 above. See also below on 2ApocJas 55.8ff. and on DialSav. Whether there is any direct relationship between these texts is not certain. There is clearly a close connection between the saying in the Gospel of the Hebrews and GTh (though only in the Greek version of the latter: the Coptic text has no reference to 'rest'). The versions in ThomCont are less close. The saying in 140.41f. may only indicate a common milieu of ideas. However, the saying in 145.10-14 shows more striking similarities, especially with the additional reference to 'reigning'. However, if there is a link between ThomCont and GTh here, it must be at a relatively early stage in the development of the saying, i.e. prior to the present Coptic version of GTh (which omits the 'rest' motif). Whether there is primitive tradition here (cf. Koester, 'Gnostic Writings', 242-4) is more doubtful. This saying appears to reflect a secondary development, perhaps of the synoptic saying: see Jeremias, *Unknown Sayings*, 14f.; Ménard, *Thomas*, 79; Vielhauer, in Hennecke, *NT Apocrypha I*, 162.

found in ThomCont. Matthaean material is echoed, and on one occasion LkR seems to be presupposed. This may show that ThomCont has knowledge of Matthew's and Luke's gospels, but in many ways it seems to be a very indirect relationship that is involved. What is perhaps surprising is the contrast between GTh and ThomCont. GTh uses what may be primitive traditions of the sayings of Jesus (whether the author derived them from the canonical gospels or elsewhere). ThomCont either does not know these traditions, or is unconcerned to use them. Whether ThomCont knows GTh is also unclear.[312] Turner considers the whole Thomas literature as in some sense a discrete unity, with ThomCont occupying a medial position between GTh and the Acts of Thomas.[313] However, ThomCont is much further along the 'trajectory' of developing Jesus-traditions than GTh, and the author seems almost oblivious to the original form of the tradition. As Turner says: 'Whatever may have been the original saying has been all but obliterated by the accretion of (ascetic) interpretation . . . The Jesuanic formulae are only an atavism designed to legitimatize the message of the interpretation by designating Jesus the Savior as its source.'[314]

There are three texts in the Nag Hammadi Library where James plays an important role. The first of these is

[312] The connection between 145.10-14 and the Greek version of GTh 2 suggests some connection. However, it is also worth noting that the apparent allusions to the canonical beatitudes in ThomCont do not overlap at all with the wording of the beatitudes which have been preserved in GTh (sayings 54, 68, 69).
[313] Op.cit., 233ff. Also his article 'A New Link in the Syrian Judas Thomas Tradition', *NHS* 3, Leiden 1972, 101-119.
[314] *The Book of Thomas the Contender*, 221.

the *Apocryphon of James*,[315] a text which presents peculiar problems in the context of the present study. Allusions to synoptic tradition appear to be present, but there may also be traditions of Jesus' sayings which are independent of the synoptic tradition, particularly in some of the parables given in ApocJas.[316] Further, many of the references which might be seen as possible allusions to the synoptic tradition are often very remote and one cannot always be sure if a definite allusion is intended.

In 8.5-10 there appears to be a list of parables which are well-known to the writer and his audience: Jesus says 'It was enough for some to listen to the teaching and understand "the Shepherds" and "the Seed" and "the Building" and "the Lamps of the Virgins" and "the Wage of the Workmen" and "the Didrachmae" and "the Woman"'. Nearly all of these can easily be seen as references to parables known from the synoptic tradition. Thus 'the Seed' could refer to various seed parables (e.g. the Sower, the mustard seed), 'the Building' could refer to Mt 7.24-27 and par., 'the lamps of the Virgins' clearly recalls Mt 25.1-13, 'the Wage of the Workmen' could refer to Mt 20.1-16, 'the Didrachmae' and 'the Woman'[317]

---

[315] For editions and translations, see especially M. Malinine–H.-C. Puech–G. Quispel–W.C. Till–R. Kasser–R.McL. Wilson–J. Zandee (eds.), *Epistula Iacobi Apocrypha,* Zürich-Stuttgart 1968; H.M. Schenke, 'Der Jakobusbrief aus den Codex Jung', *OLZ* 66 (1971) 117-130; D. Kirchner, *Epistula Jacobi Apocrypha. Die erste Schrift aus Nag-Hammadi-Codex I* (Codex Jung), Dissertation, Humbolt University,.Berlin 1977.

[316] Cf. especially J. Sevrin, 'Paroles et Paraboles de Jésus dans des écrits gnostiques coptes', in *Logia, BeThL* 59, Leuven 1982, 517-528; C.W. Hedrick, 'Kingdom Sayings and the Parables of Jesus in the *Apocryphon of James:* Tradition and Redaction', *NTS* 29 (1983) 1-24.

[317] In the *NHLE* punctuation the implication is that these are two parables, but this is unnecessary.

recalls Lk 15.8-10.[318] 'The Shepherds' is slightly more problematical: the parable of the lost sheep may be in mind,[319] though this refers to only one shepherd. Jn 10 speaks of other rivals to the true shepherd but does not explicitly call them shepherds. Thus either this is a rather loose reference to one of these parables, or it is evidence of another parable known to the writer.[320]

The remaining parallels in ApocJas pose more problems for the present discussion. The parable of the date palm which pours forth fruit and then withers (7.22ff.) is probably the most likely to be independent of the synoptic tradition.[321] The parable of the ear of grain which scatters its fruit and fills the field with ears for another year (12.22ff.) may be another independent parable,[322] though in this case the parallels with the parable of the seed growing secretly (Mk 4.26ff.) are

---

318 Cf. Malinine et al., op.cit., 58; Perkins, *Gnostic Dialogue*, 149; Sevrin, op.cit., 523. Koester ('Dialog', 547) is generally rather skeptical about whether written gospels are reflected in ApocJas, and he sees the reference in the last case to the parable of the woman and the meal jar in GTh 97.

319 So Malinine et al., op.cit., 58; Perkins, op.cit., 149.

320 Cf. Sevrin, op.cit., 523.

321 See Sevrin, op. cit., 524f.; Koester, 'Dialog', 549; Hedrick, op.cit., 13-19, who also claims that the parable may be dominical. Perkins, op.cit., 149 lists it as an example of a 'specific interpretation of the NT', and says that it is 'a growth parable composed of Mk 4.26; 12.20/Jn 12.24; Mt 3.10; 7.16ff.; 12.33; Mk 11.14; Jn 15.2ff.' Some of these texts may have contributed to the present form of the parable (Sevrin points out that it is really two parables): e.g. Jn 12.24 may be the source of the reference to the date palm 'withering', thus providing an allusion to the death of Jesus. (This seems preferable to Hedrick's claim that this feature gives an 'unexpected twist' to the story, characteristic of Jesus' parables, but simply referring to the once-for-all nature of the coming of the Kingdom (op. cit., 18)). Nevertheless the 'date palm' image is still unexplained, and it is difficult to see how it is derived from the NT texts alone. There may well, therefore, be independent tradition here, even if it is not necessarily dominical.

322 Cf. Sevrin, op.cit., 525f.; Koester, op.cit., 549; Hedrick, op.cit., 9-13, who again sees the parable as possibly dominical.

stronger.[323] Nevertheless there is still the unusual feature of the wheat providing not only an abundant harvest, but also sufficient for a re-seeding of the field next year. As Sevrin points out, this is a feature of the parables peculiar to ApocJas but which is *not* taken up in the subsequent interpretation.[324] It looks as though the author of ApocJas is thus using a parable from his tradition. This parable *may* be an elaboration of Mk 4.26-29 (the reference to re-seeding could then be an allusion to the missionary work of the church in the post-Easter situation), or it could represent a tradition quite independent of the synoptic parables. The saying about the word which is like a grain of wheat (8.16ff.) may also preserve an independent tradition. Sevrin refers to the feature (similar to that noted above) that when the grain is picked and used for food, there is still some left to sow again: this is not taken up in the interpretation appended and hence may be part of the tradition received by the author.[325] If so, it would point to the existence of another parable with no clear parallel in the synoptic gospels. This same parable appears to have an allegorical interpretation about faith, love and works embedded into

---

[323] Cf. Perkins, op.cit., 150; the parallel is also noted by Malinine et al., 69, who also refer to GTh 21. Hedrick's interpretation is perhaps suspect: he interprets the subject of the verbs 'scattered its fruit' and 'filled the field with ears for another year' as an unspecified farmer, since he claims that it would be totally exceptional for this to be due to the natural broadcasting of grain. Nevertheless, the enormous harvest from a single spike of wheat is regarded by Hedrick as an unnatural element in the story which is thereby regarded as characteristic of Jesus' parable. May it not be that the broadcasting of the grain from the wheat itself is another such unexpected feature which has just as much claim to be regarded as characteristic of Jesus' parables? But if so, then the story-line becomes considerably closer to that of Mk 4.26-29, where part of the point of the story is that the process involved takes place without any human intervention.

[324] Sevrin, op.cit., 526.

[325] Ibid., 525.

it in the text, thus providing further confirmation of the fact that we have here a redacted tradition.[326] The redaction itself may however show links with the synoptic tradition. In the interpretation, the 'word' which is like the grain of wheat is equated with the kingdom of heaven (cf. 8.25). The parable of the grain of wheat can clearly be seen as similar to the synoptic parable of the sower (both involve seed being sown). In the interpretation of the parable of the sower in Mt 13.19, the sowing and reception of the seed is compared to the acceptance or otherwise of the word of the kingdom. Further, it is only in Matthew's account here that there is explicit mention of the kingdom. Thus it looks as if the interpretation of the parable of the wheat in ApocJas presupposes knowledge of *Matthew's* interpretation of the parable of the sower.[327] This may also be indicated by the reference at the start of the section in ApocJas 8.5f., where Jesus says 'it was enough for some to listen to the teaching and understand . . . '. The language is very general, but again Mt 13.23 uses the same vocabulary of 'listening and understanding', and the latter verb is almost certainly MtR[328] Thus, whatever the status of the actual parable reflected here, its interpretation suggests that, in its final version, ApocJas is presupposing Matthew's finished gospel as well.

There is at least one clear echo of synoptic tradition elsewhere in ApocJas. At 4.25-31, James says: 'We have forsaken our fathers and our mothers and our villages and followed you. Grant us not to be tempted by the devil, the evil one.' The first half of this clearly echoes the saying in

[326] Ibid.

[327] Malinine et al., op.cit., 58; Perkins, op.cit., 150.

[328] Cf. Malinine et al., ibid. For the importance of συνιέναι in Matthew, see Barth, *Tradition and Interpretation in Matthew*, 105ff.

Mk 10.28f. and pars.[329] It seems impossible to say precisely which version is in mind. Malinine et al. claim that 'il paraît s'être inspiré plutôt de *Marc*, en raison de l'allusion que cet Évangile est seul à faire aux "persécutions" et de l'addition qui lui est propre: *μετὰ διωγμῶν*.[330] However, the allusion to persecution comes rather later in the text (line 40), and it is not certain that this particular synoptic saying is still in mind. In fact, Jesus' reply in 4.32ff. ('What is your merit if you do the will of the Father and it is not given to you from him as a gift while you are tempted by Satan? But if you are oppressed by Satan and persecuted and you do his will, I say that he will love you') is rather more reminiscent in its structure of another synoptic context, viz., Mt 5.39ff./ Lk 6.27ff. (cf. especially Mt 5.46/ Lk 6.32-34), where there is a similar construction; perhaps the passage in 1 Pet 2.20 is even closer to ApocJas here. Further, both passages refer to persecution in their contexts (cf. Mt 5.44/ Lk 6.27; 1 Pet 2.20). There is thus no need to see the persecution reference in ApocJas as necessarily inspired by Mk 10.30, and so one cannot really say anything more precise about the origin of the 'forsaking' saying here. The second half of the saying ('Grant us not to be tempted by the devil, the evil one') seems to be a clear echo of the conclusion of the Lord's Prayer.[331] The qualification that the temptation is by 'the devil, the evil one' may indicate that a version of the prayer which included the clause 'Deliver us from (the) evil (one)' is presupposed here. This clause is absent from what are considered the best MSS of Luke here, but (not very surprisingly) the clause does appear in a large

[329] Cf. Malinine et al, op.cit., 48; Koester, op.cit., 548.

[330] Malinine et al., ibid.

[331] Koester, op.cit., 549; Perkins, op.cit., 150; Malinine et al., op.cit., 48f., refer to Jas 1.12f., but this seems a much more remote parallel.

number of MSS of Luke.[332] One cannot say for certain that the language of ApocJas presupposes that of the synoptic gospels themselves: the influence of liturgy must also be taken into account and any allusion to the Lord's Prayer is probably derived as much from the writer's own use of the prayer as from a particular version of a written document.

Other possible allusions to synoptic material are not so clear. The dialogue between Jesus and the disciples in 2.26-28 (Jesus says 'If you wish to come with me, come!', to which the disciples reply 'If you bid us, we come') may be inspired by the story of Jesus calling Peter to come to him on the water in Mt 14.28;[333] but the language is not really distinctive enough to be certain. In the prediction of the persecutions ahead for the disciples in 5.9-20 ('Do you not know that you have yet to be abused (*ὑβρίζειν*) and to be accused (*κατηγορεῖν*) unjustly, and have yet to be shut up in prison, and condemned unlawfully, and crucified without reason, and buried shamefully, as was I myself, by the evil one?') there is clearly some knowledge presupposed of the passion of Jesus. Janssens claims that the closest links here are with the Lukan passion narrative.[334] However, the evidence for this is rather weak. Janssens points to the common use of *ὑβρίζω* here and in Lk 18.32 (LkR of Mk 10.34). She also refers to the use of the Coptic root ϫⲓ ⲛϭⲁⲛⲥ which can mean not only 'unjustly' but can also be related to *βία*, 'force' (cf. Crum's *Dictionary*, 822b). She therefore suggests that one should translate the text here by 'be accused with force', and see a parallel in *εὐτόνως κατηγοροῦντες* in Lk 23.10. All this is

---

332 ℵ^{1} A C D W Θ f^{13} it $syr^{c,p,h}$ $boh^{p.t}$.

333 Malinine et al., op.cit., 41.

334 Y. Janssens, 'Traits de la passion dans l'Epistula Iacobi Apocrypha', *Muséon* 88 (1975) 97-101.

however rather speculative. As Janssens herself admits, it is impossible to make the linguistic bridge between ϫⲓ ⲛϭⲁⲛⲥ and εὐτόνως on the basis of the Coptic NT.[335] In fact ϩⲛⲟⲩϫⲓⲛϭⲁⲛⲥ is attested in the Bohairic NT as the translation of ἀδίκως in 1 Pet 2.19.[336] In view of the possible link with 1 Pet 2 in Jesus' predictions of persecution for the disciples (cf. above) it would probably be more convincing if one postulated an echo of 1 Pet 2.19 rather than of Lk 23.10. The ὑβρίζω reference must be allowed some weight, but in any case, the word is used in Luke in the third passion prediction, not in the passion narrative itself. It looks as if this section in ApocJas is referring to Jesus' passion only in very general terms, and one cannot really determine the form of the passion narrative presupposed.[337]

James' rejection of the idea of Jesus' passion in 5.36-38 ('Lord, do not mention to us the cross and death, for they are far from you') seems to be an echo of Peter's protest at Caesarea Philippi (Mt 16.22/Mk 8.32).[338] No such incident is recorded in Luke. Further, it is only in Matthew's redaction of Mark that any words are explicitly put on the lips of Peter ('God forbid, Lord. This shall never happen to you'). It is most probable that ApocJas reflects Matthew's version here, and hence again presupposes Matthew's finished gospel (though it is not impossible that it is Mark's brief reference to Peter's 'rebuking' Jesus which has been expanded here independently). Jesus replies to James' protest with the words 'None will be saved unless they believe in my cross.

---

335 Nor are they listed as equivalents by Crum.

336 Crum, *Dictionary*, 822a.

337 Indeed the reference is so general that one could see this section as simply a development out of the very simple kerygma of 1 Cor 15.

338 Malinine et al., op.cit., 52; Perkins, op.cit., 149.

But those who have believed in my cross, theirs is the kingdom of God' (6.3-7). A similar beatitude form with an identical second half occurs in 3.30-34 ('Blessed will be those who have not been ill, and have known relief before falling ill: yours is the kingdom of God').[339] It is possible that the first beatitude in the canonical gospels (Mt 5.3/Lk 6.20) is reflected in the final part of these sayings. Further, the use of 'kingdom of God', rather than 'kingdom of heaven', is closer to the Lukan version. This may be significant here, since elsewhere ApocJas uses the phrase 'kingdom of heaven',[340] and hence the use of 'God' here may be indicative of the use of source material. On the other hand, the first half of the saying in 6.3f. has a very close parallel in AscIs 3.18 ('those who believe in his cross will be saved'), and the expression 'believing in the cross' is not easy to parallel elsewhere.[341] The presence of the same saying in both AscIs and ApocJas suggests the existence of an underlying common tradition.[342] It could be the case, therefore, that the reference to 'kingdom of God' in ApocJas comes from the same tradition (though there is no parallel to this phrase in AscIs). Thus whilst the form of the saying in ApocJas may well be due to dependence on prior source material, one cannot be certain if this is due to direct dependence on synoptic tradition: in view of the parallel in AscIs, the possibility of

339 For the possibility that 'relief' should rather be translated 'rest' in a more technical Gnostic sense, see J. Helderman, 'Anapausis in the Epistula Jacobi Apocrypha', *NHS* 14, Leiden 1978, 34-43.

340 See 7.22; 8.25; 9.35; 12.22f.; 13.18, 29f.

341 The parallel is noted by van Unnik, 'The Origin of the Recently Discovered "Apocryphon Jacobi"', 155. I am grateful to Dr. R.J. Bauckham for bringing my attention to the significance of this in a forthcoming study of the Ascension of Isaiah, kindly made available to me prior to its publication. For other links between AscIs and the Nag Hammadi texts, see Helmbold, 'Gnostic Elements'.

342 Direct dependence of AscIs on ApocJas, or vice versa, seems very unlikely.

the use of independent Jesus-traditions must remain open.[343]

The saying in 6.30f. ('Do you not know that the head of prophecy was cut off with John?') and its subsequent interpretation in terms of teaching in parables and teaching openly clearly presupposes the tradition of John's execution, but one cannot be more precise. Possibly too the Q saying Mt 11.13/Lk 16.16 is in mind.[344] The saying in 8.35f. ('I have taught you what to say before the archons') may be an echo of synoptic tradition (cf. Mk 13.11 and pars.; Lk 12.12), though it is too remote for one to be able to be more precise.[345] 10.32-34 ('Invoke the Father, implore God often and he will give to you') is close to Mt 7.7/Lk 11.9, though Jn 16.23f. is equally close.[346] 13.3-8 ('I am revealed to you building a house which is of great value to you since you find shelter beneath it, just as it will be able to stand by your neighbours' house when it threatens to fall') may presuppose the parable of the two houses in Mt 7.24-27/Lk 6.47-49 (which is probably alluded to anyway in 8.7), though other details may have overlaid as well.[347]. Finally, at 14.31 Jesus predicts his ascension, saying 'Today I must take my place at the right hand of the Father'. One can produce synoptic parallels for this (e.g. Mt 26.64),[348] but the idea of the risen Christ

---

343 Whether such a saying is dominical must remain very doubtful: it probably represents a secondary expansion of a statement such as Rom 10.9.

344 Malinine, op.cit., 55f.; Perkins, op.cit., 149. For the significance of the subsequent discussion about teaching in parables/openly, see Robinson, 'Gnosticism and the New Testament', 135f.

345 The absence of any reference to the Holy Spirit means that the saying is closest to Lk 21.15, but arguments from silence are clearly suspect here.

346 Malinine et al., op.cit., 63.

347 Perkins, op.cit., 150, referring to Jn 14.2. But see also Kirchner, *Epistula Jacobi Apocrypha*, 189: 'M.E. steht hinter dem Bild von Offenbaren als Bauen eines Hauses eine weisheitliche Tradition, die in Sir 14, 22-27 eine Parallele besitzt.'

348 Cf. Malinine et al., op.cit., 75.

seated at God's right hand is so ubiquitous in early Christianity that one cannot deduce too much about the source of the language used here.

In conclusion, ApocJas seems to presuppose Matthew's finished gospel. Lukan material (e.g. Lk 15.8-10) is also known and this is probably due to knowledge of Luke's gospel itself.[349] There is no evidence to suggest that Mark's gospel was known, but equally nothing to suggest that it was unknown.[350] However, the probable existence of independent traditions of the sayings of Jesus here must make one cautious before accepting some of the vaguer parallels with the synoptic tradition as evidence of an explicit allusion to that tradition.

The two other texts associated with James show affinities with Jewish Christianity. These are the two apocalypses of James from Codex V.[351] In the case of the *First Apocalypse of James* (V.3),[352] the prominent position given to James, together with the reference to Addai (the reputed founder of Syrian Christianity) as the recipient of the revelation given to James (36.15, 22), have suggested to many that this text has close links with Syrian Jewish Christianity.[353]

---

349 This is rendered more likely if the reference to ὑβρίζω is derived from Luke.

350 The argument from silence is extremely dangerous. E.g. Malinine et al, op.cit., 42, conclude from the note in 2.40 of a 550 day period between Jesus' resurrection and ascension that Acts (which specifies a 40 day period for this) cannot have been known to the author of ApocJas. But such an extended period is a standard Gnostic theme (cf. the 545 days mentioned in AscIs 9.16), providing the necessary time for the risen Christ to give his secret teaching to the disciples. It is just as easy to envisage a deliberate change of the Acts timetable by a Gnostic writer as ignorance of it.

351 Cf. A. Böhlig, 'Der judenchristliche Hintergrund in gnostischen Schriften von Nag Hammadi', *Mysterion und Wahrheit*, *AGSV* 6, Leiden 1968, 102-112.

352 Main editions of the text are in Böhlig-Labib, *Apokalypsen*; and by Schoedel in Parrott (ed.), *Codices V & VI*.

353 Cf. too W.R. Schoedel, 'Scripture and the Seventy two Heavens of the First Apocalypse of James', *NT* 12 (1970) 118-129 as well as his introduction in *Codices V & VI*, 65ff.

Despite the fact that much of the discussion apparently centres on the sufferings of Jesus, very little synoptic material seems to be echoed here. Jesus' prediction to James of his coming arrest also refers to his subsequent rescue with the words 'But my redemption will be near' (25.8f.). Schoedel compares Mk 13.29 here,[354] though a closer parallel might be Lk 21.8 ('your redemption is near'), where (perhaps significantly) the reference to 'redemption' is due to LkR.[355] However, the word 'redemption' (ⲥⲱⲧⲉ) is used very frequently in this tractate (cf. 24.12; 25.9,20; 29.8,13; 33.1; the verb is used at 25.20; 36.9) so that there is no necessity to see any synoptic reference here at all: the phrase may be simply due to the author writing freely, and the verbal agreement with Lk 21.8 may be purely coincidental. The saying of Jesus to James about Jerusalem as 'she who always gives the cup of bitterness to the sons of light' (25.16-18) also has affinities with synoptic tradition (cf. Mk 10.38; 14.34, 36 and pars.).[356] However, the synoptic use of the 'cup' metaphor itself has a background in the OT (cf. Ps 75.9; Is 51.17-22; Jer 25.15). It is thus not possible to say whether the language of 1ApJas has been derived from the synoptic tradition or simply shares a common background with that tradition; there is certainly nothing in the text to demand the former alternative. Jesus' later words about his coming passion in 28.2-4 ('There shall be within me a silence (σιγή) and a hidden mystery. But I am faint-hearted before their anger') have been compared with Jesus' silence at his trial as reported in the synoptic

---

354 Schoedel, in *Codices V & VI*, 70.

355 ⲥⲱⲧⲉ (used here) translates ἀπολύτρωσις 10 times in the Sahidic NT (cf. Wilmet's *Concordance*, 826f.), including Lk 21.8, and otherwise always corresponds to some other word in the λυτρο-group.

356 Referred to by Schoedel, op.cit., 70.

gospels and with Jesus' terror in Gethsemane (cf. Mk 14.34,61; 15.4f. and pars.)[357] However, 'silence' is a technical term in Gnosticism (e.g. in some forms of Valentinianism *σιγή* is one of the aeons of the pleroma (cf. *A.H.* 1.1), though this is probably not reflected here; perhaps a closer parallel might be seen in *A.H.*1.14.1 where Marcus claims to be the receptacle of *σιγή*). There is thus no need to see any allusion to the synoptic trial scenes here. The note about being 'faint-hearted before their anger' might be inspired by the Gethsemane tradition in the synoptic gospels; but the allusion is too remote for one to be more precise about which form of that tradition is presupposed.

The end of the text is extremely fragmentary, but one further possible synoptic allusion may occur in James' words in 41.22f. ('for they have been reviled and they have been persecuted'). This is very close to the words of Mt 5.11;[358] further, the use of *διώκω* in Mt 5.11 is probably due to MtR.[359] Thus, *if* there is a synoptic allusion here, it is to Matthew's finished gospel, and not just to a source. However, the poor state of the text must make any claims to certainty suspect. Finally, at the end of the text, there appears to be an account of James' condemnation to death (and perhaps his execution, though if so it has now been lost), from which some dissociate themselves with the words 'We have no part in this blood, for a just man will perish through injustice' (43.17-21). These words may be partly inspired by the similar disassociation of Pilate

[357] Cf. Schoedel, op.cit., 74.

[358] The Coptic verbs used here are ⲥⲱϣ and ⲡⲱⲧ. ⲥⲱϣ is used at Mt 5.11 boh (but not sah, cf. Crum, *Dictionary*, 375b). ⲡⲱⲧ is used 9 times for *διώκω* in the Sahidic NT, including Mt 5.11 (cf. Wilmet's *Concordance*, 641). The theory that this is an allusion to the NT is thus possible linguistically.

[359] See my 'Beatitudes', 203.

from the blood of Jesus in Mt 27.24.[360] The latter is almost certainly due to MtR.[361] However, if this is an allusion it is at best indirect and cannot in any sense be called a quotation.

The evidence from 1ApJas for the present purposes is thus meagre. Clearly, if the text were better preserved, we might find more echoes of synoptic tradition. As it is, such evidence as there is might suggest that the author of 1ApJas knew the finished gospel of Matthew; and there is nothing to compel the belief that he knew any other form of synoptic tradition.

The *Second Apocalypse of James* (V.4)[362] is, at first sight, rather richer in synoptic material. One must, however, bear in mind, as always, the possibility of independent traditions being available to the author. This possibility is suggested in this case by the fact that the writer may have had access to independent traditions about the stoning of James: the stoning procedure presupposed here corresponds more closely to what is laid down in the Mishnah than do the other Christian accounts of James' execution.[363] This issue is, however, not of direct concern here, and with regard to the relationship between this text and the NT, widely differing views have been expressed. For example, in an

[360] Cf. Schoedel, op.cit., 102; also Böhlig-Labib, *Apokalypsen*, 53.

[361] It is almost universally agreed that Matthew's sole written source in his passion narrative is Mark's gospel, so that most of Matthew's alterations and additions are due to MtR: see N.A. Dahl, 'Die Passionsgeschichte bei Matthäus', *NTS* 2 (1955) 17-32; also D.P. Senior, *The Passion Narrative according to Matthew*, *BEThL* 39, Leuven 1982.

[362] In addition to the editions of the text in Parrott (ed.) *Codices V & VI* and Böhlig-Labib, *Apokalypsen*, see Funk, *Die zweite Apokalypse des Jakobus*.

[363] See A. Böhlig, 'Zum Martyrium des Jakobus', *Mysterion und Wahrheit*, 112-118; S.K. Brown, 'Jewish and Gnostic Elements in the Second Apocalypse of James (CG V.4)'; *NT* 17 (1975) 225-237.

early discussion, Wilson refers to 'the frequent New Testament echoes and allusions' here,[364] whereas Hedrick speaks of 'the almost total absence of allusions to the New Testament tradition' as suggesting an early date for the text.[365] I shall consider the various texts which have been regarded by some as synoptic echoes in the order in which they occur here.

At 47.19f., the speaker (perhaps James) says 'These two who see, I . . . '. The text is uncertain, and a corruption has been suspected.[366] If this is the true reading,[367] it is just possible that the 'two' are the two blind men of Mt 9.27-31 or 20.29-34,[368] possibly interpreted allegorically as referring to the two eyes. If this were established, it is significant that the doubling of the blind men in Matthew's version is MtR: the allusion would thus show dependence on Matthew's finished gospel. However, Hedrick regards it as just as likely that the reference to the 'two who see' is to two prophets, Isaiah (mentioned in line 23) and another.[369] It is thus clearly dangerous to build too much on an uncertain interpretation of such a difficult text.

The text then continues: "They have already proclaimed through these words 'He shall be judged with the unrighteous *(ἄδικος)*'" (47.21-23). This might be seen as betraying knowledge of the application of Is 53.12 to the passion of Jesus in Lk 22.37.[370] However, the use of

---

364 *Gnosis and the New Testament*, 135.
365 In his introduction to the text in *Codices V & VI*, 108.
366 So Böhlig-Labib, *Apokalypsen*, 69. Hedrick, op. cit., 61., suggests that a line may have dropped out.
367 So, e.g., Funk, op. cit., 105f., following Schenke, in his review of Böhlig-Labib, *Apokalypsen*, col.29, who takes it as a nominal sentence and translates: 'Die beiden, die wieder sehen, das bin ich'.
368 So Funk and Schenke, ibid.
369 Op. cit., 117.
370 Cf. Hedrick, ibid.

ἄδικος here does not correspond to either Is 53.12 LXX or Lk 22.37, which both use ἄνομος.[371] This application of Is 53.12 to the passion of Jesus may thus represent a use of that verse which is independent of the use of the same verse in Lk 22.[372] The text then continues: 'He who lived without blasphemy died by means of blasphemy' (47.24f.). Although reference is sometimes made to Gal 3.13,[373] the sense does not appear to be that of the curse of the cross;[374] rather, that the one who never himself blasphemed was brought to death by others who did blaspheme.[375] The thought is not dissimilar to 1 Pet 2.23. If one wishes to search for synoptic parallels, one can find examples of Jesus' opponents 'blaspheming' (cf. Lk 22.65 or Mt 27.39/Mk 15.29 or Lk 23.39). However, the allusion is too remote for one to be able to say which tradition, if any, is reflected here.

At 48.22-24, the speaker says (according to the *NHLE* translation): 'I am the brother in secret who prayed to the Father'. The text is again uncertain. The verb here translated as 'pray' is ἄρασθαι, but the middle α and σ have to be supplied.[376] Böhlig-Labib and Funk fill the lacuna with νι and so read 'deny'.[377] Further, the reference to 'Father' here is not absolutely certain.[378] *If* the NHLE

---

[371] Though one should be slightly cautious: the presence of a Greek loan word in Coptic does not necessarily imply the use of the same word in a Greek *Vorlage*.

[372] Cf. Funk, op. cit., 107: 'Das Schriftzitat selbst besteht in einer freien Wiedergabe von Jes 53, 12.'

[373] So Böhlig-Labib, op. cit., 69; Hedrick, op. cit., 117.

[374] Funk, op. cit., 107f., points out that the Coptic here ⲟⲩⲁ corresponds to βλασφφμία not κατάρα which corresponds to Coptic ⲥⲁϩⲟⲩ

[375] Funk, ibid.

[376] Hedrick, op. cit., 118f.

[377] Böhlig-Labib, op. cit., 70; Funk, op. cit., 111f.

[378] Funk, op. cit., 112, takes the ⲡⲉⲓ of ⲡⲉⲓ[...]ⲧ as the demonstrative adjective and thus produces a translation '. . . who denied this pitiless . . .' (making further conjectures for the lacuna which follows).

translation is accepted, the text may be reminiscent of Mt 6.6,[379] a verse which is also echoed in GPh 68.9-13. However, the uncertain nature of the text must make any conclusions extremely tentative.

At 50.8f. Jesus is referred to as 'that one whom you hated and persecuted'. (The same two verbs are used together in 2LogSeth 59.22f.) It may be that the language is inspired by the canonical gospels; however, the reference is probably too general to be certain, and certainly not specific enough for one to be able to say for sure that a synoptic allusion is in mind (e.g. the language could be derived from Jn 15.18ff.).

At 52.9ff., the speaker (presumably Jesus) says: 'Your father, whom you consider to be rich, shall grant that you inherit all things that you see.' Funk compares the devil's promise in the Q Temptation story (Mt 4.8f./Lk 4.5-7), though, as he also points out, there is no question here of this promise being a temptation to be rejected.[380] There is no suggestion that the 'father' here is the evil Demiurge, or that the promise is seen as anything other than thoroughly positive. It may well be, therefore, that the agreement in wording with the Q account is purely coincidental. (There is in any case nothing very distinctive about the language used here.) A little later on the same page there is the general exhortation 'When you hear, therefore, open your ears and understand' (52.16-18), which may be reminiscent of texts like Mt 11.15 and pars.[381] However, such an exhortation is extremely common in these Gnostic texts, and is often used where a saying or piece of teaching requires further elucidation.[382] There is thus no

---

[379] Cf. Hedrick, op. cit., 118.
[380] Op. cit., 29.
[381] Cf. Böhlig-Labib, op. cit., 74.
[382] Cf. Robinson, 'Gnosticism and the New Testament', 135f., and see pp.34 and 38 above, on SJC and GMary respectively.

need to see any direct reference to synoptic language in the use of what is clearly, in part, a stereotyped exhortation.

At 55.2 there is a reference to the 'small children', which may be reminiscent of Mk 10.13-16 and pars., and Mt 18.1ff.[383] However, the use of this language, referring to the true Gnostic, is widespread,[384] and there is no need to assume that the biblical language is explicitly in mind here. The text at 55.8ff. ('Those who seek to walk in the way that is before the door open the good door through you') correlates 'way' and 'door'; Mt 7.13f. uses similar imagery, but so also do other texts,[385] and there is nothing here to compel the view that the gospel passage has determined the language here. Similarly 55.14 says of those who enter the door that James will 'give a reward to each one who is ready for it'. Böhlig-Labib compare Mt 20.1-16 here;[386] but the only common feature is the general idea of reward, and hence again there is probably not enough for one to be able to deduce the existence of a definite allusion. In fact this whole section from 55.8 comes to a climax in 56.2-5 ('For your sake they will be told these things and will come to rest. For your sake they will reign and will become kings'). This is clearly reminiscent of the saying associated with the sequence seek–find–marvel–rest–reign attested elsewhere, notably in the Gospel of the Hebrews.[387] In view of the Jewish-Christian natures of both 2ApJas and GHeb, it is

383 Cf. Funk, op. cit., 141f.

384 Funk himself refers to GTr 19.27-30; *Exc.Theod.* 41.1f.; ApPet 80.11 (where, however, an allusion to Matthew is more likely: see below).

385 Cf. Funk, op. cit., 145f.

386 Op. cit., 77.

387 In Clement, *Strom.* II.9.45; V.14.96; cf. Brown, op.cit., 234. See too GTh 2 (in the POxy version), ThomCont 145.10-14 (cf. p.86 above), and DialSav passim (see below). Brown shows how that 'seek–find–marvel' part of the sequence is presupposed in 55.8; 55.13f. and 55.22f. respectively.

tempting to see some relationship between the two documents here, with perhaps GHeb being the source of 2ApJas. However, one cannot be more than tentative in view of the lack of other evidence. In any case the version in GHeb and elsewhere is probably a secondary development of the synoptic seek–find saying in Mt 7.7/Lk 11.9.[388] Thus 2ApJas shows no direct knowledge of synoptic tradition here.

At 57.20-22, the speaker (whose identity is not clear) says: 'I tell you, judges, you have been judged'. This is similar to the synoptic saying in Mt 7.1/Lk 6.37, though the saying was probably proverbial,[389] and hence one cannot be certain that any synoptic allusion is intended. At 60.7ff. James says: 'The Lord has taken you captive from the Lord, having closed your ears, that they may not hear the sound of my word.' The double reference to 'Lord' is very difficult, and some corruption of the text has been suspected.[390] Böhlig-Labib refer to Mt 13.13 and pars.;[391] Funk refers to Is 6.9f. and its citations in the NT.[392] Whatever one does with the second 'Lord' in the passage, the first 'Lord', who is also the subject of the 'closing your eyes', must be the Demiurge.[393] If so, then the allusion may be intended to be to the words of the God of the OT, and hence Is 6 itself is more likely to be the direct source of the language used.

---

388 See n.311 above.

389 Funk, op. cit., 133f., refers to 1 Clem 13.2; Sent Sext 183,184; GMary 15.17f.; Thunder 20.11f.; TeachSilv 102.11-13; Polycarp 2.3. Some of these may be related to the synoptic saying, but 1 Clem 13 may not be directly dependent on the synoptic gospels: cf. above on p.39 on GMary 15.17f.

390 Schenke, op.cit., col.31, followed by Funk, op.cit., 169, transposes the second 'Lord' reference to line 14 of the same page.

391 Op.cit., 82.

392 Op.cit., 169.

393 Funk, ibid., and Hedrick, op.cit., 140, refer to the similarities with 54.10ff. and what is said of the Demiurge there.

The text at 61.20-23 refers to the martyrdom of James himself: 'And they were there and found him standing beside the columns of the temple beside the mighty corner stone.' There is doubt about the correct translation here, and one should perhaps read 'pinnacle' for 'columns'.[394] Funk says: 'Natürlich erinnert die ganze Szene an Matth 4,5f. Par und damit an das erwartete Flugwunder des Messias.'[395] Whether there was such an expectation in pre-Christian Judaism is unclear,[396] and it may be that any such references to the 'Flugwunder' are ultimately derived from this Q tradition. On the other hand, the motif of James standing on the pinnacle of the temple also occurs in Hegesippus' account of James' martyrdom.[397] Thus this feature seems to be a well-established element in the James tradition, and one cannot necessarily see any direct reference to synoptic tradition at this point.

A few final possible allusions to synoptic tradition have been noted in James' final prayer. The text at 63.15-19 ('Do not give me into the hand of a judge who is severe with sin. Forgive me all my debts of the days of my life') may be compared with the end of the Lord's prayer.[398] Perhaps the petition for forgiveness affords the closest parallel; on the other hand, a prayer for forgiveness is hardly surprising in a Jewish-Christian document, and such a prayer is specifically ordained for a man about to be stoned in M.Sanh. 6.2. Finally, the text at 63.22 ('you I have confessed') migh be compared with Lk 12.8f.,[399] but again the parallel is only a very general one.

In conclusion there is no clear evidence of direct

394 So Böhlig-Labib, op. cit., 83; Funk, op. cit., 174f.; cf. Hedrick, op. cit., 142f.
395 Op. cit., 175.
396 Cf. the doubts raised by Manson, *Sayings*, 44; Marshall, *Luke*, 173.
397 In Eusebius, *E.H.* II.23.11ff.
398 Hedrick, op.cit., 147.
399 Hedrick, ibid.

dependence of 2ApJas on synoptic tradition. There are several stock phrases and ideas which the tractate shares with the gospels, but there is virtually nothing which is distinctive enough to suggest direct knowledge and use of the synoptic tradition. The text at 47.23 (the use of Is 53.12) might suggest that the document is independent of the synoptic gospels, and the use of the seek–find–marvel–rest–reign saying may suggest more direct links with Jewish-Christian tradition traditions as preserved in GHeb. Thus 2ApJas may provide a witness to a trajectory within early Christianity which preserved Christian traditions independently of the trajectories on which our present synoptic gospels lie.

Another sub-group of texts associated with an individual apostle centres on the figure of Peter. *The Acts of Peter and the Twelve Apostles* (VI.1)[400] is one text within the subgroup. For the most part synoptic tradition is not very prominent. However, in at least one passage, it is clearly presupposed. This occurs on p.9 of the tractate in the conversation between Lithargoel (=Jesus) and Peter concering Peter's name. Lithargoel addresses Peter by name, whereupon Peter expresses surprise that his name should be known to an apparent stranger. The text continues: 'Lithargoel answered, "I want to ask you who gave the name Peter to you?" He said to him, "It was Jesus Christ, the son of the living God. He gave this name to me." He answered and said, "It is I! Recognise me."' (9.8-14). This seems to be quite clearly based on Matthew's version of the confession of Peter at Caesarea Philippi, where Jesus, in his praise of Simon, gives him the name

400 For editions, see Parrott, in *Codices V & VI*; Krause-Labib in *Codex II und Codex VI*; also H.M. Schenke, 'Die Taten des Petrus und der zwölf Apostel', *ThLZ* 98 (1973) 13-19.

Peter (Mt 16.17-19).[401] The origin of this tradition is much disputed, so that one cannot decide from this alone whether the text in AcPet12 is based on Matthew's gospel or Matthew's source. However, Peter's initial reply ('It was Jesus Christ, the son of the living God') clearly reflects the Matthaean version of Peter's actual confession (Mt 16.16), where the phrase 'the son of the living God' is unquestionably due to MtR of Mark's version (whatever one decides about the origin of Mt 16.17-19). Thus AcPet12 here is almost certainly dependent on Matthew's finished gospel and not just on Matthew's source.[402]

The scene which immediately follows is also full of reminiscences of Matthew's gospel. Lithargoel loosens his garment revealing his true identity to the disciples. To this the reaction is: 'We prostrated ourselves on the ground and worshipped him. We comprised eleven disciples' (9.19-21; cf. also 12.16f.). This may well be based on Matthew's resurrection account: the explicit reference to 'eleven' disciples determines the scene as a resurrection appearance, and Mt 28.16 explicitly mentions 'eleven' disciples; further, the worship of the risen Jesus is also mentioned in Mt 28.17. It is thus very probable that the Matthaean account has provided the basis for the language used by AcPet12 here.

Other possible synoptic allusions in the text are not so clear. At the start of the text, the apostles say: 'We agreed to fulfil the ministry to which the Lord appointed us' (1.10-12). Several NT passages could be given as possible

---

[401] Cf. Parrott, op. cit., 222; Krause-Labib, op. cit., 117.

[402] See too the similar results of the analysis of J. Sell, 'Simon Peter's "Confession" and *The Acts of Peter and the Twelve Apostles*', *NT* 21 (1979) 344-356 who concludes that this section 'reflects knowledge of Mt xvi 13-19 and that, in fact, both the pericope as a whole and the "I am" statement itself are based upon Simon Peter's confession in its *Matthaean* form' (356).

parallels here, e.g. Mk 3.13-19 and pars., Mt 28.19f.; Acts 1.8,[403] but the reference is too general for one to be able to be more precise. Similarly the section about the rich rejecting Lithargoel's offer to sell pearls (3.14-27) may have been inspired in part by the negative attitude to riches in some gospel texts,[404] though again one cannot say more. At 3.23-25 it is said that Lithargoel had 'no pouch (πήρα) on his back, nor bundle inside his cloth and napkin'. This may reflect the synoptic mission instructions, where the disciples are told not to take anything for their journey, including a πήρα.[405] However, once again there is no way of distinguishing between the gospel traditions in this particular case. The reference to the 'napkin' may be significant. Here it is said that Lithargoel had no napkin (ⲙⲛ ⲡⲓⲥⲟⲩⲇⲁⲣⲓⲟⲛ), whereas 2.14 mentions a σουδάριον as part of Lithargoel's magnificent attire. A napkin is mentioned at Lk 19.20, but it is very improbable that this is the source of the allusion here.[406] It is more likely that, if a biblical allusion is intended, it refers to the σουδάριον around Jesus' head in the tomb (cf. Jn 20.7). This may therefore be a veiled allusion to Jesus' death.[407] It would thus suggest knowledge of Johannine tradition,[408] and so is probably

---

[403] Cf. Krause-Labib, op. cit., 107; Parrott, op. cit., 205.

[404] Cf. Mt 6.19-21; Mk 10.17-25 and pars.; cf. Parrott, op. cit., 209 (his reference to 'Mt 7.19-21' is presumably a misprint). At 3.17 ('they (the rich) came out of their hidden store-rooms (ταμεῖον)'), Krause-Labib (op. cit., 110) refer to 'Mt 6.6; 24.26; but the agreement in the use of ταμεῖον can scarcely be regarded as significant.

[405] Cf. Mt 10.10/Mk 6.8/Lk 9.3; 10.4. Parrott, op. cit., 210; Krause-Labib, op. cit., 110.

[406] Contra Krause-Labib, who give this verse as a parallel to 3.25.

[407] Cf. Parrott, op. cit., 202, 207. The stress on the fact that four parts of Lithargoel's body were visible, including the soles of his feet and the palms of his hands (2.21-24), may also allude to the resurrection appearance tradition and the Thomas scene (cf. Jn 20.25-27).

[408] For other possible allusions to the fourth gospel, see Sell, 'A Note on a striking Johannine motif found at CGVI: 6,19', *NT* 20 (1978) 232-240; and

not of direct relevance to the present study despite its intrinsic interest. When Lithargoel is rejected by the rich, it is said that 'He did not reveal himself to them' (3.28). Again there is a general parallel in the synoptic tradition (cf. Mt 11.27/Lk 10.21),[409] but one cannot say more.

In the instructions which Lithargoel gives to the twelve, Lithargoel says: 'No one is able to go on that road, except one who has forsaken (ἀποτάσσεσθαι) everything' (5.22f.), and these words are twice echoed later by Peter: 'We forsook(ἀποτάσσεσθαι)everything as he said' (7.24-26), 'Lord, you have taught us to forsake (ἀποτάσσεσθαι) the world and everything in it' (10.15f). Whilst this can be paralleled in general terms at a number of points in the gospels,[410] the use of ἀποτάσσεσθαι may point to a connection with Lk 14.33.[411] This verse is probably due to LkR,[412] and this may therefore indicate knowledge of Luke's gospel.

After Peter's echo of the ἀποτάσσεσθαι command, Peter continues: 'What we are concerned about is the food for a single day' (10.18f.). It is just possible that the Q tradition about freedom from cares is in mind (cf. Mt 6.25,31 and par.),[413] though the reference is again very general. Jesus replies to Peter by telling him that the needs of the poor which the disciples are to satisfy are not material needs, and the means to be used are not material

'Jesus the "Fellow-Stranger". A study of CG VI 2,35-3,11', *NT* 23 (1981) 173-192.

409 Cf. Krause-Labib, op. cit., 110; Parrott, op. cit., 210.

410 E.g. Parrott, op. cit., 215, refers to Mk 8.34 and pars.

411 Krause-Labib, op. cit., 113. For the further development of this theme, see Y. Haas, 'L'Exigence de renoncement au monde dans les *Actes de Pierre et des Douze Apôtres, les Apophtegmes des Pères du Désert,* et la *Pistis Sophia', BCNH* Études 1 Quebec-Louvain 1981, 295-303.

412 Cf. Marshall, *Luke*, 594; and see below on TestTr 41.7-9.

413 Also alluded to in GPh 57.7f. (see p.74 above). Cf. Perkins, *Gnostic Dialogue*, 127.

medicines but the name of Jesus: '"Do you not understand that my name, which you teach, surpasses all riches, and the wisdom of God surpasses gold and silver and precious stones?" He gave them the pouch of medicine and said "Heal all the sick of the city who believe in my name"' (10.25-11.1).[414] Whilst the general instruction to 'heal the sick' is reminiscent of the mission instructions in the gospels (Mt 10.8/ Lk 10.9),[415] the whole passage is remarkably close to the context of the scene in Acts 3. There Peter and John heal the lame man in Jerusalem by the 'name' of Jesus which is, by implication, more valuable that any gold or silver (cf. Acts 3.6: 'Silver and gold I do not have, but what I have I give you: in the name of Jesus Christ of Nazareth, walk!'). The connection between the two passages is also supported by the fact that John, who is Peter's companion in Acts 3, is suddenly brought on the scene at this point in AcPet12 (11.3ff.). Thus the common collocation of the insignificance of 'silver and gold', the power of the 'name' of Jesus enabling the apostles to heal the sick, and the explicit mention of John as Peter's companion, all serve to bind the two texts firmly together. AcPet12 shows knowledge of the tradition in Acts 3, and hence probably of the Lukan writings as well as Matthew's gospel. (One could argue that AcPet12 presupposes only Luke's tradition in Acts 3; however, the use of the 'forsaking' saying suggests knowledge of Luke's gospel, and so a theory of the knowledge of only Luke's source in Acts 3 seems unnecessary.)[416]

---

414 The whole section which follows on p.11 is also relevant.

415 Cf. Krause-Labib, op. cit., 119.

416 This passage follows closely on the revelation of Lithargoel's identity as the risen Jesus on p.9 (see above). It may be that the stress here on the 'name' of Jesus as the healing power is being linked with the charge of the risen Jesus in Mt 28.19 to baptise in the 'name' of the Father, Son and Holy Spirit. The

The conclusion of this section, therefore, is that the author of AcPet12 betrays direct use of the finished works of both Matthew and Luke.

A second text in which Peter plays a leading role is the *Letter of Peter to Philip* (VIII.2),[417] which is well-known for being replete with NT allusions. Above all there is clear dependence on the Lukan resurrection account in Lk 24 and Acts 1.[418] Thus the command of the risen Jesus to the disciples to assemble (132.16-133.1; 133.6-8) recalls Lk 24.49 and Acts 1.4ff. (the explicit command does not occur in the other synoptic traditions); the assembly on the Mount of Olives (133.13-15) may be derived from Acts 1.12;[419] the references to the 'promise' and the 'power' given by the risen Jesus (132.21-23; 137.24-27) recall Lk 24.49; Acts 1.4,8; the debate on the road (138.10ff.) may be inspired by the Emmaus tradition in Lk 24;[420] the return of the disciples to the Jerusalem temple (138.9f.; 139.4-6) recalls Lk 24.52f.; Acts 1.12; the

---

common reference to the 'name' may have led the author to bring the two texts together and to allow them to interpret each other.

417 This text has attracted a great deal of interest. For the text and translations, see H.G. Bethge, 'Der sogenannte "Brief des Petrus an Philippus" Die zweite Schrift aus Nag-Hammadi-CodexVIII', *ThLZ* 103 (1978) 161-170; J.-É. Ménard, *La Lettre de Pierre à Philippe;* M.W. Meyer, *The Letter of Peter to Philip*, *SBLDS* 53, Chico 1981; for the present discussion the following articles are also important: K. Koschorke, 'Eine gnostische Pfingstpredigt. Zur Auseinandersetzung zwischen gnostischem und kirchlichem Christentum am Beispiel der "Epistula Petri ad Philippum" (NHC VIII,2)', *ZThK* 74 (1977) 323-343; G.P. Luttikhuizen, 'The Letter of Peter to Philip and the New Testament', *NHS* 14, Leiden 1978, 96-102.

418 See especially Koschorke, op.cit., 326f. for details.

419 So also in SJC 91.1ff. and elsewhere in Christian literature (cf. Meyer, op. cit., 98f.). Whilst allusion to Acts 1 must remain doubtful in the case of SJC, the clear dependence on Luke-Acts elsewhere in EpPetPhil means that Acts 1.12 is probably the source here.

420 This parallel is perhaps more remote at first sight, but is not impossible in view of the extensive use of Lk 24 elsewhere.

reference to 'witnesses' (135.4-6) may be derived from Lk 24.48; the account of the ascension of Jesus (138.5-7) probably shows knowledge of the ascension tradition in Luke-Acts. A final possible allusion occurs in 140.15-17, where the risen Jesus appears again and says 'Peace to you all and everyone who believes in my name . . . Be not afraid.' The situation is complicated by the fact that Lk 24.36, which could clearly be the source of the language used here, is a 'Western non-interpolation' in Luke with a parallel in Jn 20.19,26. The same problem arises with the 'peace' greeting in SJC, though here the extensive use of the Lukan narrative makes it perhaps more plausible to see Lk 24.36 as the basis of the language used. *If* the allusion is to Lk 24, then this indicates that the text form available to the author of EpPetPhil was not that of the Western text. It may also be significant that the words *μὴ φοβεῖσθε* appear in Lk 24.36 in some MSS.[421] Again one cannot build too much on this as the words appear elsewhere in the gospels,[422] and are in any case hardly very distinctively Jesuanic. It *may* provide a further clue to the text form known to the author, but one cannot be certain.

In addition to the Lukan resurrection tradition, it would appear that the author of EpPetPhil knows Matthew's resurrection account as well. The text at 134.17f. ('I am Jesus Christ who is with you for ever') appears to be inspired by Mt 28.20. The same verse also seems to be echoed in the final words of Jesus here: 'Behold I am with you for ever' (140.22f.).[423] Further, the note in 137.13f. ('then the apostles worshipped him') may

---

421 P W 1230 1241 1253 it$^{aur, c, f}$ syr^{p,h} boh eth arm.

422 Cf. Jn 14.1 etc. Meyer, op.cit., 158f., in fact sees the closest parallels here with the mini-'Pentecost' scene in Jn 20.19-23.

423 Cf. Bethge, op.cit., col.169; Luttikhuizen, op.cit., 96; Meyer, op.cit., 112.

also be derived from the Matthaean resurrection scene, viz., Mt 28.17.[424]

Other synoptic allusions are rather harder to establish with any degree of certainty. The fact that the Mount of Olives is 'the place where they used to gather with the blessed Christ when he was in the body' (133.15-17) may derive from Lk 21.37.[425] 137.7-9 ('You will become illuminators (φωστήρ) in the midst of dead men') has been compared with Mt 5.14,[426] though Phil 2.16 would seem to be a closer parallel,[427] if indeed any Biblical parallel is in mind at all: at 139.15 Jesus is the φωστήρ and such language is common in Gnostic literature.[428] The overlap with Biblical language may be purely coincidental.

Jesus' words at 137.26 ('Gird yourselves with the power of my Father') use metaphorical language which occurs also in the Bible (cf. Lk 12.35; 1 Thess 5.8; Eph 6.14; 1 Pet 1.13, all probably reflecting Exodus imagery).[429] The clear knowledge of Luke's gospel elsewhere in the text might suggest that it is Luke's language which is being reflected here. On the other hand, the immediate context in EpPetPhil is that of the spiritual warfare against the Archons, and this is very similar to that of Eph 6. It may therefore be that Eph 6 is the source of the imagery

---

424 The explicit reference to the disciples' worshipping Jesus is somewhat extraneous to the general context of replies by Jesus to the disciples' questions. Meyer, op.cit., 141, postulates a seam here in the tractate. It is possible that the note is a secondary (possibly Christianising) addition to a prior source.

425 Cf. Koschorke, op. cit., 327. Cf. also the discussion (p. 33 above) on the apparent identification in SJC of the Mount of the Transfiguration as the Mount of Olives.

426 Cf. Koschorke, op. cit., 327.

427 Also mentioned by Koschorke, ibid.

428 Cf. Meyer, op. cit., 104.

429 Cf. Bethge, op. cit., col.168.

here.[430] EpPetPhil then continues with the exhortation to 'let your prayer be known. And he, the Father, will help you' (137.28f.). Koschorke compares Mt 5.16a.[431] However, the meaning is more probably that one should make one's prayers known to God, rather than that one's prayers to God should be publicised before other men. In this case Phil 4.6 would be closer biblical parallel. The promise of help from the Father in answer to prayer could recall a number of biblical parallels, and one cannot really say which, if any, is in mind.[432]

The prediction of sufferings in store for the disciples in 138.25f. ('It is necessary that they bring you to synagogues (*συναγωγή*) and governors (*ἡγεμών*) so that you shall suffer') clearly reflects some form of synoptic tradition. Koschorke calls this an 'ausdrückliche Zitierung' of Lk 21.12.[433] This is perhaps too optimistic a claim. Lk 21.12 has synoptic parallels in Mt 10.17 and Mk 13.9. 'Synagogues' and 'governors' are separated by 'prisons' and 'kings' in Lk 21.12. 'Synagogues' and 'governors' do occur rather closer together in Mk 13.9, though attached to different verbs ('they will hand you over to councils and synagogues, and you will stand before governors and kings . . . '); a similar (but not identical) situation occurs in Mt 10.17f. ('they will scourge you in their synagogues and you will be led before governors and kings . . . '). Luttikhuizen claims that Matthew's verb *ἀχθήσεσθε*

---

430 Meyer, op. cit., 142, refers to Eph 6 only at this point. For the use of Eph 6 elsewhere, see Hyp Arch 86.20-27; Exeg Soul 131.9-12, and E. Pagels. *The Gnostic Paul*, Philadelphia 1975, 119, 128f. (cited by Meyer, but not available to me).

431 Op. cit., 327.

432 Bethge, col.168, refers to Lk 11.9 and par.; Koschorke, 327, to Lk 12.11f.; Meyer, op. cit., 181, also refers to Mt 18.19; 21.22 and pars.; Jn 14.13f.; 15.7; 16.23f.; 1 Jn 5.14f.; Jas 1.5,8.

433 Op. cit., 327.

could explain the Coptic form of the verb here, but he gives no further details.[434] He may be referring to the fact that the form of the verb ⲉⲓⲛⲉ used here (ⲉⲧⲣⲉⲩⲛⲧⲏⲩⲧⲛ) may be a passive form,[435] but then, as Meyer points out, this could reflect either Matthew's *ἀχθήσεσθε* or Luke's *ἀπαγομένος*.[436] It is thus difficult to be certain precisely which synoptic version is in the author's mind.

The references to Jesus' passion in Peter's 'Pentecost' sermon include the words 'he bore a crown of thorns and he put on a purple garment' (139.16-18). This could reflect synoptic tradition as in Mk 15.17-20,[437] and if so, it is noteworthy that only Mark of the synoptic gospels mentions the 'purple' robe. On the other hand, both the crown of thorns and the purple robe are mentioned in Jn 19.2. Further, the order here (crown of thorns–purple robe) corresponds to Jn 19.2 as against Mk 15.17 which has them in reverse order. It is clearly dangerous to press such detailed comparisons too far in what is clearly only an allusion to the gospel tradition and not an explicit citation, but it may indicate that it is Johannine tradition which is in mind at this point.[438]

A final point which may be relevant to the present discussion is the end of the text which reads (in the *NHLE* translation): 'The apostles separated from each other into

---

434 Op. cit., 101.

435 Meyer, op. cit., 149.

436 Ibid. Meyer claims that Matthew and Luke are closer to EpPetPhil here than Mark (though he gives no reasons, unless it is the passive form of the verb). He concludes (n.192 on 183) that Luke's version may be the source in view of the numerous parallels elsewhere with the Lukan writings. This may, however, be a somewhat circular argument.

437 Cf. Bethge, op. cit., col.169.

438 For the theory that John's gospel is definitely presupposed elsewhere, see K. Koschorke, 'Eine gnostische Paraphrase des johanneischen Prologs: Zur Interpretation von "Epistula Petri ad Philippum" (NHC VIII,2) 136,14-137,4', *VigChr* 33 (1979) 383-392, the title of which is self-explanatory. See, however, the doubts on this raised by Meyer, op.cit., 132f.

four words in order to preach' (140.23-27). The meaning of the reference to 'four words' is uncertain and emendations have been proposed. Bethge suggests an original ⲛⲥⲁ ϫⲉ 'to four directions', which was corrupted via a dittography ⲛⲥⲁϫⲉ ϫⲉ to the present ⲛϣⲁϫⲉ ϫⲉ[439] It may be, however, that the 'four words' are the 'four gospels', in which case EpPetPhil would here be showing clear knowledge of the four-fold Gospel canon.[440] It is a curious reference and tantalisingly allusive, but its precise interpretation must remain unclear.

Amongst the 'Petrine' literature in the Nag Hammadi Library, it is perhaps the *Apocalypse of Peter* (VII.3)[441] which is the most positive in its evaluation of the person of Peter. At the same time it gives some of the clearest insights into the conflicts between Gnostic communities and the 'orthodox' Christian churches. It is also very interesting for the present discussion in that the text is full of synoptic-like material. The main argument of this section will be that all the synoptic material in ApPet can be seen as deriving from Matthew's gospel.

The opening section of the text (70.20ff.) gives an adulation of Peter and clearly seems to be built on the Petrine saying in Mt 16.[442] Thus 70.20ff. ('blessed are those above belonging to the Father . . . ') uses a beatitude

---

[439] Op. cit., col.169f.

[440] Cf. Ménard, op. cit., 47, though he prefers the meaning 'quatres points cardinaux' (however, he does not say if he is interpreting ϣⲁϫⲉ in this way, or if he is implicitly emending the text). Meyer, op. cit., 160f., seeks to combine both interpretations via Irenaeus' discussion of the four-fold gospel canon (*A.H.* III.11.8), where the four gospels are said to correspond to, amongst other things, the four zones (κλιματα) of the world.

[441] A. Werner 'Die Apokalypse des Petrus–Die dritte Schrift aus Nag-Hammadi-Codex VII', *ThLZ* 99 (1974) 575-584; see also the very important study of Koschorke, *Polemik*, 11-90.

[442] See Koschorke, op. cit., 27-29.

form as in Mt 16.17, and the references here to 'Father' (70.22) and, a little later, to Jesus as the 'Son of man' (71.12) (both of which are slightly unusual in this tractate) can both be explained on the basis of the Matthaean context (Mt 16.13,17). Those who receive the true teaching are described as 'they who are built on what is strong, that they may hear my word . . . ' (70.26-28). This appears to be an interpretation of the saying in Mt 16.18 about the church 'built upon the rock' combined with the small parable in Mt 7.24f., where the one who builds his house upon the rock is the person who hears Jesus' words.[443] Jesus' words at 71.15ff. ('But you yourself, Peter, become perfect in accordance with your name with myself, the one who chose you, because from you I established a base for the remnant whom I have summoned to knowledge') seems to provide further interpretation of the Mt 16 passage, where the giving of Peter's name and the establishment of the community are closely related.[444]

Several points of contact are clear between the accounts of the crucifixion here and in the synoptics,[445] though for the most part it is impossible to say precisely which synoptic version is presupposed. The very first words of the text in 70.14f. ('as the Saviour was sitting in the temple') set the scene in agreement with Mt 26.55 and pars. At 71.22-72.4, Jesus warns Peter of a three-fold testing to come, and the most natural allusion would seem to be to the denial of Jesus by Peter in Mt 26.69ff. and pars.[446] The threatening attack mentioned in 72.5-9 ('I

[443] See also P. Perkins, 'Peter in Gnostic Revelation', in *SBL 1974 Seminar Papers Vol.2*, Cambridge, Mass. 1974, 5f.; also *Gnostic Dialogue*, 119.

[444] See Koschorke, ibid.; Perkins, ibid.

[445] See especially Koschorke, op. cit., 19f.

[446] See, however, Koschorke, op. cit., 29-32, who interprets this difficult passage as a reference to the conversation between Jesus and Peter in Jn 21.15-17.

saw the priests and the people running up to us with stones, as if they would kill us') can be paralleled in general terms from the gospel story.[447] The note in 73.1-4 ('I listened to the priests as they sat with the scribes. The multitudes were shouting with their voices') seems to be a combination of the cry of the crowds (Mt 27.22f. and pars.) and the plot by the authorities. At first sight the reference to 'scribes' is not so easily derivable from Matthew's gospel, since the 'scribes' are mentioned in Mk 14.1/Lk 22.2, but not in Matthew's parallel here, Mt 26.3.[448] On the other hand, 'scribes' are explicitly mentioned in Matthew's account of the actual trial of Jesus, rather than the initial plotting, by the authorities (26.57). This could, therefore, be the source of the allusion here. In any case it would probably be wrong to place too much weight on this detail: the presence of scribes throughout the gospel story means that it would hardly be surprising were an extra reference to 'scribes' to be inserted secondarily into a re-telling of the story.

When the text resumes its account of the passion of Jesus on p.80, there is probably a reference to the end of the Gethsemane story, as Jesus says to Peter 'Come, therefore, let us go on with the completion of the will of the incorruptible Father. For behold, those who will bring them judgement are coming, and they will put them to shame' (80.23-29). This is parallel to Mt 26.46/Mk 14.42 (Luke has nothing corresponding here). The arrest of Jesus (here interpreted as only an apparent arrest, 81.3-10) corresponds to Mt 26.50/Mk 14.46. The peculiar interpretation of the crucifixion itself follows: 'Who is this

---

447 Koschorke, op. cit., 19, suggests quite plausibly that the note may be more due to the Johannine narrative in Jn 7-10.

448 There is a little, albeit rather weak, MSS support for reading *καὶ οἱ γραμματεῖς* at Mt 26.3 (0133 0255 it $sy^{p,h}$).

one, glad and laughing on the tree? And is it another one whose feet and hands they are striking? . . . (81.12ff.).[449] The crucifixion is, of course, common to all the gospels, though the hands and feet explicitly are mentioned only in Lk 24.39 and Jn 20.20ff. However, the detail could be easily supplied independently by an author. Peter's words to Jesus in 81.26-28 ('Lord, no one is looking at you. Let us flee this place.') may derive from the flight of the disciples (Mt 26.56/Mk 14.50). Jesus' reply ('Leave the blind alone. And you, see how they do not know what they are saying', 81.30-32) is regarded by Koschorke as an instance where the text only makes sense if the canonical account is presupposed.[450] However, precisely what is presupposed is not clear. Presumably it is the belief by the authorities that they have captured the true Saviour.[451] But such a claim is nowhere explicitly made in the biblical narrative, even though some details of the canonical account could clearly be in mind. Finally, the mission charge in 83.15ff. ('These things which you saw you shall present to those of another race who are not of this age') is too general for one to be able to see more than a vague reference to synoptic tradition; but the promise of the risen Jesus in 84.8f. ('I will be with you') clearly reflects Mt

[449] Koschorke, op. cit., 44, points out that this is not strictly 'docetic', in the sense that the sufferings are only imaginary. Rather, it is that the (real) sufferings do not affect the true Saviour. He also (p. 24) sees here an allusion to the substitution of Simon of Cyrene for Jesus (thus alluding to Mk 15.21-24 and par.), as in the very closely related 2LogSeth. However, Tröger distinguishes the Christology of the two documents: whilst a substitutionary doctrine is present in 2LogSeth, in ApPet a trichotometric division of the Saviour is assumed, and the point is simply that only the lowest part of him suffers. See his discussion in *Die Passion Jesus in der Gnosis nach den Schriften von Nag Hammadi*, Dissertation, Humbolt University, Berlin 1978. His argument seems persuasive.

[450] Op.cit., 20.

[451] 'Der Fortsetzung nach geht es um die irrige Ansicht, den Soter selbst ergriffen zu haben: Jn 18,4-8 (cf. Mt 26,63 par 27,54)', (ibid.).

28.20. With the exception of the last example, all the allusions mentioned could be derived from either Matthew or Mark (though not Luke); there is thus nothing inconsistent in the theory that they are all derived from Matthew.

The intervening paraenetic section is couched in part in apocalyptic terms and again it seems likely that the synoptic gospels have provided the basis for much of the language used. The reference to 'the multitudes that will mislead other multitudes of living ones' (80.3f.) is similar to Mt 24.11 (where the use of πλανάω is probably due to MtR). 70.31 refers to 'transgression of the law', which is comparable to the ἀνομία of Mt 24.12 (which again is probably MtR). Jesus' words at 74.27f. ('they will speak evil things against each other') may reflect Mt 10.21 / Mk 13.12. The text at 73.32-74.9, referring to persecution, possibly even to death (cf. 'the guileless, good, pure one they push to the worker of death' 74.4-6) may reflect Mt 24.9 (where καὶ ἀποκτενοῦσιν ὑμᾶς is probably MtR). 74.10f. ('the men of the propagation of falsehood') and 77.22-24 ('others who oppose the truth') may derive from the description of false prophets in Mt 24.11.[452] Although none of this is unique to the synoptic tradition, it is likely that, in view of the clear dependence elsewhere in the text, that tradition has also been used here. Further, all these allusions are most easily seen as derived from Matthew's gospel, and the links with Matthew's redactional work demand that theory at times.

A very similar picture emerges when one looks at the more hortatory parts as well as the more polemical sections of the document. The reference to the true Gnostics as 'little ones' (78.22; 79.19; 80.11) may well

[452] For all these, see Koschorke, op. cit., 42f.

derive from Matthew's gospel (cf. Mt 18.6,10,14) where the motif is redactionally developed (though not confined to Matthew in the synoptics).[453] The polemic against the 'orthodox' church leaders, accusing them of 'striving after the first places' (79.28f.) almost certainly alludes to Mt 23.6[454] Further use of Mt 23, now applied to the opposing church leaders, can be seen elsewhere.[455] The taunt that they take names for themselves (of bishop and deacon, cf. 79.24-26) reflects Mt 23.6-10. The text at 78.26-30 ('for neither will they enter, nor do they permit those who are going up to their approval for their release') clearly alludes to Mt 23.12.[456] 72.12f. ('they are blind ones who have no guide') is similar to Mt 23.16,17,19,26; 15.14, where the charge of 'blindness' is thoroughly Matthaean.

Other exhortations include the saying 'Evil cannot produce good fruit' (75.7-9) which is close to Mt 7.18/ Lk 6.43 (though Matthew and Luke are similar and one cannot really distinguish them). In the same vein, at 76.4-8 Jesus says 'For people do not gather figs from thorns or from thorn trees if they are wise, nor grapes from thistles', quoting the saying found in Mt 7.16/ Lk 6.44. This could be said to be closer to the Lukan version: Matthew's version has grapes from thorns and figs from thistles, whereas Luke's version has figs from thorns (as here) and grapes from a bramble. However, Matthew alone has the 'thistles' and there is little difficulty in seeing Mt 7.16 as the source here: the interchange of the 'grapes' and the 'figs' between the two halves of the saying is very easy to

[453] Cf. Koschorke, op. cit., 61,83; Perkins, 'Peter', 6.
[454] Koschorke, op. cit., 64f.; Perkins, op. cit., 6. Literally 'they bend themselves under the judgement of the first places'. The *NHLE* translation has 'the judgement of the leaders'. For the translation given here and the interpretation, see Koschorke, op. cit., 65.
[455] Koschorke, op. cit., 66f.
[456] Cf. also GTh 39 (which may also be related to the synoptic saying).

envisage. An explicit quotation appears in 83.26-29 and 84.5f.: 'Everyone who has, it will be given to him and he will have plenty. But he who does not have . . . it will be taken from him and be added to the one who is.'[457] Various synoptic sayings are similar to this, but Mt 13.12 and 25.29 are probably closest in view of the additional καὶ περισσευθήσεται there.[458] Futher, the note about giving what is taken away from one who lacks (here, life) to another who already has seems to allude to the parable of the talents (cf. Mt 25.28). Thus the allusion seems to be clearly to Mt 25.29, and presupposes both the form and the context of that saying, both of which are due to MtR.

Virtually all the synoptic allusions can be adequately explained on the basis of Matthew's gospel alone. There is nothing here which demands a belief that other synoptic tradition was known to the author; further, the links with some elements of MtR which have been noted suggest that it is Matthew's finished gospel, not just Matthew's traditions, which were used here. Perkins too observes the dominance of Matthaean allusions here (though she does not give a full list of such allusions), and comments:

> Allusions to *Matthew* scattered thoughout that material may indicate that exegesis of *Matthew* played an important role in the controversy over authority to which the author of ApPet is addressing himself. Perhaps the image of Peter held by his adversaries was formulated in Matthaean terms.[459]

457 The use of the verb 'is' (Coptic ϣωπε) at the end is slightly unusual: one might have expected 'has' rather than 'is'. Cf. Werner, col.582, who feels obliged to add a supplement in his translation: '. . . um zu hinzufügen dem, das (bei dem anderen schon) ist'.

458 Koschorke, op. cit., 73; Werner, op. cit., col.584; Perkins, op. cit., 6 and *Gnostic Dialogue*, 119. (On both occasions, she refers to 15.29: presumably this is a misprint.).

459 'Peter', 5.

This may go beyond the evidence. There is not very much to indicate that, in his use of Matthew, the author of ApPet is consciously trying to correct an alternative interpretation of the same text. It appears rather that the author knows what he wants to say and can naturally use Matthaean vocabulary to express it. It may well be that rival claims about the position of Peter are at stake (and presumably this is one reason why the text is couched in the form of an Apocalypse to *Peter*), but that is a slightly different problem.

Certainly this text has been used to illustrate the continuing existence of a specifically Matthaean 'trajectory' in the early church.[460] The polemical nature of the text may account for the extraordinarily large amount of synoptic material present. It may indicate that use of the NT was part of the Gnostic armoury in its self-conscious opposition to orthodox Christianity, and that this was for many Gnostics its primary function. Nevertheless, whatever one may decide about that, the conclusion here seems clear: ApPet presupposes and uses Matthew's gospel alone for the synoptic tradition which it wishes to appropriate.

A tractate having close theological affinities with ApPet is the *Second Treatise of the Great Seth* (VII.2).[461] Although the manuscript itself provides one of the best preserved of all the Nag Hammadi texts, it seems likely that the final form of the text represents a conglomeration

---

[460] Cf. E. Schweizer, 'The "Matthaean" Church', *NTS* 20 (1974) 216.

[461] H.G. Bethge, '"Zweiter Logos des grossen Seth"—Die zweite Schrift aus Nag-Hammadi—Codex VII', *ThLZ* 100 (1975) 97-110; J.A. Gibbons, *A Commentary on the Second Logos of the Great Seth*, Dissertation, Yale University 1972.

of various traditions which do not always fit together very happily.[462]

The most interesting passages of the text for the present purposes are the references to the passion of Jesus. The longest section is that in 55.9-56.20 which includes the famous piece about the Saviour, watching and laughing as Simon of Cyrene is crucified in his place. This interpretation of the passion story is attributed to Basilides by the church fathers.[463] It is however possible that this substitutionary section (55.15-56.13) is itself an insertion into the present context, since the rest of the section appears to presuppose a more simple, docetic passion.[464] It is in the section dealing with the substitutionary passion that allusions to the gospels are most numerous: 'It was another, their father, who drank the gall and the vinegar; it was not I. They struck me with the reed. It was another, Simon, who bore the cross on his shoulder. It was another upon whom they placed the crown of thorns.' (56.6-13). The somewhat unnecessary reference to Simon as 'their father' may well allude to Mk 15.21,[465] which alone of the gospels states that Simon was 'the father of Alexander and Rufus'. This is usually taken as implying that Simon's sons were well known in Mark's community,[466] and hence the note is probably due to MkR. So 2LogSeth here presupposes Mark's redactional

[462] See Gibbons, op. cit.; also his 'The Second Logos of the Great Seth: Considerations and Questions', in *SBL 1973 Seminar Papers Vol.2*, Cambridge Mass. 1973, 242-261.

[463] Irenaeus, *A.H.* I.24.4; Epiphanius, *Pan.* 24.3. Whether this is quite the same as the 'laughing Saviour' of ApPet is more doubtful: see n.449 above.

[464] See Gibbons, *Commentary*, 203ff., and 'Considerations and Questions' 249. He thinks that 56.4-13 is an insertion into a docetic passion account (cf. 55.16-19). Further, there is no indication elsewhere in the tractate of a substitutionary idea.

[465] So Bethge, op.cit., col.98; Gibbons, *Commentary*, 211; also K.W. Tröger, 'Der zweite Logos des grossen Seth', *NHS* 6, Leiden 1975, 269.

[466] Cf. Taylor, *Mark*, 558.

work and thus Mark's finished gospel. It thus affords a rare example of the clear use of Mark in the early church.

The drinking of the 'gall and vinegar' is also revealing. 'Vinegar' is mentioned in Mt 27.48/Mk 15.36 and Jn 19.28; however, 'gall' appears only in Mt 27.34, where it is Matthew who has added the reference to Mark to make the allusion to Ps 69.21 clearer.[467] It is just possible that 2LogSeth derived the gall and vinegar from Ps 69 directly, and independently of the gospels. It is more likely that the words are derived from the accounts of the crucifixion of Jesus, and the reference to 'gall' pin-points Matthew's gospel as the version presupposed here. The other details of the account here also reflect the canonical gospels (for the beating with the reed, cf. Mt 27.29/Mk 15.19; for the crown of thorns, cf. Mt. 27.29/Mk 15.17; Jn 19.2). If the synoptic (rather than the Johannine) tradition is indeed reflected here, one can only say that that tradition cannot be Luke's gospel, but one cannot be more precise. Thus this account of the passion presupposes both Matthew's and Mark's finished gospels.

A second version of the passion narative is given in 58.17-59.9, but this time with no hint of a substitution of Simon for Jesus.[468] Further, this section appears to give an allegorical interpretation of *Matthew's* passion narative, with the main emphasis on Christ as the deliverer of the dead souls:[469] 'When they had fled from the fire of the

---

[467] Cf. B. Lindars, *New Testament Apologetic*, London 1961, 101f.

[468] Hence it may be of different origin: see Gibbons.*Commentary*. 227ff., and 'Considerations and Questions'. 251, who argues that it probably represents a prior source (cf. the very unusual allegorical exegesis, and also the transition into a narrative in the third person). The coherence of the references of the passion in the final form of the tractate at one level (cf. Painchaud. 'Polémique') does not preclude the possibility of their having different origins in the tradition.

[469] See Gibbons. ibid.; also Ménard. 'Normative Self-Definition', 142.

seven Authorities, and the sun of the power of the Archons had set, darkness took them (cf. Mt 27.45 and pars.). And the world became poor when he was restrained with a multitude of fetters (cf. Mt 26.50; 27.2 and pars.). They nailed him to the tree and they fixed him with four nails of brass (cf. Mt 27.35 and pars.). The veil of his temple he tore with his hands (cf. Mt 27.51 and pars.). It was a trembling which seized the chaos of the earth (Mt 27.51), for the souls which were in the sleep below were released. And they arose (Mt 27.52). They went about boldly having shed zealous service of ignorance and unlearnedness beside the dead tombs (Mt 27.53).' Although the early part of the section could be paralleled in all the Gospels, the allusions to the earthquake, the resurrection of the dead saints fom the tombs and their subsequent preaching, make it quite clear that it is Matthew's account which is in mind. Since these extra details are almost certainly due to MtR, it is Matthew's *gospel* which is again presupposed.

In the second half of the tractate, attention is turned to the present experience of the Gnostic community suffering persecution. The wording *may* at times owe something to synoptic tradition. For example, the text at 59.22-32 says: 'We were hated and persecuted, not only by those who are ignorant, but also by those who think they are advancing the name of Christ . . . They persecuted those who have been liberated by me, since they hate them.' Predictions of persecution occur at various places in the gospels. It might be simplest to see this as deriving loosely from Mt 24.9/Mk 13.13. though one could equally well argue that one has here a compression of Jn 15.18-20 and/or a free paraphrase of Jn 16.2. The note that the opponents 'lead astray' others (61.18) may be inspired by Mt 24.11 (where πλανάω is probably MtR). At 60.2, the writer attacks those who are persecuting the community, claiming that 'they served two masters'. This seems to be a negative application of the Q saying in Mt 6.24/ Lk 16.13, though the two canonical versions are indistinguishable. Finally, at 65.18-20, the text has Jesus say 'I am Christ, the Son of Man, the one from you who is among you'. Gibbons suggests that this may be an allusion to Lk 17.21, the presence of the term 'Son of Man' here being perhaps influenced by the fact that the immediate sequence in Lk 17 is a series of 'Son of Man' sayings.[470] If this were the case it would show knowledge of Luke's redactional arrangement,[471] and hence of Luke's gospel. Nevertheless the parallel is not certain, and the text could just as well be a loose reference to Mt 28.20, or it could have no biblical parallels in mind at all.

2LogSeth clearly uses synoptic tradition. Most of the allusions can be traced back to Matthew's gospel and some can only be derived from there. The fact that the text almost certainly has a long tradition-history makes it difficult to draw conclusions which presuppose that the text is unitary. Clearly Matthew's gospel provides the major source for the synoptic tradition used; but Mark's gospel is also clearly presupposed on one occasion and it is possible (though not certain) that Luke's gospel is also echoed. Such a pattern of synoptic allusions must probably preclude an early date for the text, at least in its present form.

The *Dialogue of the Saviour* (III.5) is potentially a very important text in the present discussion. According to Koester, this text may enable us to reach behind the

---

470 *Commentary*, 268f. Cf. also GMary 8.18f. (see p. 37 above).
471 Lk 17.22ff. is mostly Q material; v.21 is Lukan *Sondergut*.

present synoptic gospels to earlier forms of the tradition.[472] He claims that there are many allusions to synoptic tradition: ten of these allusions appear in Matthew (most of which also appear in Luke), one in Luke only, as well as sixteen in GTh;[473] however, Koester claims 'auf der anderen Seite fehlen redaktionelle Stücke dieser Schriften völlig'.[474] Thus 'eine Bekanntschaft mit den synoptischen Evangelien lässt sich allerdings auch hier noch nicht nachweisen'.[475] Koester dates the older Dialogue (which he believes is a major source used in the present text) at the end of the first century, with the final redaction of the document in the first half of the second century.[476] Parallels between sayings in DialSav, GTh, 1 Cor 1-4, John and Q lead him to postulate a common source, similar to, but not identical with, Q and GTh.[477] If such a theory were established it would be extremely important for the present discussion. It is, however, not easy to maintain.

The Achilles heel for such a theory would appear to be the words placed on the lips of Mariam in 139.9-11: 'Thus about "the wickedness of each day" and the "labourer being worthy of his food (τροφή)" and "the disciple resembling his teacher". All three of these sayings have parallels in Matthew's gospel (6.34; 10.8; 10.25), the first and last being peculiar to Matthew in the synoptic gospels. On the other hand, one could reasonably argue that these sentiments are typical Wisdom-type sayings

[472] See Koester, 'Dialog'.
[473] Ibid., 550; cf. also E. Pagels and H. Koester, 'Report on the *Dialogue of the Saviour* (CG III,5)', *NHS* 14, 67, though here two parallels with Luke alone are mentioned. However, in neither instance is an exhaustive list of parallels given.
[474] 'Dialog', 550.
[475] Ibid., 554.
[476] Ibid.
[477] Cf. his 'Gnostic Writings', 243f.; also 'Dialog', 551.

with nothing particularly Christian about them.[478] Thus the mere fact of the presence of these maxims here does not necessarily imply dependence on Matthew's gospel. Far more significant here is the second allusion which echoes the command of Jesus to the disciples in the synoptic mission charge. However, it is plain that the reference to 'food' (τροφή) means that it is *Matthew's* version which is in mind (Luke has μισθός) and, further, Matthew's τροφή here is probably due to MtR.[479] Thus DialSav here presupposes knowledge of Matthew's redacted form of the saying and thus of Matthew's finished gospel. Further, the way in which all three phrases are placed together suggests that they are all derived from the same source. One may therefore conclude that the parallels between the other two maxims and Matthew mean that they also have been derived from Matthew's gospel.[480] DialSav thus appears to show clear knowledge of Matthew's finished gospel, and this makes it generally more likely that echoes of synoptic tradition elsewhere are due rather to knowledge of the finished gospels (certainly where the link is with Matthew's gospel) than to links with pre-synoptic traditions.

Further echoes of synoptic tradition can certainly be found in DialSav. At 125.18-21, the Saviour says 'the lamp of the body is the mind; as long as you are upright of heart which is (. . .) then your bodies are lights.' This

[478] For example, for Mt 6.34, Ber 9a ('there is enough trouble in its hour') is frequently cited as a parallel; for Mt 10.25, cf. Ber 58b ('it is enough for a slave if he is as his master').

[479] See my '1 Corinthians and Q', *JBL* 102 (1983) 612.

[480] Thus agreeing with Sevrin, 'Paroles et Paraboles', 523 (though Sevrin argues only on the basis of the fact that the first and last maxims occur in Matthew alone; this seems methodologically dangerous and excludes the possibility of the use of independent traditions available to DialSav and Matthew.) Cf. too M. Krause, *Der Dialog des Soter* in Codex III von Nag Hammadi', *NHS* 8, Leiden 1977, 26.

clearly appears to be reflection of the 'light' saying in Mt 6.22/Lk 11.34, with the interpretative replacement of 'eye' by 'mind'.[481] However, Matthew and Luke are almost identical here and it is not really possible to say which version precisely is reflected. 127.17f. says 'there will be weeping and gnashing of teeth at the end of all these things'. Again this is a clear reflection of the synoptic saying about weeping and gnashing of teeth. The phrase is often regarded as a Matthaean favourite and most of its occurences in Matthew are usually taken as MtR (Mt 13.42,50; 22.13; 24.51; 25.30). However, according to the standard two-document hypothesis, the phrase appears once in Q (Mt 8.12/Lk 13.28). Thus one cannot be certain if the phrase here reflects the usage in Q, Luke or Matthew (or indeed if it does not simply reflect the common use of standard terminology). The frequent occurrence of the phrase in Matthew perhaps makes it more likely that that gospel is the source of the language used, but one can probably say no more than this. At 134.14f., Jesus says 'He who does not know the Son, how will he know the Father?.' This may be intended to echo synoptic tradition (cf. Mt 11.27/Lk 10.22), although one could also refer to various texts in the fourth gospel as equally good parallels (cf. Jn 8.19; 14.7).[482] Finally, in 144.6 there is a clear reference to the parable of the mustard seed, though there is no indication of which version is presupposed.

Other possible allusions to the synoptic tradition are less immediately obvious. Koester claims that the whole text (or at least the dialogue source which takes up the greater part of the present text) is based on the sequence

[481] Cf. Koester, 'Dialog', 551; Sevrin, op. cit., 522; also the similar adaption of the same saying in TeachSilv 99.16-20.

[482] According to Koester, op. cit., 550 n.86, it is a clear example of a Christianising interpolation.

of events attested in the saying, found in GHeb and elsewhere, of seek–find–marvel–rule–rest.[483] This seems very plausible.[484] However, it is doubtful if this saying represents a tradition which is independent of the synoptic gospels: it is just as likely that the five-fold saying is a secondary development from the simple two-fold synoptic saying 'seek and you shall find'.[485] The synoptic saying itself may well be in mind at 129.14-16: 'And he who (knows, let him) seek and find and (rejoice)'. It would seem more probable then that one of the synoptic gospels is reflected directly here, or that this is a witness to a *post*-synoptic development, as in GHeb, GTh and elsewhere.

The text at 122.5-7, referring to the 'time of the dissolution', urges the listener 'Do not be afraid and say "Behold the time has come"'. It is possible (though not certain) that this reflects Lk 21.8. If so, it is significant that ὁ καιρὸς ἤγγικεν in Lk 21.8 is LkR, and hence DialSav, if it is indeed reflecting this synoptic passage, here presupposes knowledge of Luke's finished gospel. The same may be implied at 144.14f. where Judas asks 'When we pray, how should we pray?' This may be based on the introduction to the Lord's prayer in Lk 11.1,[486] which in turn is probably due to LkR.[487] Thus DialSav again appears to presuppose Luke's finished gospel. A further link with Luke's gospel may be seen in 128.2-5 (as for what you seek after and enquire about, behold it is within you').

---

[483] Koester, 'Dialog', 551; 'Gnostic Witnesses', 242f.; Pagels & Koester, op. cit., 242f. The saying is also reflected in ThomCont and 2ApJas (see above pp. 86, 104.).

[484] For 'seeking and finding', cf. 125.11-17; 126.6-10; 128.2-5; 129.14-16; for 'marvelling', cf. 136.2-4; for 'ruling', cf. 138.7-20; for 'resting', cf. 141.3-12.

[485] See n.311 above.

[486] Cf. Krause, op.cit., 26.

[487] Cf. Schulz, *Q*, 84 n.185; J. Jeremias, *Die Sprache des Lukasevangeliums*, Göttingen 1980, 195, points to the large number of Lukanisms in the verse.

This may well be related to Lk 17.20f. (and also GTh3),[488] though it is probably easiest to see the form of the saying in DialSav and GTh as a secondary, gnosticising interpetation of the original synoptic saying.[489]

Other possible allusions to synoptic tradition are less clear. The text at 129.12-14 ('but I say to you, he who is able, let him deny himself and repent') may echo the 'deny' sayings in Mk 8.34 and pars,[490] though the link is via the single word 'deny', and there is nothing in the synoptic saying about 'repenting'. Allusions to the final attainment of the Gnostic as 'rest' (e.g. 120.6f.; 121.8; 141.4 etc.) might have the synoptic saying Mt 11.30 in mind;[491] however, the motif of 'rest' is a very important Gnostic theme and one does not need the synoptic saying to explain its presence in a Gnostic text.[492] The discussion in 126.18ff. ('Mariam said "O Lord, behold, when I am bearing the body, for what reason do I weep and for what reason do I laugh?" The Lord said "If you weep because of its deeds, you will abide, and the mind laughs . . . "') may be inspired in part by the beatitude in Lk 6.21, though the weep-laugh antithesis is a widely used motif (cf. Eccles. 3.4) and does not necessarily imply use of synoptic tradition. The semi-stereotyped formula which introduces many of the sayings in DialSav ('But I say to you . . . ') may be intended to imitate the introductions to the antitheses in Mt 5.21ff.,[493] but this cannot be certain. There is nothing corresponding to the first half of each antithesis in Mt 5, i.e. an equivalent to 'you have heard

[488] Cf. Koester, 'Gnostic Writings', 240f.
[489] Contra Koester.
[490] Koester, ibid., 239.
[491] So Koester, ibid., 246, who sees this as evidence of a common tradition.
[492] Cf. n.120 above.
[493] So Krause, op.cit., 26, referring to 120.8f.; 128.1f.; 129.12; 133.13f.; 137.22; 140.4f.; 143.21f.; 147.13f., 19f.

that it was said...' and in any case the Coptic form varies slightly.[494] Sevrin sees a reflection of Mt 11.8/Lk 7.25 in the text at 143.15-17 ('the archons and the governors have garments which are given them for a time, which do not abide'),[495] but this seems a very remote parallel. (The saying in Mt 6.30, about the transient nature of clothing, is an equally close parallel.) Finally, Jesus' words at 140.1-3 ('You have asked me for a word about that which eye has not seen, nor have I heard about it...') may be related to the (apocryphal) saying in 1 Cor 2.9, which in turn is quoted as a saying of Jesus in GTh 17.[496] Whether there is any link with specifically synoptic tradition is, however, uncertain. Koester refers to Mt 13.16f./Lk 10.23f. as a related Q saying, but I have argued elsewhere that the sayings are quite unrelated.[497] DialSav may well presuppose the development which has placed the saying of 1 Cor 2.9 on the lips of Jesus, as in GTh. But this says something about the relationship between DialSav and GTh (or their tradition-histories), and not necessarily anything about the relationship between DialSav and the synoptic tradition.

The conclusion of this section is that DialSav appears to presuppose certainly Matthew's, and probably Luke's, finished gospels. There is no support here for Koester's theories about links between DialSav and synoptic tradition being at a pre-redactional stage as far as the

---

494 An emphatic ⲁⲛⲟⲕ appears only in 120.8f.; 128.1f.; 133.13f.; 137.22; 147.19f. ⲅⲁⲣ (not ⲇⲉ ⲁⲗⲗⲁ) appears in 147.13f.

495 Sevrin, op. cit., 522.

496 Cf. Koester, 'Gnostic Writings', 248. For later use of this logion, see P. Prigent, 'Ce que l'oeil n'a pas vu, 1 Cor. 2,9', *ThZ* 14 (1968) 416-429.

497 See my '1 Corinthians and Q', 616. Koester's theories of a sapiential source lying behind 1 Corinthians and GTh here are also criticized by B. Dehandschutter, 'L'Évangile de Thomas comme collection de paroles de Jésus' in *Logia*, *BEThL* 59, Leuven 1982, 513.

synoptic gospels are concerned. There is no evidence that the author had access to synoptic tradition in a form other than the finished gospels of Matthew and Luke.

One tractate which has little significance in the present context is the *Concept of Our Great Power* (VI.4).[498] The text is, at least in its present form, relatively late: the mention of the Anomoean heresy (40.7) implies a date of writing in the fourth century. It is thus a priori highly probable that any synoptic tradition presupposed will be in the form of the completed synoptic gospels. In fact, suggested allusions to the NT often turn out either to be very indirect and remote, or to involve the use of standard imagery or phraseology with nothing distinctive enough for one to be able to infer the existence of an explicit allusion. For example, at 40.32 ('He will proclaim the aeon that is to come') Wisse and Williams in their edition of the text refer to Mt 12.32; Mk 10.30 and pars.;[499] but the phrase is standard Jewish terminology and does not necessarily need a particular verse in the synoptic tradition to explain its presence here.

The coming of the redeemer figure (who is clearly Jesus but not actually named as such) is described in more detail on p.41: e.g. 'he raised the dead' (41.10f.). This could reflect a number of different gospel stories (cf. Mk 5.21; Lk 7.14; Jn 5.21 etc.).[500] At 41.18ff., there is a reference to Judas' betrayal of Jesus ('they (the archons) knew one of his followers. A fire took hold of his soul. He handed him over') which is probably based ultimately on the betrayal stories in the gospels. At 41.29f. it is said: 'they handed

498 For editions of the text, see Wisse and Williams in Parrott (ed.), *Codices V & VI*; also Krause and Labib, *Codex II und Codex VI*.

499 Op.cit., 306; also Krause-Labib, op.cit., 156.

500 Krause-Labib, op. cit., 156; Wisse-Williams, op. cit., 307.

him over to Sasabed for nine bronze coins'. A specific sum of money is mentioned by Matthew only of the evangelists though the sum involved is different (thirty silver pieces in Mt 26.15; 27.3). Further, this extra detail in Matthew's passion narrative is probably due to MtR.[501] This may imply that the writer of the text presupposes knowledge of Matthew's finished gospel. 42.15-17 ('the sun set during the day; the day became dark') also probably alludes to the passion narrative in the gospels (cf. Mk 15.33 and pars.);[502] however the allusion is again too indirect for one to be able to be any more precise about which particular version is presupposed. Further synoptic parallels in the apocalyptic section of the tractate (e.g. p.44) are noted by Krause and Labib, and by Wisse and Williams, in their editions of the text. However, it is doubtful whether one can infer the existence of any deliberate synoptic allusion here since the motifs in question (e.g. 'the earth trembled and the cities were troubled') are widespread in apocalyptic imagery and the synoptic passages themselves are drawing on this background of ideas.

A little later in the tractate there is reference to the work of the redeemer figure at the End-time. The language is again very allusive but it is probable that the gospel tradition is again echoed.[503] Thus the sending of the 'imitator' (45.2) is probably a reference to Jesus' temptation by the Devil.[504] The text at 45.5-7 ('they were

[501] Most of Matthew's alterations to Mark in the passion story are probably MtR (cf. n.361 above; for this detail as MtR, see Senior, *Passion Narrative,* 47,373ff.) The Matthaean parallel is noted by Krause-Labib, op. cit., 156f.; and Wisse-Williams, op. cit., 308.

[502] Krause-Labib, op. cit., 157; Wisse-Williams, op. cit., 309.

[503] According to Tröger (ed.), *Gnosis und Neues Testament*, 52, the figure is not Jesus, since Jesus' activity has already been treated earlier. However, the text is generally very confused, and one should probably not expect too much consistency here.

[504] Cf. Wisse-Williams, op. cit., 315.

expecting from him that he would perform for them a sign') may reflect the synoptic story of the request for a sign (Mt 12.38; 16.1 and pars.); the following words ('and he bore great signs') may echo Mk 13.22 or they may be simply a summary of the whole gospel story, as is probably the case at 45.14f. ('he will perform signs and wonders').[505] At 45.12f., it is not clear who the subject is, but the words ('I will make you god of the world') may be intended to echo the Devil's offer to Jesus in the Q temptation story (Mt 4.9/Lk 4.6). However, in all these cases one cannot be more precise about which version is in mind. Finally, 47.31,34 says about the souls being punished that 'they will see the saints and cry out to them "Have mercy on us"'. This may be an echo of the scene in Lk 16.22-24,[506] though the motif of the unrighteous seeing the righteous after death and pleading with them can also be paralleled elsewhere.[507]

This tractate thus shows knowledge of Matthew's gospel, and perhaps of Luke's, but most of the allusions are indirect and unclear in what is in any case a very confused text.

The tractate *Melchizedek* (IX.1)[508] is of great interest from a number of different points of view. The text is part of the 'trajectory' of Melchizedek speculations, apparently identifying the figure of Melchizedek with the figure of Jesus,[509] and it almost certainly presupposes the epistle to the Hebrews.[510] There is too a notable section on

[505] Cf. also Acts 2.22.
[506] Krause-Labib, op.cit., 164; Wisse-Williams, op. cit., 322.
[507] Cf. Bar 51.4ff.; 1 En 108.15; cf. 62.9, and generally G.W.E. Nickelsburg, *Resurrection, Immortality and Eternal Life in Intertestamental Judaism*, *HThS* 26, Cambridge, Mass. 1972, 82ff.
[508] The main edition is by Pearson, *Codices IX & X*.
[509] Pearson, op. cit., 28f.
[510] Ibid., 34f.

p.5 which is concerned to reject any form of docetism and to underline the reality of the humanity (and suffering) of Jesus. For the present purposes, the evidence afforded by the tractate is fairly meagre in that synoptic allusions are not numerous.

In his edition of the text, Pearson notes a few parallels, but on examination they turn out to be rather remote and not readily identifiable as clear references to a synoptic passage.[511] More important are the references to Jesus' passion on p.25 (though unfortunately the text here is extremely fragmentary).[512] The text at 25.2 has 'you struck me', presumably reflecting either of the mockery accounts in Mk 14.65 pars. or Mk 15.19 par.[513] At 25.12 there is a brief reference to the empty tomb tradition with the words 'they did not find anyone'. Pearson compares Lk 24.3, which alone of the synoptic gospels has the verb 'find' here, presumably due to LkR. However, one cannot base too much on this use of a very common verb since the text of Melch could equally well be a general summary of the empty tomb narrative.

More significant is the note in 25.5-7: '(you crucified me) from the third hour (of the sabbath-eve [προσάββατον]) until (the ninth hour)'. Once again the text is very fragmentary, but the reference to 'third' is

511 At 5.1 ('. . . will come in his name') Pearson compares Mt 7.22 (p.48); but the text is too fragmentary to be certain, and anyway Mk 13.6 and pars. is an equally close parallel. In the anti-docetic section which follows, the author corrects the opposing view, saying that they say 'he does not eat, even though he does eat, he does not drink, even though he does drink'. Pearson refers at this point to Mt 11.19/Lk 7.34 (p.48), but this seems unnecessary to explain the author's assertion about Jesus' full humanity: the parallel with the Q saying is purely formal.

512 See the references in Pearson, op. cit., 80f.

513 Pearson suggests filling the following lacuna with 'with the reed', thus referring to the later mockery scene of Mk 15.19 and par.; but there is no firm evidence for this.

clearly there;[514] also the brackets in the *NHLE* English translation are slightly misleading if they imply that the whole word 'sabbath-eve' is a conjectural restoration, since the ⲥⲁⲃⲃⲁ ⲟⲛ are clearly visible. The significance of these details is that both occur only in Mark's passion narrative (cf. Mk 15.33, 42) and not in the other gospels. Thus Melch here betrays knowledge of the Markan passion narrative. Although there is much debate on the issue, there seems to be a growing consensus that Mark in his gospel may have been responsible for putting together the passion narrative into a connected form, and, in particular, that the time references in the passion narrative may be due to MkR.[515] If this could be established, it would show that Melch is here presupposing Mark's finished gospel, rather than Mark's source, though the echoes of other NT works (e.g. Hebrews) make this theory more probable in any case.

Thus although the quantity of relevant evidence here is relatively limited, this tractate is of great interest in the present discussion (as well as for the other reasons mentioned already) in that it provides another rare example of the clear use of Mark's gospel in the early church.[516]

The final two tractates to be considered are of interest in that they reveal something of Gnostics' ideas about their communities, both in themselves and in relation to other Christian groups. The first of these is the *Testimony of Truth* (IX.3).[517] There are numerous echoes of synoptic

---

[514] ϫⲓⲛ ⲛϫⲡ-ϣⲟⲙⲧⲉ

[515] See, for example, the essays in W.H. Kelber (ed.), *The Passion in Mark*, Philadelphia 1976, with references to earlier literature.

[516] The other example in the Nag Hammadi Library is in 2LogSeth: see p.125 above.

[517] Editions and translations of the text in Pearson, *Codices IX & X*; K. Koschorke, 'Der gnostische Traktat "Testimonium Veritatis" aus dem Nag-Hammadi-Codex IX', *ZNW* 69 (1978) 91-117; see also the important section in Koschorke's study *Polemik*, 91-174.

tradition in this tractate and it seems simplest to consider the possible allusions in the order in which they occur in the test.

29.12-15 ('there has taken hold of them the old leaven of the Pharisees and of the scribes of the Law') uses the language of Mt 16.16/ Mk 8.14/ Lk 12.1, though there is no clear indication as to which of these three may be in mind.[518] (In any case the fact that the leaven is 'old' suggests that 1 Cor 5.7 is also in mind.) The text at 29.24f. ('they will not be able to serve two masters') recalls Mt 6.24/ Lk 16.13. Luke here has an additional *οἰκέτης*, which may well be secondary,[519] TestTr is thus marginally closer to Matthew's version than to Luke's, though this could be due to use of Matthew's source and in any case the difference is very insignificant;[520] 30.17 (' . . . until they pay the last penny (*κορδάντης*) recalls Mt 5.26.[521] Luke's parallel here (Lk 12.59) has *λεπτόν*. It is not certain which version is more original here.[522] TestTr thus shows links with Matthew's gospel, and it is possible that the writer here shows knowledge of MtR.

The text at 31.18-22 quotes words of Jesus: 'I have said to you "Do not build nor gather for yourselves in the place where brigands *λῃστής* break open, but bring forth fruit to the Father"'. The first half of this recalls Mt 6.19f. Luke has a parallel version (Lk 12.33f.) but there the *λῃστής* only 'draws near' and does not 'break through' as in Matthew. This thus shows another link with Matthew's gospel

[518] TestTr defines the 'leaven' as 'the errant desire of the angels and the demons and the stars' (19.15-17), which agrees with neither Matthew (the leaven is the teaching) nor Luke (the leaven is hypocrisy).

[519] So Schmid, *Matthäus und Lukas*, 239; Schulz, *Q*, 459.

[520] The saying was widely used: see Koschorke, *Polemik*, 112 n.1.

[521] Pearson, op. cit., 125; Koschorke, 'Traktat', 98.

[522] Matthew is more original according to Schulz, *Q*, 422; Luke is more original according to Marshall, *Luke*, 552.

or his source). The final phrase may be alluding to Jn 15.5-8.[523] However, the reference to 'building' in the first phrase may indicate that the parable of the two houses(Mt 7.24-27/Lk 6.47-49) is in mind.[524] If so, then it is significant that just before this in the Great Sermon is the section about the tree and its fruits (Mt 7.16-20/Lk 6.43f.). It may well be that the whole sentence cited here is an allusion to synoptic (rather than Johannine) tradition with material taken from the Great Sermon. However, one cannot be more precise about which source is being used.

The text at 33.5-8 ('the lame, the blind, the paralytic, the dumb and the demon-possessed were granted (χαρίζεσθαι) healing') looks very similar to the summary in Lk 7.21f.[525] Further, this summary, including the use of χαρίζεσθαι, is probably due to LkR.[526] The parallel here is not exact, but it is fairly close and, if it is accepted, betrays knowledge of LkR and hence of Luke's gospel. There now follows a reference to Jesus' walking on the water (33.8f.). Although an allusion to the synoptic account of the miracle is possible,[527] the sequel makes it more probable that the Johannine version of the story is in mind; a few lines later there is the note 'they boarded the ship and at about 30 stades they saw Jesus walking on the sea' (33.22-24), where the reference to the 30 stadia indicates that the Johannine account is being used (Jn 6.19).

The text at 37.5-8 ('they do not know the power of God nor do they understand the interpretation of the

---

[523] So Pearson, op.cit., 127; Koschorke, op.cit., 99.
[524] So Koschorke, ibid.
[525] So Pearson, op.cit., 131; Koschorke, op.cit., 100.
[526] See Schürmann, *Lukasevangelium*, 410; Jeremias, *Sprache des Lukasevangeliums* 162.
[527] Pearson, op.cit., 131; Koschorke, op.cit., 100.

scriptures') clearly echoes the language of Mt 22.29/ Mk 12.24, though one cannot say whether it is Matthew or Mark (or a prior source) which is in mind since their versions are identical here. 37.22f. says of the blessed that 'they dwell before God under the light yoke'. This is perhaps a reminiscence of Mt 11.29f., which is part of Matthew's M material, though not clearly MtR. The text at 39.24-28 says of Jesus that 'when he came to John at the time he was baptized, the Holy Spirit came down upon him as a dove'. This recalls the synoptic accounts of Jesus' baptism, but only Luke's account qualifies the Spirit as 'holy', and this is presumably due to LkR. Thus TestTr may once again show knowledge of LkR (though the addition of the word 'holy' is easy to envisage by any later Christian writer).

39.29f. says that Jesus 'was born of a virgin', indicating some knowledge of the birth stories, though at this stage one cannot be more precise. The text at 41.7-9 speaks of the man 'who will forsake all of the things of the world having renounced (ἀποτάσσειν) the whole place'. This may well echo Lk 14.33,[528] a verse which has no exact parallel in the other gospels (though similar ideas occur in e.g. Mk 10.29 and pars.) and which may be LkR.[529] Thus once again TestTr seems to presuppose knowledge of Luke's gospel. 41.10 then speaks of the man who has forsaken all 'having grasped the fringe of his garment'. This recalls Mt 9.20/ Lk 8.44.[530] Mark's parallel here (Mk 5.27) has no κρασπέδον, so, assuming that this 'minor

[528] So Pearson, op.cit., 147, who also refers to Lk 5.28. (Koschorke notes no biblical parallel.) The use of ἀποτάσσειν in the text here and in Lk 14.33 suggests that there is a link here.

[529] Cf. Marshall, *Luke,* 594, and p. 110 above on the allusion in AcPet12.

[530] Koschorke, op. cit., 104.

agreement' is due to independent redaction,[531] TestTr shows a link with either MtR or LkR. More decisive for the present discussion is the text at 44.16-18 which says 'that which anyone wants he brings to him in order that he might become perfect (τέλειος)'. There is probably an allusion to Mt 5.48 here;[532] further, it is significant that the use of τέλειος in Mt 5.48 is probably due to MtR,[533] so that TestTr here shows dependence on MtR.

45.7f. ('John was begotten by the Word through a woman, Elizabeth') and 45.13f. ('John was begotten by means of a womb worn with age') show knowledge of the birth stories in Lk 1; the continuation in 45.14-17 ('but Christ passed through a virgin's womb. When she conceived she gave birth to the Saviour') probably alludes to Lk 2, especially Lk 2.11.[534] The only remaining clear synoptic allusion appears to be at 68.4 ('they are gratified by unrighteous mammon'). This recalls Lk 16.9 which is material peculiar to Luke (though not clearly LkR). Other allusions are noted by Pearson and Koschorke but they seem too remote to be certain.[535]

---

531 There is some textual uncertainty here: κρασπέδου is omitted in some MSS in Luke and is present in some MSS in Mark. Although the shorter Lukan text is accepted by some (e.g. J.M. Creed, *The Gospel according to St. Luke*, London 1930, 123), an independent change of Mark seems equally likely (perhaps under the influence of Mk 6.56): see Schürmann, *Lukasevangelium* 490f.

532 So Pearson, op. cit., 155; Koschorke, op.cit., 106.

533 Cf. n.219 above.

534 Pearson, op. cit., 157, also refers to Mt 1.21, but the whole context is explicable on the basis of the use of Luke alone.

535 The text at 29.7-9 ('ears of the mind') may allude to Mt 11.15 and pars. (so Pearson, 122), but this is only a very general parallel. 30.12f. ('he came by the Jordan river') may echo Mt 3.13 (Pearson, 125), but Jn 1.32 is equally close. 33.25 ('empty martyrs') is seen by Koschorke (100), as an allusion to Lk 7.21f., but this seems very remote. 36.23f. ('to know the Son of man') *may* allude to Mt 11.27 (Pearson, 136), but the reference is very general. 37.27f. ('they have become manifest to the Son of man') is compared by Pearson (139) to Mk 4.22 and pars.; but again this is very general language. 39.4f. ('now will they reach to

There are no clear allusions to Mark's gospel in TestTr.[536] The majority of the allusions are to Q sayings, sometimes in the more original form of the tradition. However, TestTr clearly depends upon both MtR and LkR, so that knowledge of both Matthew's and Luke's finished gospels is implied. This pattern of synoptic allusions is certainly consistent with a relatively late date of the 3rd century (or end of the 2nd century) postulated by Pearson and Koschorke as the date of writing. (A date later than c.180 is in any case demanded by the polemic against 2nd century gnostic teachers in the second half of the text.)[537]

The distribution of synoptic allusions in the document may also be significant. Most occur in the opening section 29.6-45.6; the remaining allusions on p.45 occur in a section (45.7ff.) which may be separable from what precedes using different criteria,[538] and the allusion in 68.4 is quite isolated. Pearson suggests that the section 29.6-45.6 had a separate existence as a tract or homily before being incorporated into the present document.[539] The uneven distribution of synoptic allusions in TestTr would be consistent with this theory. For although TestTr uses biblical language freely throughout (cf. the long

heaven') is compared by Koschorke (103) to Lk.20.34f, but this too is only a very general parallel. At 39.18 ('unquenchable') Pearson (143) sees an allusion to Mk 9.44; but there are large lacunae here and in the absence of the full text a conclusion must remain conjectural. 44.7-9 ('he rejects for himself loquacity and disputations') may allude to Mt 6.7 (so Pearson, 154), but not clearly so.

[536] Unless it be 39.18 (see previous note).

[537] Koschorke, 'Traktat', 96, and *Polemik*, 109, dates the document to mid-3rd century; Pearson, op.cit., 118-120, suggests that Julius Cassianus was the author, which would imply a slightly earlier date. However, specific ascriptions of authorship must remain conjectural.

[538] Koschorke, *Polemik*, 92, points to the apparent contradiction between 45.7ff., where Jesus is born of a virgin, and 30.18-30, where Jesus comes directly from heaven to earth, as perhaps indicating the presence of different strata in the text.

[539] Op. cit., 102f.

Genesis midrash starting at 45.22, the use of Jewish haggadic traditions about David and Solomon in 70.1-23,[540] and the explicit citation of Gal 1.8 in 73.18-22), synoptic allusions do seem to disappear and this *may* suggest that the early part of the document had a different origin from the rest. (However, it must also be said that the extremely fragmentary state of the text in the second half makes any such arguments from silence of uncertain value.)

The only text remaining to be examined is the *Interpretation of Knowledge* (XI.1).[541] This is an important text in that it enables us to see something of a Gnostic's ideas about the church. It is clearly written for a situation not dissimilar to that at Corinth when Paul wrote 1 Corinthians, i.e. a situation in which the variety and validity of different spiritual gifts have become a source of contention. The writer uses many of Paul's own arguments in dealing with the situation, and Paul's letters are clearly a source used by the writer.[542] For the purposes of the present discussion, this evidence can be put to one side. However, whilst the Pauline allusions dominate the second half of the text, there are a number of synoptic allusions in the first half. The first few pages of the manuscript have suffered a great deal, but on p.9 there is a series of sayings which seem to be direct quotations: 'Now this is his teaching: Do not call out to a father upon the

[540] On these passages, see B.A. Pearson, 'Jewish Haggadic Traditions in the *Testimony of Truth* from Nag Hammadi (CG IX,2)', in *Ex Orbe Religionum* Leiden 1972, 457-470

[541] Apart from the *NHLE* translation, see the article by K. Koschorke, 'Eine neugefundene gnostische Gemeindeordnung. Zum Thema Geist und Amt im frühen Christentum', *ZThK* 76 (1979) 30-60.

[542] Koschorke, op.cit., 39, suggests that the interpretation of scripture was itself regarded as an important charismatic activity.

earth. Your Father, who is in heaven, is one (cf. Mt 23.9). You are the light of the world (Mt 5.14). They are my brothers and my fellow companions who do the will of the Father (cf. Mt 12.50). For what use is it if you gain the world and you forfeit your soul (cf. Mt 16.26/ Mk 8.36).' (9.27ff.).[543] This appears to be a deliberate quotation of texts. All the texts occur in Matthew's gospel (though certainly the last has synoptic parallels as well). Moreover, the 'light' saying is probably Matthew's own introduction added as a preface to his adapted version of the Markan light saying (Mk 4.21) in Mt 5.15. Thus the verse is probably due to MtR. Similarly, the saying in Mt 12.50 has a synoptic parallel in Mk 3.35, and Matthew has redacted Mark's 'the will of God' to 'the will of my Father'. IntKnow here appears to quote Matthew's text rather than Mark's, and thus again presupposes Matthew's redactional activity.[544] Thus the text here shows dependence on Matthew's gospel, and not just on Matthew's source material(s).

In an earlier passage, which is unfortunately very damaged in the manuscript, there is clearly a reference to the parable of the sower with an interpretation of it (5.14ff.). However, the text which has survived is too fragmentary for one to be able to say more precisely which version of the parable is presupposed.[545] In another

---

543 Koschorke, ibid.

544 One must, however, register a certain amount of caution here, since 'Father' is a favourite description of God in IntKnow itself. The reference to 'Father' here might thus be due to a change of the Markan text by the Gnostic author himself. Nevertheless, the fact that all the other quotations here are from Matthew probably makes this hypothesis unnecessary.

545 J.D. Turner's English translation (*NHLE*, 429) supplies '(fell in the rocks)' at 5.16. If the plural form could be established, it would reflect Mt 13.5, where the plural τὰ πετρώδη is due to MtR of Mark. However, there seems no justification for such precision from the Facsimile edition of the text, where the words in question are missing.

passage, which is also very damaged, there is an interpretation of the parable of the Good Samaritan (6.19ff., cf. the references to 'thieves' and 'Jericho'). The passage in 6.26ff. is slightly better preserved, and speaks of men being 'brought down' and 'bound in the flesh'. This may well be part of the interpretation of the parable, since such an interpretation appears to have been current in Gnostic circles.[546] Whether this shows that the author knew the full gospel of Luke must remain undertermined from this piece of evidence alone, since the parable might have been known as an independent unit of tradition.[547]

Further possible allusions to the synoptic tradition include the text at 10.27-30: 'I became very small so that through my humility I might take you up to the great height, whence you had fallen'. This may reflect an adaptation of the synoptic logion found in Mt 23.12; Lk 14.11; 18.14. However, one cannot be certain of this: the ideas expressed fit very well with the overall argument of the text, so that one does not need a source to explain what is said here; further, the synoptic saying itself is scarcely original and can be paralleled elsewhere, e.g. in Jewish Wisdom literature.[548] Perhaps more significant are the words which immediately follow: 'You were taken to this pit. If you now believe in me, it is I who shall take you above through this shape that you see. It is I who shall bear you on my shoulders . . . ' (10.30-34). This seems to be a conflation of the imagery and language of the saying about the sheep fallen into the pit (Mt 12.11f.) and the

---

[546] See pp. 34, 56 above.

[547] The widespread use of the parable suggests that this may be the case in GPh, where all the other synoptic allusions can be explained as due to dependence on Matthew's gospel alone. Here, however, further evidence may suggest that Luke's gospel was known (see below on 10.30-34).

[548] E.g. Ezek 21.26; Prov 29.23; see p. 46 above.

parable of the lost sheep (Mt 18.12-14/ Lk 15.4-7).[549] The note about laying the lost sheep on the 'shoulders' is peculiar to Luke's version of the parable, and may be due to LkR.[550] Further, the two passages in the gospels can only be linked via the implied reference to 'sheep' in both contexts; however, in the 'pit' saying, it is only Matthew's gospel which refers to the 'sheep' in this context and this is almost certainly due to MtR.[551] Thus the text here probably betrays knowledge of MtR and LkR.

IntKnow thus shows clear knowledge of Matthew's gospel and probably also of Luke's (though the evidence for this is not quite so strong).

---

[549] The two sayings are alluded to in close proximity also in GTr 31.35-32.24.
[550] So Schulz, *Q*, 388.
[551] See n.194 above.

III. CONCLUSIONS

One important, albeit negative, result of the analysis undertaken here is that there appears to be no evidence for the use of pre-synoptic sources by the authors of the texts studied.[552] Insofar as they reflect synoptic tradition at all, the texts examined here all seem to presuppose one or more of the finished gospels of Matthew, Mark or Luke.[553] It would therefore appear that the texts of the Nag Hammadi Library (with the possible exception of GTh) will not be of any assistance in dealing with the problem of the development of synoptic tradition at a pre-redactional stage. Rather, these texts are witnesses of the post-redactional development of that tradition. There is thus no evidence here for the existence of texts earlier than probably the second century;[554] there is also no evidence for the continuing survival and use of a Q source (or any other pre-redactional synoptic source) by Gnostic communities.

Of all the synoptic allusions noted here, by far the greatest number show affinities with Matthew's gospel. In some instances, a decision about which synoptic version is reflected is not possible since the synoptic gospels agree amongst themselves (e.g. in double- or triple-tradition passages). Nevertheless, in the majority of the passages considered, Matthew's gospel could be the source of the language used; and in several other passages, features of MtR appear so that Matthew's gospel is clearly

[552] The present study has, of course, excluded consideration of GTh: the results here should not prejudice the discussion with regard to that text.

[553] This should not exclude the possibility of the existence of tradition lying on trajectories which are independent of those leading to and from the synoptic gospels: such traditions may be present in, for example, ApocJas and 2ApJas.

[554] Though the analysis undertaken here proves nothing about the date of those texts which do not reflect synoptic tradition at all.

indicated as the source in question (whether directly or indirectly). This fits well with the general popularity of Matthew's gospel in the early church.[555] Luke's gospel is alluded to rather less often, though not infrequently (but there are no instances where Luke, and *not* Matthew, has been used). Clear allusions to Mark's gospel are rarer. Only two instances seem certain (in 2LogSeth 56.6 and Melch 25.5f.). However, one should also note the existence of a number of allusions to triple tradition passages in the synoptic gospels where Matthew and Mark (and sometimes Luke) are almost identical. Such passages could be regarded as allusions to Mark's gospel, though often the fact that the text in question makes clear allusions to Matthew's gospel elsewhere has been taken as an indication that the allusion is probably to Matthew's gospel in these cases as well. The overall pattern of synoptic allusion is thus reasonably clear, and consistent with the pattern of allusions in other patristic sources: Matthew's gospel is widely favoured, Luke's gospel is sometimes used, whilst there are relatively few instances of Mark's gospel being clearly echoed.

The extent to which one may make deductions from the pattern of synoptic allusions in any one document is uncertain. By the start of the third century, the four canonical gospels appear to have been accepted by all. It is also the case that both the gospels of Mark and Luke may have been regarded with a certain amount of reserve by some Christians in the second century.[556] It might be

---

555 Cf. Massaux, *Influence de Matthieu*, 651: 'De tous les écrits néotestamentaires, l'évangile de *Mt.* est celui dont l'influence littéraire est la plus généralisée et la plus profonde dans la littérature chrétienne jusqu'aux dernières décades du deuxième siècle.'

556 Papias' defence of Mark's gospel (Eusebius, *E.H.* III.39) may well be apologetic in part. With regard to Luke, the claim has been made that Luke's gospel had some difficulty in being accepted into the canon: see W.

tempting to assume that a document which refers to only one synoptic gospel, e.g. Matthew, was written earlier than another document which alludes to more than one synoptic gospel.[557] Further, it must also presumably have been the case that all the gospels were initially used only in the communities for which they were written, and that universal usage was a later development. The ubiquitous influence of Matthew's gospel in the early church makes it difficult to make deductions from allusions to Matthew in other texts; but the existence of allusions in a document to, say, Luke's gospel might indicate that that document emanated from a geographical area where Luke's gospel was respected and used. The difficulty here is in delineating such an area with any precision. Massaux claims that, in the first two centuries, 'l'influence lucanienne paraît plus forte dans les écrits d'origine alexandrine que dans les documents palestiniens'.[558] However, precisely because of the fact that allusions to Luke are outnumbered by allusions to Matthew, the quantity of evidence is relatively small, and hence such global assertions must be treated with caution. It may be that the Nag Hammadi evidence itself will provide further

---

Schneemelcher, in Hennecke, *NT Apocrypha I*, 33, among others, following W. Bauer, *Orthodoxy and Heresy in Earliest Christianity*, London 1972, 184f. But Bauer's only argument was based on the lack of any mention of Luke by Papias in Eusebius' account; from this Bauer deduced that Papias must have spoken so disparagingly of Luke that Eusebius deliberately omitted what he had said. But this reads a lot into Eusebius' silence. In any case, see now F. Siegert, 'Unbeachtete Papiaszitate bei armenischen Schriftstellern', *NTS* 27 (1981) 605-614 who gives a fragment of Papias' commentary on Revelation where Papias quotes the words of Lk 11.18: Papias' attitude to Luke's gospel cannot thus have been wholly negative. Nevertheless, a certain amount of reserve about Luke's gospel may be implicit in Irenaeus' defence of Luke in *A.H.* III.14.3 ('if any man set Luke aside as one who did not know the truth . . . '). The Muratorian Canon's long defence of Luke's reliability may also reflect some doubts about Luke.

[557] Cf. the tentative suggestions made above (p.68) about the date of GTr.

[558] Op.cit., 654.

data here, in indicating the extent of the influence of Mark and Luke within early Christianity. But for such data to be provided, one would need to establish the date and provenance of the Nag Hammadi texts themselves, using criteria independent of arguments based on the use of biblical tradition in these texts.[559]

However, any arguments from silence, based on the absence of allusions to one particular gospel, must remain of very limited value. As has already been said, the fact that a writer does not appear to allude to one particular gospel in the fragment of his work which happens to survive cannot show that that gospel was unknown to the writer concerned, or that it was considered of doubtful authority in some way. The absence of allusions may be due to chance, to lack of an appropriate context into which such an allusion could be worked, or simply to the fact that such allusions occurred in the parts of the text which are now lost. Arguments based on the pattern of synoptic allusions in a text may provide some contributory evidence in assessing the date and provenance of a text when coupled with other considerations, but they must be used with care.

One striking feature of the allusions noted in the Nag Hammadi Library is their great variety. The actual synoptic passages referred to vary considerably. It is true that there is some overlap between the different texts, but perhaps less than might be expected. One text referred to frequently is the saying in Mt 7.16 about trees and their fruits. This appears to be alluded to in a number of texts (cf. TriTrac 118.23f.; GTr 33.30,38f.; ApPet 75.7-9;

---

559 For example, an Alexandrian origin for TestTr has been proposed on other grounds, and this would fit the pattern of dependence on Luke's gospel and Massaux's claim above. On the other hand, TeachSilv, which also probably stems from an Alexandrian milieu, does not appear to reflect use of Luke.

TestTr 31.21f; ValExp 36.32ff.; *perhaps* also ApAdam 76.15), and indeed according to Origen (*De Princ.* I.8.2) it was a favourite Valentinian text. The resurrection appearance traditions of Matthew and Luke are also frequently used (allusions to the Matthaean account occur in TreatRes, ApocJohn, SJC, AcPet12, EpPetPhil and ApPet; allusions to the Lukan narratives occur in SJC and EpPetPhil). However, the fact that some Gnostic writers present their teachings in the form of discourses by the risen Jesus in what is, implicitly or explicitly, another resurrection appearance scene, makes this result hardly surprising. Another synoptic complex which recurs relatively frequently is the sequence in Mt 6.19ff. The saying about 'treasure' (Mt 6.19-21) is reflected, directly or indirectly, in AuthTeach 38.23-27; TeachSilv 88.13-17; TestTr 31.20; SentSext 316; GMary 10.15f.; GTr 33.15f. also alludes to the same passage, though in a quite different way. The 'light' saying which follows in Mt 6.22f. is also alluded to in the same context in TeachSilv 88.13f. and at 99.16-20 and also in DialSav 125.18-21. Clearly these texts differ greatly: at the very least, TeachSilv and SentSext are not Gnostic works, whereas GMary is. One cannot then assume without more ado that these texts come from the same milieu or from the same Gnostic school. Nevertheless, it is a slightly unusual phenomenon which *may* be purely coincidental but which may have further significance.[560] The Q saying 'Seek and you shall find' (Mt 7.7/Lk 11.9) is alluded to a number of times (e.g. GTr 17.3f.; GMary 8.20f.; perhaps too ThomCont 140.41f. and AuthTeach passim); the

[560] It is noteworthy that the passage does not appear to have been particularly popular in other circles: e.g. Massaux cites only Justin (*1Apol.* 15.11,12,16) and Tatian (in Clement, *Strom.* III.12.86) amongst patristic authors prior to Irenaeus using Mt 6.19-21; he notes no authors alluding to Mt 6.22f.

appended sayings 'ask and you shall receive' and 'knock and it will be opened to you' may be echoed in ApocJas 10.32-34 and TeachSilv 117.5-9,19,22 respectively; further, the longer saying involving the sequence 'seek-find-marvel-reign-rest', which may represent a development of the more simple synoptic saying, is reflected in ThomCont, 2ApJas, DialSav amongst the texts examined here (as well as GHeb and GTh). Nevertheless, the simple synoptic saying is perhaps not used in these texts as frequently as one might have expected from the remarks of Tertullian (*De Praescr.* 8-13, 43) or Irenaeus (*A.H.* II.13.10; 18.6; 30.2).[561]

Other overlaps in texts referred to are less extensive. Both AcPet12 and ApPet refer to the Petrine saying in Mt 16, perhaps because for the authors of both texts the position of Peter was a matter of direct concern. GTr and IntKnow show some similarity in correlating the saying about the sheep fallen into the pit (Mt 12.11f.) and the parable of the lost sheep (Mt 18.12-14/Lk 15.4-7). Lk 10.19 is alluded to by both SJC 119.4-8 and ValExp 40.10-16. The parable of the two houses built upon the sand/rock (Mt 7.24-27 and par.) is echoed in ApocJas 8.7; 13.3-8; ApPet 70.26-28; TestTr 31.18f. The saying in Lk 17.21 may be echoed in GMary 8.17f., and possibly DialSav 128.2-5 and 2LogSeth 65.20, though the saying in GTh 3 should also be noted as possibly indicating a wider use of this saying (or a developed form of it). It is perhaps surprising that some synoptic texts are *not* used more frequently. For example, the famous *Jubelruf* in Mt 11.25-27/Lk 10.21f. (which might be considered as potentially very congenial to Gnostic interpreters) seems

[561] On the use of this text, see N.Brox, 'Suchen und Finden. Zur Nachgeschichte von Mt 7,7b/Lk 11,9b', in *Orientierung an Jesus*, Freiburgh-Basel-Wien 1973 17-36; also Koschorke, 'Suchen und Finden'.

to be echoed only in GTr 19.22ff.; SJC 94.9-13 and DialSav 134.14f. There are thus not many synoptic texts which are alluded to frequently here. Rather, the Nag Hammadi Library presents a great variety in this respect.

If there is a wide variation in the actual texts alluded to here, it is also the case that there is great variety between the different tractates concerning the *extent* to which synoptic tradition is reflected. One might have expected that synoptic tradition would be echoed to a greater extent in texts where the speaker is identified as Jesus than in texts where the author speaks directly. But this is not the case. For example, GPh and TeachSilv do not claim for the most part to be giving the words of Jesus himself, and yet both texts exhibit some close allusions to synoptic tradition. On the other hand, ThomCont and ApocJohn are both couched in the form of discourses of the risen Jesus, and yet both texts betray only minimal influence from synoptic tradition. In the course of a discussion of GTh and of the possibility that that gospel might preserve primitive traditions of the sayings of Jesus, R.M. Grant argued that the nature of the GTh was not in fact surprising. He said that any author, wishing to compose a document which purported to give the esoteric teaching of Jesus as the Gnostic Revealer, would have had to ensure that his Gnostic Jesus 'proclaimed doctrines which were in some respects close to those set forth in the Church's gospel; otherwise he cannot be recognised as Jesus'.[562] Whether this is a sufficient explanation of the similarities between GTh and the synoptic tradition (as Grant was arguing here) cannot be discussed here. However, Grant's argument is by no means self-evident

[562] 'Two Gnostic Gospels', *JBL* 79 (1960) 3. Grant was assuming that GTh is a Gnostic text; this too is an issue which must be left on one side here.

and not necessarily justified by the evidence (now more fully available than when Grant's article was written) from the rest of the Nag Hammadi Library. The authors of these texts appear to have differed greatly over the question of how important they believed it to be that the central figure in their writings be 'recognised as Jesus', or how important it was for them to relate what they wanted to say to what 'orthodox' Christians were saying. For some writers, this was clearly not an issue. For example, the author of TriTrac is generally content to expound his argument in his own words with little *direct* reference to synoptic tradition. At the other end of the scale, the author of ApPet gives what might loosely be described as a 'midrashic' exposition of Matthew's gospel to present his message. In some cases it seems to have been considered sufficient for the Gnostic writer simply to name the speaker in his text 'Jesus' in order to claim continuity with the Christian tradition (cf. ThomCont). In other instances it appears that a conscious effort was made to make this identification at a deeper level, by ensuring that the Gnostic Jesus said things which were recognisable from elsewhere as Jesus' words (cf. the catena in GMary 8).[563]

This whole issue is also connected with the problem of the relationship between the texts of the Nag Hammadi Library and the accounts of Gnostics which are given by the Church Fathers. Prior to the discovery of the Nag Hammadi Library, one had to rely for information about Gnostic Christians almost entirely on the patristic reports. One was assisted in this by the fact that many of the Fathers gave extensive quotations of the writings of

[563] This issue can, of course, only be fully discussed when the results of a study of the use of Johannine and other (possibly non-canonical) Jesus-traditions in these texts have been correlated.

their opponents, e.g. the letter of Ptolemy to Flora, recorded by Epiphanius (*Pan.* 33.3-7), or the Naassene hymn, quoted by Hippolytus (*Ref.* V.10.2). The accuracy of the descriptions of Gnostic thinkers by the Church Fathers is a subject which cannot be fully discussed here, though most would accept that Irenaeus at least is generally reasonably accurate in his reporting. However, the overwhelming impression given by the patristic reports of Gnostic thinkers is that the NT tradition and its proper interpretation was extremely important for them. In a famous passage, Tertullian contrasts Valentinus with Marcion, claiming that whilst Marcion mutilates the NT text (by cutting some bits out), Valentinus uses the whole text, albeit (according to Tertullian) perversely misinterpreting its meaning (*De Praescr.*38). A similar picture emerges from the accounts of Irenaeus and Hippolytus. For example Irenaeus gives many instances of the way in which (according to him) the Gnostics twist the scriptures to their own ends, 'striving as they do to adapt the good words of revelation to their own wicked inventions' (*A.H.* I.3.6; cf.II.10.1; V.26.2). According to Irenaeus, they see great significance in several of the numbers given in the gospel narrative (e.g. the number of years of Jesus' life prior to his ministry, the numbers of the hours of the day mentioned in the parable of the labourers in the vineyard: cf. *A.H.* I.1.3; 3.2-3). They interpret parables such as the lost sheep, the lost coin (*A.H.* I.8.4; 16.1) and the leaven (I.8.3); they see the Demiurge reflected in figures of the gospel story such as the centurion of Mt 8.9 (*A.H.* 1.7.4) or Simeon in Lk 2 (I.8.4) etc. etc. Indeed Irenaeus himself clearly regards it as extremely important to be able to counter his opponents' interpretation of the NT text.[564]

[564] Cf. Pagels, *The Johannine Gospel in Gnostic Exegesis*, 40ff.

A similar picture emerges from some of the more extended quotations given by the Church Fathers: here too NT exegesis plays an important role. The *Excerpts of Theodotus*, however precisely they are divided into different strata of tradition,[565] clearly show the Gnostic writers could and did give extensive quotations from the NT. Finally one may refer to Ptolemy's Letter to Flora which is full of explicit citations and references to the Bible. At the conclusion of the letter, the author claims that 'we can prove all our statements from the teaching of the Saviour' (Epiphanius, *Pan.* 33.7.9).[566] It is clearly regarded as vitally important by the writer that he should be able to show that his teaching is consistent with, and derivable from, the teachings of Jesus and the OT Law. Thus C. Barth, writing solely on the basis of patristic reports about Gnostics could write of Valentinian Gnosticism thus:

> Wie ernst es aber dennoch der valentinianischen Schule mit ihrem Christentum war, lehrt uns bereits ein Blick auf die Fülle neutestamentlicher Zitate, die ihre Schriften enthalten. Augenscheinlich war man bemüht, die Lehre auf die Schrift zu gründen, und war stolz im Bewusstsein, auf die Autorität des Neuen Testaments sich berufen zu können.[567]

Now all this is very different from the pattern which emerges from the vast majority of the Nag Hammadi texts. Very rarely do these texts explicitly cite a text (with, for example, some kind of introductory formula) which is then interpreted. In fact the only Nag Hammadi text to

---

565 Cf. the rather different conclusions about the extent of Clement's own comments by C.Barth, *Die Interpretation des neuen Testaments in der valentinischen Gnosis, TU* 37.3 Leipzig 1911 (who attributes very little to Clement), and R.P. Casey *The Excerpta ex Theodoto of Clement of Alexandria StD* 1, London 1934; also the extracts given by Foerster, *Gnosis I*, following Sagnard's *Sources Chrétiennes* edition, who attribute much more to Clement.
566 Cited from Foerster, *Gnosis I*, 161.
567 Op.cit., 44.

come near to this kind of use of the NT is ExegSoul.[568] Elsewhere, anything approaching an explicit citation is the exception rather than the rule. At times NT language is echoed, but often with no authority claims being made implicitly by the use of the language. Rather, it often seems to be the case that a writer is using language and terminology which is familiar to him, in the same way as some preachers might preach sermons using slightly archaic English reflecting the language of the Authorised Version of the Bible. Thus when the authors of ThomCont or 1ApJas refer to persecutions of the disciples and use language which is reminiscent of the canonical beatitudes (cf. ThomCont 145.3ff.; 1ApJas 41.22f.) there is probably no more significance to be seen in this than the fact that this language was familiar to the author concerned. Similarly, the author of GTr is clearly steeped in the language of the NT; yet many of the echoes of the NT in that text do not require the reader to recognise their background in order to appreciate the force of what is said. Not much, if anything, would be lost from the context if the allusion were not recognised.

There is too a remarkable lack of correlation between the use of synoptic tradition in the Nag Hammadi Library and the patristic reports of the use of synoptic tradition by Gnostic Christians. This is not to say that there is no correlation at all. The use of the 'seek and you shall find' saying corresponds with the remarks of Irenaeus and Tertulian, and Origen's remark about the popularity of the saying about the tree and its fruits is also confirmed here (see above). There is a close correlation between the interpretation of the parable of the lost sheep in GTr 31.35ff. and Irenaeus' report in *A.H.* I.16.1-2 and II.24.6.

[568] Cf. Wisse, 'The Nag Hammadi Library and the Heresiologists', 216.

The interpretation of the crucifixion narrative in 2LogSeth 56.6ff., whereby Simon of Cyrene takes the place of Jesus who stands by watching and laughing, corresponds closely with the reports of Basilides' teaching in Irenaeus (*A.H.* I.24.4) and Epiphanius (*Pan,* 24.3). Lk 10.19, alluded to in SJC and ValExp, is also quoted in *Exc.Theod.* 76.2. Allusion is made in passing in the Nag Hammadi texts to various synoptic parables. Occasionally these match patristic references. For example, the parable of the mustard seed is alluded to in DialSav 144.6f. and in *Exc. Theod.*1.3;[569] the parable of the labourers in the vineyard is referred to briefly in ApocJas 8.8f., whilst Irenaeus gives an account of the significance seen in the numbering of the hours in the parable (*A.H.* I.3.1). But in general, with the exception of the use of the parable of the lost sheep in GTr, it is remarkably difficult to match up references to the parables in the Nag Hammadi texts with patristic accounts of Gnostic interpretation of the parables.

How this is to be explained is not certain. It is not known for sure whether patristic writers actually knew any of the Gnostic texts which have now come to light in the Nag Hammadi Library. It is not clear whether Irenaeus' reference to Valentinus' *Gospel of Truth* (*A.H.* III.11.9) is an allusion to the text of that name from the Nag Hammadi Library. 2LogSeth was probably known to Epiphanius,[570] and ParShem may have been known in some form to Hippolytus.[571] It is widely accepted that

[569] According to Casey and Foerster (following Sagnard) this is part of Clement's own comments; but Barth argues strongly (op.cit., 2) that the close connection between 1.3 and 2.1 (which is clearly Valentinian) implies that they should not be separated.

[570] *Pan.* 24.3.2. Cf. Gibbons, *Commentary,* 210f.

[571] Cf. Wisse, op.cit., 216.

Irenaeus in his account of the beliefs of the Barbelognostics in *A.H.*1.29 is describing the same system as appears in part in ApocJohn. But the fact that Irenaeus' account is much shorter, as well as differing in some details, indicates that Irenaeus probably did not know ApocJohn itself, but rather a related source.[572] There is thus little evidence that the patristic writers had direct access to many of the texts which have now come to light in the Nag Hammadi Library.

It may be, therefore, that the reports of Gnostics given by patristic writers were based on different kinds of Gnostic texts. This is essentially the thesis of Wisse[573] who argues that the Gnostic sources available to people like Irenaeus were not necessarily texts which would have been produced for internal consumption within Gnostic communities: rather, they were the sort of material which would have been used by Gnostic propagandists in their missionary efforts to gain adherents from th more 'orthodox' Christian communities. NT exegesis would therefore be appropriate in such a missionary context, whereas, when writing for their own communitie, the Gnostic writers would not have felt the need to bolster their claims by reference to the NT.

This is an attractive thesis, though it perhaps needs some expansion and correction. We do not know the extent to which Gnostic Christians tried to propagate their faith and to gain new adherents, though the letter of Ptolemy to Flora (*with* its great stress on the importance of 'correct' biblical interpretation) would support Wisse's thesis. However, it is not clear whether other Nag Hammadi texts were ever written with such a missionary aim in view. Some clearly seem not to have been: e.g.

[572] Cf. Krause, in Foerster, *Gnosis I,* 100ff.
[573] Op. cit., 216.

ApPet and 2LogSeth appear to have been written in polemical situations for Gnostic Christians suffering persecution at the hands of the 'orthodox'. One could extend Wisse's theory to suggest that NT exegesis was important when Gnostics and 'orthodox' Christians came into contact with each other, whether that contact was friendly or not. Nevertheless even this will not work as an overall explanation. A text like IntKnow appears to have been written to deal with a situation entirely with*in* the Gnostic community, and yet devotes some considerable space to interpreting the NT. On the other hand, a text like AuthTeach witnesses to a very similar *Sitz im Leben* to that reflected in ApPet (i.e. a community experiencing persecution) and yet it is a text where allusions to synoptic, and biblical, tradition are far from numerous.[574]

It is probably impossible to make any sweeping generalisations about the place of NT exegesis within Gnosticism. Gnostic thought is famed neither for its uniformity nor its logical consistency, and any single over-arching explanation of the place of the NT in Gnosticism would perhaps by its very nature be suspect. One can probably say that the contact which some Gnostic Christians had with other Christian groups led them to attempt to give what they regarded as the 'true'[575] interpretation of the Christian tradition which they, in part at least, claimed to share with other Christians. Yet it is also probably the case that other Gnostics, writing solely for a Gnostic audience and without direct relation to outsiders, also regarded it as desirable to appropriate and use the Christian tradition. (Unless, of course, one could turn this line of reasoning on its head and claim that

---

574 Indeed some have said that the text is non-Christian: see above.

575 Though 'true' does not imply 'only': cf.Barth, op.cit., 98.

any use of NT traditions in a Gnostic text implies a *Sitz im Leben* of contact, friendly or otherwise, with non-Gnostic Christians: but that would seem to be methodologically highly suspect.)

It is hoped that the analysis offered here may be of some assistance in the continuing research into the Nag Hammadi texts in seeking to solve some of the many problems which still remain unanswered.

ABBREVIATIONS

(Where possible, abbreviations used for journals etc. have been those in S. Schwertner, *Theologische Realenzyklopädie Abkürzungsverzeichnis*, Berlin–New York 1976)

ADAI.K	Abhandlungen des Deutschen Archäologischen Instituts zu Kairo. Koptische Reihe.
AGSU	Arbeiten zur Geschichte des Spätjudentums und Urchristentums
APF	Archiv für Papyrusforschung
BCNH	Bibliothèque Copte de Nag Hammadi
BEThL	Bibliotheca Ephemeridum Theologicarum Lovaniensum
BGBE	Beiträge zur Geschichte der biblischen Exegese
Bib	Biblica
BJRL	Bulletin of the John Rylands Library
BSt(F)	Biblische Studien, Freiburg
BZ	Biblische Zeitschrift
BZNW	Beihefte zur Zeitschrift für die neutestamentliche Wissenschaft
CSCO	Corpus Scriptorum Christianorum Orientalium
Eng.Tr.	English Translation
EThL	Ephemerides Theologicae Lovanienses
FRLANT	Forschungen zur Religion und Literatur des Alten und Neuen Testaments
FS	Festschrift
FzB	Forschung zur Bibel
HeyJ	Heythrop Journal
HThK	Herders Theologischer Kommentar zum Neuen Testament

HThR	Harvard Theological Review
HThS	Harvard Theological Studies
JAC	Jahrbuch für Antike und Christentum
JAC.E	Jahrbuch für Antike und Christentum. Ergänzungsband
JBL	Journal of Biblical Literature
JEH	Journal of Ecclesiastical History
JThS	Journal of Theological Studies
LkR	Lukan redaction
MtR	Matthaean redaction
MkR	Markan redaction
MSSNTS	Monograph Series. Society for New Testament Studies
Muséon	Le Muséon
NHLE	J.M. Robinson (ed.), *The Nag Hammadi Library in English*, Leiden 1977
NHS	Nag Hammadi Studies
NT	Novum Testamentum
NT.S	Novum Testamentum. Supplements.
NTA	Neutestamentliche Abhandlungen
NTS	New Testament Studies
OLZ	Orientalische Literaturzeitung
Or.	Orientalia
PTS	Patristische Texte und Studien
SBL	Society of Biblical Literature
SBLDS	Society of Biblical Literature. Dissertation Series
SBLMS	Society of Biblical Literature. Monograph Series
SBLTT	Society of Biblical Literature. Texts and Translations
StD	Studies and Documents
StEv	Studia Evangelica
StPatr	Studia Patristica

TaS	Texts and Studies
ThLZ	Theologische Literaturzeitung
ThWNT	Theologisches Wörterbuch zum Neuen Testament
ThZ	Theologische Zeitschrift
TU	Texte und Untersuchungen
VigChr	Vigiliae Christianae
WMANT	Wissenschaftliche Monographien zum Alten und Neuen Testament
WUNT	Wissenschaftliche Untersuchungen zum Neuen Testament
ZNW	Zeitschrift für die neutestamentliche Wissenschaft
ZThK	Zeitschrift für Theologie und Kirche

The following abbreviations for the Nag Hammadi texts themselves have been used (with the standard conventions for numbering the codices and the tractates within each codex):

PrPaul	The Prayer of the Apostle Paul (I.1)
ApocJas	The Apocryphon of James (I.2)
GTr	The Gospel of Truth (I.3 and XII.2)
TreatRes	The Treatise on Resurrection (I.4)
TriTrac	The Tripartite Tractate (I.5)
ApocJohn	The Apocryphon of John (II.1, III.1, IV.1 and BG 8502.2)
GTh	The Gospel of Thomas (II.2)
GPh	The Gospel of Philip (II.3)
HypArch	The Hypostasis of the Archons (II.4)
OrigWorld	On the Origin of the World (II.5 and XIII.2)
ExegSoul	The Exegesis on the Soul (II.6)
ThomCont	The Book of Thomas the Contender (II.7)

ABBREVIATIONS

GEg	The Gospel of the Egyptians (III.2 and IV.2)
Eug	Eugnostos the Blessed (III.3 and V.1)
SJC	The Sophia of Jesus Christ (III.4 and BG 8502.3)
DialSav	The Dialogue of the Saviour (III.5)
ApPaul	The Apocalypse of Paul (V.2)
1ApJas	The First Apocalypse of James (V.3)
2ApJas	The Second Apocalypse of James (V.4)
ApAdam	The Apocalypse of Adam (V.5)
AcPet12	The Acts of Peter and the Twelve Apostles (VI.1)
Thunder	The Thunder, Perfect Mind (VI.2)
AuthTeach	Authentic Teaching (VI.3)
GtPower	The Concept of Our Great Power (VI.4)
Rep	Plato's Republic (VI.5)
8th and 9th	The Discourse on the Eighth and Ninth (VI.6)
Prayer	The Prayer of Thanksgiving (VI.7)
Ascl	Asclepius 21-29 (VI.8)
ParShem	The Paraphrase of Shem (VII.1)
2LogSeth	The Second Treatise of the Great Seth (VII.2)
ApPet	The Apocalypse of Peter (VII.3)
TeachSilv	The Teachings of Silvanus (VII.4)
3StSeth	The Three Steles of Seth (VII.5)
Zost	Zostrianos (VIII.1)
EpPetPhil	The Letter of Peter to Philip (VIII.2)
Melch	Melchizedek (IX.1)
Norea	The Thought of Norea (IX.2)
TestTr	The Testimony of Truth (IX.3)
Mar	Marsanes (X.1)
IntKnow	The Interpretation of Knowledge (XI.1)
ValExp	A Valentinian Exposition (XI.2)

Allog	Allogenes (XI.3)
Hypsi	Hypsiphrone (XI.4)
SentSext	The Sentences of Sextus (XII.1)
TriProt	Trimorphic Protennoia (XIII.1)
GMary	The Gospel of Mary (BG 8502.1)

BIBLIOGRAPHY

Allen W.C., *A Critical and Exegetical Commentary on the Gospel according to St Matthew*, Edinburgh 1907.

Arai S., 'Zur Christologie des Apokryphons des Johannes', *NTS* 15 (1969) 302-318.

---'Simonianische Gnosis und die *Exegese über die Seele*', M. Krause (ed.), *Gnosis and Gnosticism, NHS* 8, Leiden 1977, 185-203.

Barth C., *Die Interpretation des neuen Testaments in der valentinischen Gnosis, TU* 37.3, Leipzig 1911.

Bauer W., *Orthodoxy and Heresy in Earliest Christianity*, London 1972.

Bellinzoni A., *The Sayings of Jesus in the Writings of Justin Martyr, NT.S* 17, Leiden 1967.

Bethge H.G., '"Nebront"—Die zweite Schrift aus Nag-Hammadi-Codex VI', *ThLZ* 98 (1973) 97-104

---'"Zweiter Logos des grossen Seth"—Die zweite Schrift aus Nag-Hammadi-Codex VII', *ThLZ* 100 (1975) 97-110.

---'Die Exegese über die Seele', *ThLZ* 101 (1976) 93-104.

---'Der sogenannte "Brief des Petrus an Philippus" -Die zweite Schrift aus Nag-Hammadi-Codex VIII', *ThLZ* 103 (1978) 161-170.

Bornkamm G., Barth G., Held H.J., *Tradition and Interpretation in Matthew*, London 1963.

Böhlig A., *Mysterion und Wahrheit, AGSU* 6, Leiden 1968.

---'Zur Frage nach den Typen des Gnostizismus und seines Schriftums', in *Ex Orbe Religionum. Studia Geo Widengren Oblata I*, Leiden 1972, 389-400.

Böhlig A. and Labib P., *Koptisch-gnostische Apokalypsen aus Codex V von Nag Hammadi im koptischen Museum zu Alt-Kairo*, Halle-Wittenberg 1963.

---*Die koptisch-gnostisch Schrift ohne Titel aus Codex II von Nag Hammadi*, Berlin 1962.

Böhlig A., and Wisse F., *Nag Hammadi Codices III,2 and IV,2: The Gospel of the Egyptians, NHS* 4, Leiden 1975.

Broek R. van den, 'The Authentikos Logos: A New Document of Christian Platonism', *VigChr* 33 (1979) 260-286.

Brown S.K., 'Jewish and Gnostic Elements in the Second Apocalypse of James (CG V.4)' *NT* 17 (1975) 225-237.

Brox N., 'Suchen und Finden. Zur Nachgeschichte von Mt 7,7b/Lk 11,9b', in P. Hoffmann (ed.), *Orientierung an Jesus*. FS for J. Schmid, Freiburg—Basel—Wien 1973, 17-36.

Bruce F.F., 'Some Thoughts on the Beginning of the New Testament Canon', *BJRL* 65 (1983) 37-60.

Bullard R.A., *The Hypostasis of the Archons, PTS* 10, Berlin 1970.

Campenhausen H. von, *The Formation of the Christian Bible*, London 1972.

Carlston C.E., 'Transfiguration and Resurrection', *JBL* 80 (1961) 233-240.

Casey R.P., *The Excerpta ex Theodoto of Clement of Alexandria, StD* 1, London 1934.

Catanzaro C.J. de, 'The Gospel according to Philip', *JThS* 13 (1962) 35-71.

Chadwick H., *The Sentences of Sextus, TaS* 5, Cambridge 1957.

Chilton B.D., '"Not to Taste Death". A Jewish, Christian and Gnostic Usage', in E.A. Livingstone (ed.), *Studia Biblica 1978 II. Papers on the Gospels*, Sheffield 1980, 29-36.

Colpe C., 'Heidnische, jüdische und christliche Überlieferung in den Schriften aus Nag Hammadi. III', *JAC* 17 (1974) 109-125.

Creed J.M., *The Gospel according to St. Luke*, London 1930.

Crum W.C., *A Coptic Dictionary*, Oxford 1939.

Dahl N.A., 'Die Passionsgeschichte bei Matthäus', *NTS* 2 (1955) 17-32.

Dehandschutter B., 'L'Évangile de Thomas comme collection de paroles de Jésus', in J. Delobel (ed.), *LOGIA. Les Paroles de Jésus—The Sayings of Jesus*, *BEThL* 59, Leuven 1982, 507-515.

Delling G., 'Zur Hellenisierung des Christentums in den "Sprüchen des Sextus"', in *Studien zum Neuen Testament und zur Patristik*. FS for E. Klostermann, *TU* 77, Berlin 1961, 208-241.

Denaux A., 'Der Spruch von den zwei Wegen im Rahmen des Epilogs der Bergpredigt (Mt 7,13-14 par. Lk 13,23-24). Tradition und Redaktion', in J. Delobel (ed.), *LOGIA. Les Paroles de Jésus—The Sayings of Jesus*, *BEThL* 59, Leuven 1982, 305-335.

Dodd C.H., 'The Appearances of the Risen Christ: An Essay in Form-Criticism of the Gospels', in D.E. Nineham (ed.), *Studies in the Gospels. Essays in Memory of R.H. Lightfoot*, Oxford, 1955, 9-35.

Dupont J., *Les Béatitudes*, Paris 1969.

Edwards R.A. and Wild R.A., *The Sentences of Sextus, SBLTT* 22, Chico 1981.

Evans C.A., 'On the Prologue of John and the *Trimorphic Protennoia*', *NTS* 27 (1981) 395-401.

Fallon F.T., *The Enthronement of Sabaoth, NHS* 10, Leiden 1978.

Farrer A., 'On Dispensing with Q', in D.E. Nineham (ed.), *Studies in the Gospels. Essays in Memory of R.H. Lightfoot*, Oxford 1955, 55-88.

Fischer K.M., 'Die Paraphrase des Seem', in M. Krause (ed.), *Essays on the Nag Hammadi Texts. In Honour of Pahor Labib*, *NHS* 6, Leiden 1975, 255-266.

Foerster W. (ed.), *Gnosis*, Oxford 1972.

Frankemölle H., 'Die Makarismen (Mt 5,1-12; Lk 6,20-23): Motive und Umfang der redaktionellen Komposition', *BZ* 15 (1971) 52-75.

Frickel J., 'Naasener oder Valentinianer?', in M. Krause (ed.), *Gnosis and Gnosticism*, *NHS* 17, Leiden 1981, 95-119.

Funk W.-P., '"Authentikos Logos"—Die dritte Schrift aus Nag-Hammadi-Codex VI', *ThLZ* 98 (1973) 251-259.

——— '"Die Lehren des Silvanus"—Die vierte Schrift aus Nag-Hammadi-Codex VII', *ThLZ* 100 (1975) 7-23.

——— *Die zweite Apokalypse des Jakobus aus Nag-Hammadi-Codex V*, *TU* 119, Berlin 1976.

Gärtner B., *The Theology of the Gospel of Thomas*, London 1961.

Gibbons J.A., *A Commentary on the Second Logos of the Great Seth*, Dissertation, Yale University 1972.

——— 'The Second Logos of the Great Seth: Considerations and Questions', in G. MacRae (ed.), *SBL 1973 Seminar Papers Vol.2*, Cambridge Mass. 1973, 242-261.

BIBLIOGRAPHY

Giversen S., *Apocryphon Johannis*, Copenhagen 1963.
Grant R.M., 'Two Gnostic Gospels', *JBL* 79 (1960) 1-11.
--- 'The Mystery of Marriage in the Gospel of Philip' *VigChr* 15 (1961) 129-140.
--- *Gnosticism. An Anthology*, London 1961.
Grobel K., *The Gospel of Truth*, New York 1960.
Guillaumont A., 'Une Citation de l'Apocryphe d'Ezéchiel dans l'Exégèse au sujet de l'âme', in M. Krause (ed.), *Essays on the Nag Hammadi Texts. In Honour of Pahor Labib*, *NHS* 6, Leiden 1975, 35-39.
Haardt R., '"Die Abhandlung über die Auferstehung" des Codex Jung aus der Bibliothek gnostischer koptischer Schriften von Nag Hammadi', *Kairos* 11 (1969) 1-5, and 12 (1970) 241-269.
Haas Y., 'L'Exigence de renoncement au monde dans les *Actes de Pierre et des Douze Apôtres*, les *Apophtegmes des Pères du Désert*, e5 la *Pistis Sophia*', in B. Barc (ed.), *Colloque International sûr les Textes de Nag Hammadi, BCNH* Etudes 1, Quebec—Louvain 1981, 295-303.
Hedrick C.W., *The Apocalypse of Adam. A Literary and Source Analysis, SBLDS* 46, Chico 1980.
--- 'Gnostic Proclivities in the Greek Life of Pachomius and the Sitz im Leben of the Nag Hammadi Library', *NT* 22 (1980) 78-94.
--- 'Christian Motifs in the *Gospel of the Egyptians*', *NT* 23 (1981) 242-260.
--- 'Kingdom Sayings and the Parables of Jesus in the *Apocryphon of James:* Tradition and Redaction', *NTS* 29 (1983) 1-24.
Helderman J., 'Anapausis in the Epistula Jacobi Apocrypha', in R. McL. Wilson (ed.), *Nag Hammadi and Gnosis, NHS* 14, Leiden 1978, 34-43.
Helmbold A.K., *The Nag Hammadi Gnostic Texts and the Bible*, Grand Rapids 1967.
--- 'Translation Problems in the Gospel of Philip', *NTS* 11 (1964) 90-93.
--- 'Gnostic Elements in the "Ascension of Isaiah"', *NTS* 18 (1972) 222-226.
Hennecke E., *New Testament Apocrypha*, London 1963.
Hoffmann P., *Studien zur Theologie der Logienquelle*, *NTA* 8, Münster 1972.
Janssens Y., 'L'Apocryphon de Jean', *Muséon* 83 (1970) 157-165.
--- 'Le Codex XIII de Nag Hammadi', *Muséon* 87 (1974) 341-413.
--- 'Traits de la passion dans l'Epistula Iacobi Apocrypha', *Muséon* 88 (1975) 97-101.
-- *La Protennoia Trimorphe BCNH* Textes 4, Quebec 1978.
Jeremias J., *Unknown Sayings of Jesus*, London 1957.
--- *The Parables of Jesus*, London 1963.
--- *Die Sprache des Lukasevangeliums*, Göttingen 1980.
Jonas H., *The Gnostic Religion*, Boston 1958.
Jülicher A., *Die Gleichnisreden Jesu*, Tübingen 1899.
Kasser R.—Malinine M.—Puech H.-C.—Quispel G.—Zandee J.—Vycichl W.—Wilson R. McL. (eds.), *Tractatus Tripartitus*, Bern Pars I 1973, Pars II 1975.
Kelber W. (ed.), *The Passion in Mark*, Philadelphia 1976.
Kirchner D., 'Das Buch des Thomas. Die siebte Schrift aus Nag-Hammadi-Codex II', *ThLZ* 102 (1977) 794-804.
--- *Epistula Jacobi Apocrypha. Die erste Schrift aus Nag-Hammadi-Codex I* (Codex Jung), Dissertation, Humbolt University, Berlin 1977.

Kilpatrick G.D., *The Origins of the Gospel according to St. Matthew*, Oxford 1946.

Kline L.L., *The Sayings of Jesus in the Pseudo-Clementine Homilies, SBLDS* 14, Missoula 1975.

Koester H., *Synoptische Überlieferung bei den apostolischen Vätern, TU* 65, Berlin 1957.

--- 'One Jesus and Four Primitive Gospels', in H. Koester—J.M. Robinson *Trajectories through Early Christianity*, Philadelphia 1971, 158-204.

--- 'Dialog und Spruchüberlieferung in den gnostischen Texten von Nag Hammadi', *EvTh* 39 (1979) 532-556.

--- 'Apocryphal and Canonical Gospels', *HThR* 73 (1980) 105-130.

--- 'Gnostic Writings as Witnesses for the Development of the Sayings Tradition', in B. Layton (ed.), *The Rediscovery of Gnosticism I. The School of Valentinus*, Leiden 1980, 238-261.

Koschorke K., '"Suchen und Finden" in der Auseinandersetzung zwischen gnostischem und kirchlichem Christentum', *Wort und Dienst* 14 (1977) 51-65.

--- 'Eine gnotische Pfingstpredigt. Zur Auseinandersetzung zwischen gnostischem und kirchlichem Christentum am Beispiel der "Epistula Petri ad Philippum" (NHC VIII,2)', *ZThK* 74 (1977) 323-343.

--- *Die Polemik der Gnostiker gegen das kirchliche Christentum, NHS* 12, Leiden 1978.

--- 'Der gnostische Traktat "Testimonium Veritatis" aus dem Nag-Hammadi-Codex IX', *ZNW* 69 (1978) 91-117.

--- 'Eine gnostische Paraphrase des johanneischen Prologs. Zur Interpretation von "Epistula Petri ad Philippum" (NHC VIII,2) 136,16—137,4', *VigChr* 33 (1979) 383-392.

--- 'Eine neugefundene gnostische Gemeindeordnung. Zum Thema Geist und Am5 im frühen Christentum', *ZThK* 76 (1979) 30-60.

Krause M., 'Das literarische Verhältnis des Eugnostosbriefes zur Sophia Jesu Christi', *Mullus.* FS for T. Klausner, *JAC.E* 1, Münster 1964, 215-223.

--- 'Zur Bedeutung des gnostisch-hermetischen Handschriftenfunds von Nag Hammadi', in M. Krause (ed.), *Essays on the Nag Hammadi Texts. In Honour of Pahor Labib, NHS* 6, Leiden 1975, 65-89.

--- 'Die Sakramente in der *Exegese über die Seele*', in J.-É. Ménard (ed.), *Les Textes de Nag Hammadi, NHS* 7, Leiden 1975, 47-55.

--- 'Der *Dialog der Soter* in Codex III von Nag Hammadi', in M. Krause (ed.), *Gnosis and Gnosticism, NHS* 8, Leiden 1977, 13-34.

--- 'Die Texte von Nag Hammadi', in B. Aland (ed.), *Gnosis.* FS for H. Jonas, Göttingen 1978, 216-243.

Krause M.—Labib P., *Die drei Versionen des Apokryphon des Johannes im koptischen Museum zu Alt-Kairo, ADAI.K* 1, Wiesbaden 1962.

--- *Gnostische und hermetische Schriften aus Codex II und Codex VI, ADAI,K* 2, Glückstadt 1971.

Layton B., 'The Hypostasis of the Archons', *HThR* 67 (1974) 351-425, and 69 (1976) 31-101.

--- *The Gnostic Treatise on Resurrection from Nag Hammadi, Harvard Dissertations in Religion* 12, Missoula 1979.

Lindars B., *New Testament Apologetic*, London 1961.

Luttikhuizen G.P., 'The Letter of Peter to Philip and the New Testament', in R. McL. Wilson (ed.), *Nag Hammadi and Gnosis, NHS* 14, Leiden 1978, 96-102.
Luz U., 'Der dreiteilige Traktat von Nag Hammadi', *ThZ* 33 (1977) 384-392.
Mahé J.-P., *Hermes en Haute Égypte, BCNH* Textes 3 and 7, Quebec 1978 and 1982.
Malinine M.—Puech H.-C.—Quispel G. (eds.), *Evangelium Veritatis*, Zürich 1956.
Malinine M.—Puech H.-C.—Quispel G.—Till W.C.—Wilson R. McL.—Zandee J. (eds.), *De Resurrectione (Epistula ad Rheginum), Codex Jung f.XXII^r*—f.XXV^v, Zürich—Stuttgart 1963.
Malinine M.—Puech H.-C.—Quispel G.—Till W.C.—Kasser R.—Wilson R. McL.—Zandee J. (eds.), *Epistula Iacobi Apocrypha*, Zürich-Stuttgart 1968.
Manson T.W., *The Sayings of Jesus*, London 1949.
Marshall I.H., *The Gospel of Luke*, Exeter 1977.
Massaux E., *Influence de l'Évangile de saint Matthieu sur la littérature chrétienne avant saint Irénée*, Louvain 1950.
--- 'Le Texte du Sermon sur la Montagne utilisé par Saint Justin', *EThL* 28 (1952) 411-448.
McArthur H.K., 'The Gospel according to Thomas', in H.K. McArthur (ed.), *New Testament Sidelights*, FS for A.C. Purdy, Hartford 1960, 43-77.
McNeile A.H., *The Gospel according to St. Matthew*, London 1915.
MacRae G.W., 'The Coptic Gnostic Apocalypse of Adam', *HeyJ* 6 (1965) 27-35.
--- 'A Nag Hammadi Tractate on the Soul', in *Ex Orbe Religionum. Studia Geo Widengren Oblata. I*, Leiden 1972, 471-479.
--- 'Nag Hammadi and the New Testament', in B. Aland (ed.), *Gnosis*, FS for H. Jonas, Göttingen 1978, 144-157.
Ménard J.-É., *L'Évangile de Vérité. Retroversion et Commentaire*, Paris 1962.
--- *L'Evangile selon Philippe*, Paris 1967.
--- *L'Évangile de Vérité, NHS* 2, Leiden 1972.
--- *L'Évangile selon Thomas, NHS* 5, Leiden 1975.
--- *La Lettre de Pierre à Philippe, BCNH Textes* 1, Quebec 1977.
--- *L'Authentikos Logos, BCNH Textes* 2, Quebec 1977.
--- 'Gnose paienne et gnose chrétienne: L'Authentikos Logos et L'Enseignements de Silvain de Nag Hammadi', in *Paganisme, Judaisme, Christianisme*. FS for M. Simon, Paris 1978, 287-294.
--- 'La Lettre de Pierre à Philippe', in B. Aland (ed.), *Gnosis*. FS for H. Jonas, Göttingen 1978, 449-463.
--- 'Normative Self-Definition in Gnosticism', in E.P. Sanders (ed.), *Jewish and Christian Self-Definition Vol. I*, London 1980, 134-150.
Meyer M.W., *The Letter of Peter to Philip, SBLDS* 53, Chico 1981.
Monselewski W., *Der barmherzige Samariter. Eine auslegungsgeschichtliche Untersuchung zu Lukas 10,25-37, BGBE* 5, Tübingen, 1967.
Nagel P., *Das Wesen der Archonten aus Codex II der gnostischen Bibliothek von Nag Hammadi*, Halle 1970.
--- 'Die Septuaginta-Zitate in der koptisch-gnostischen "Exegese über die Seele" (Nag Hammadi Codex II)', *APF* 22-23 (1974) 249-269.

Nickelsberg G.W.E., *Resurrection, Immortality and Eternal Life in Intertestamental Judaism, HThS* 26, Cambridge, Mass. 1972.
Pagels E.H., *The Johannine Gospel in Gnostic Exegesis, SBLMS* 17 Abingdon—New York 1973.
--- *The Gnostic Paul*, Philadelphia 1975.
Pagels E.H.—Koester H., 'Report of the *Dialogue of the Saviour* (CG III,5)', in R.McL. Wilson (ed.), *Nag Hammadi and Gnosis, NHS* 14, Leiden 1978, 66-74.
Painchaud L., 'La polémique anti-ecclésiale et l'exégèse de la passion dans le Deuxième Traité du Grand Seth', in B. Barc (ed.), *Colloque International sur les Textes de Nag Hammadi, BCNH Etudes 1*, Quebec—Louvain 1981, 340-351.
Parrott D.M. (ed.), *Nag Hammadi Codices V,2-5 and VI with Papyrus Berolinensis 8502, 1 and 4, NHS* 11, Leiden 1979.
Pearson B.A., 'Jewish Haggadic Traditions in the *Testimony of Truth* from Nag Hammadi (CG IX,2)', in *Ex Orbe Religionum. Studia Geo Widengren Oblata I*, Leiden 1972, 457-470.
--- *Nag Hammadi Codices IX and X, NHS* 15, Leiden 1981.
Peel M.L., *The Epistle to Rheginos*, London 1969.
--- 'The "Descensus ad Infernos" in "The Teachings of Silvanus" (CG VII,4)', *Numen* 26 (1979) 23-49.
Peel M.L.—Zandee J., 'The Teachings of Silvanus from the Library of Nag Hammadi', *NT* 14 (1972) 294-311.
Perkins P., 'Peter in Gnostic Revelation', in G. MacRae (ed.), *SBL 1974 Seminar Papers Vol.2*, Cambridge, Mass. 1974, 1-13.
--- *The Gnostic Dialogue*, New York 1980.
--- 'Johannine Tradition in *Ap.Jas.* (NHC I,2)', *JBL* 101 (1982) 403-414.
Perrin N., *Rediscovering the Teaching of Jesus*, London 1967.
Pesch W., 'Zur Exegese von Mt 6,19-21 und Lk 12,33-34', *Bib* 41 (1960) 356-378.
Prigent P., 'Ce que l'oeil n'a pas vu, 1 Cor.2,9', *ThZ* 14 (1968) 416-429.
Przybylski B., *Righteousness in Matthew and his World of Thought, MSSNTS* 41, Cambridge 1980.
Quispel G., 'Das Hebräerevangelium im gnostischen Evangelium nach Maria', *VigChr* 11 (1957) 139-144.
--- 'Jewish Gnosis and Mandaean Gnosticism: Some Reflections on the Writing *Brontè*', in J.-É. Ménard (ed.), *Les Textes de Nag Hammadi, NHS* 7, Leiden 1975, 82-122.
Robinson J.M., 'Logoi Sophon: On the Gattung of Q', in H. Koester—J.M. Robinson, *Trajectories through Early Christianity*, Philadelphia 1971, 71-113.
--- 'The Three Steles of Seth and the Gnostics of Plotinus', in *Proceedings of the International Colloquium on Gnosticism. Stockholm 1973*, Stockholm 1977, 132-142.
--- (ed.), *The Nag Hammadi Library in English*, Leiden 1977.
--- 'Gnosticism and the New Testament', in B. Aland (ed.), *Gnosis*. FS for H. Jonas, Göttingen 1978, 125-143.
--- 'Sethians and Johannine Thought. The Trimorphic Protennoia and the Prologue of the Gospel of John', in B. Layton (ed.), *The Rediscovery of*

Gnosticism II. Sethian Gnosticism, Leiden 1981, 643-662.
--- 'Jesus from Easter to Valentinus (or to the Apostles' Creed)', *JBL* 101 (1982) 5-37.
Robinson W.C.. 'The Exegesis on the Soul', *NT* 12 (1970) 102-117.
Säve-Söderberg T., 'Holy Scriptures or Apologetic Documentations? The "Sitz im Leben" of the Nag Hammadi Library', in J.-É. Ménard (ed.), *Les Textes de Nag Hammadi*, *NHS* 7, Leiden 1975, 3-14.
Schelke K.H., 'Das Evangelium Veritatis als kanongeschichtliches Zeugnis', *BZ* 5 (1961) 90-91.
Schenke G., '"Die dreigestaltige Protennoia"—Eine gnostische Offenbarungsrede in koptischer Sprache aus dem Fund von Nag Hammadi', *ThLZ* 99 (1974) 731-746.
Schenke H.-M., 'Das Evangelium nach Philippus', *ThLZ* 84 (1959) 1-26.
--- *Die Herkunft des sogenannten Evangelium Veritatis*, Göttingen 1959.
--- Review of Böhlig-Labib, *Apokalypsen*, *OLZ* 61 (1966) 23-34.
--- 'Exegetische Probleme der zweiten Jacobus-Apokalypse in Nag-Hammadi-Codex V', in P. Nagel (ed.), *Probleme der koptischen Literatur* (Halle, 1968), pp.109-114.
--- 'Der Jakobusbrief aus den Codex Jung', *OLZ* 66 (1971) 117-130.
--- 'Die Taten des Petrus und der zwölf Apostel', *ThLZ* 98 (1973) 13-19.
--- 'Zur Fasimile-Ausgabe der Nag-Hammadi-Schriften-Codex VI', *OLZ* 69 (1974) 229-243.
--- 'The Phenomenon and Significance of Gnostic Sethianism', in B. Layton (ed.), *The Rediscovery of Gnosticism II. Sethian Gnosticism*, Leiden 1981, 580-616.
Schmid J., *Matthäus und Lukas*, *BSt* 23.2-4, Freiburg 1930.
Schoedel W.R., 'Scripture and the Seventy two Heavens of the First Apocalypse of James', *NT* 12 (1970) 118-129.
--- 'Jewish Wisdom and the Formation of the Christian Ascetic', in R.L. Wilken (ed.), *Aspects of Wisdom in Judaism and Early Christianity*, Notre Dame-London, 1975 169-199.
Scholer D.M., *Nag Hammadi Bibliography 1948-1969*, *NHS* 1, Leiden 1971.
Schrage W., *Das Verhältnis des Thomas-Evangeliums zur synoptischen Tradition und zu den koptischen Evangelien-übersetzungen*, *BZNW* 29, Berlin 1964.
Schulz S., *Q-Die Spruchquelle der Evangelisten*, Zürich 1972.
Schürmann H., *Traditionsgeschlichtliche Untersuchungen zu den synoptischen Evangelien*, Düsseldorf 1968.
--- *Das Lukasevangelium I*, *HThK* 3/1, Freiburg 1969.
Schweizer E., 'The "Matthaean" Church', *NTS* 20 (1974) 216.
--- *The Good News according to Matthew*, London 1976.
Scopello M., 'Les "Testimonia" dans le traité de "l'exégèse de l'âme" (Nag Hammadi II,6)', *RHR* 191 (1977) 159-171.
--- 'Les citations d'Homère dans le traité de l'Exégèse de l'Âme', in M. Krause (ed.) *Gnosis and Gnosticism*, *NHS* 8, Leiden 1977, 3-12.
Senior D.P., *The Passion Narrative according to Matthew*, BEThL 39, Leuven 1982.
Sell J., 'Simon Peter's "Confession" and *The Acts of Peter and the Twelve Apostles*' *NT* 21 (1979) 344-356.

--- 'A Note on a striking Johannine Motif found at CG VI: 6,19', *NT* 20 (1978) 232-240
--- 'Jesus the Fellow Stranger. A Study of CG VI 2,35-3,11', *NT* 23 (1981) 173-192
Sevrin J., 'A propos de la Paraphrase de Sem', *Muséon* 88 (1975) 69-96.
--- 'La rédaction de l'exégèse de l'âme (Nag Hammadi II,6), *Muséon* 92 (1979) 237-271.
--- 'Paroles et Paraboles de Jésus dans des écrits gnostiques coptes', in J. Delobel (ed.), *LOGIA. Les Paroles de Jésus—The Sayings of Jesus, BEThL* 59, Leuven 1982, 517-528.
Shellrude G.M. 'The Apocalypse of Adam: Evidence for a Christian Gnostic Provenance', in M. Krause (ed.), *Gnosis and Gnosticism, NHS* 17, Leiden 1981, 82-91.
Sieber J.H., 'An Introduction to the Tractate Zostrianos from Nag Hammadi', *NT* 15 (1973) 223-240.
Siegert F., 'Unbeachtete Papiaszitate bei armenischen Schriftstellern', *NTS* 27 (1981) 605-614.
--- *Nag-Hammadi-Register, WUNT* 26, Tübingen 1982.
Steck O.H., *Israel und das gewaltsame Geschick der Propheten, WMANT* 23, Neukirchen-Vluyn 1967.
Stein R.H., 'Is the Transfiguration (Mark 9:2-8) a misplaced Resurrection Account?', *JBL* 95 (1976) 79-96.
Story C.I.K., *The Nature of Truth in "The Gospel of Truth" and in the Writings of Justin Martyr, NT.S* 25, Leiden 1970.
Strecker G., *Der Weg der Gerechtigkeit, FRLANT* 82, Göttingen 1962.
--- 'Die Makarismen der Bergpredigt', *NTS* 17 (1971) 255-275.
--- 'Eine Evangelienharmonie bei Justin und Pseudoklemens?', *NTS* 24 (1978) 297-316.
Streeter B.H., *The Four Gospels*, London 1924.
Tardieu M., *Trois Mythes Gnostiques. Adam, Éros, et les animaux d'Égypte dans un écrit de Nag Hammadi* (II.5), Paris 1974.
Taylor V., *The Gospel according to St. Mark*, London 1952.
Till W.C., *Die gnostischen Schriften des koptischen Papyrus Berolinensis 8502, TU* 60, Berlin 1955.
--- 'Bemerkungen zur Erstausgabe des "Evangelium Veritatis"', *Or.* 27 (1958) 269-286.
--- 'Das Evangelium der Wahrheit', *ZNW* 50 (1959) 165-185.
--- *Das Evangelium nach Philippos, PTS* 2, Berlin 1963.
Tröger K.W., (ed.) *Gnosis und Neues Testament*, Berlin 1973.
--- 'Der zweite Logos des grossen Seth', in M. Krause (ed.), *Essays in the Nag Hammadi Texts. In Honour of Pahor Labib, NHS* 6, Leiden 1975, 268-276.
--- *Die Passion Jesus in der Gnosis nach den Schriften von Nag Hammadi*, Dissertation, Humbolt University, Berlin 1978.
Tuckett C.M., *The Revival of the Griesbach Hypothesis, MSSNTS* 44, Cambridge 1983.
--- 'The Beatitudes: A Source-Critical Study', *NT* 25 (1983) 193-201.
--- '1 Corinthians and Q', *JBL* 102 (1983) 607-619.
Turner J.D., 'A New Link in the Syrian Judas Thomas Tradition', in M. Krause (ed.), *Essays on the Nag Hammadi Texts in Honour of Alexander Böhlig, NHS* 3, Leiden 1972, 101-119.

--- *The Book of Thomas the Contender*, *SBLDS* 23, Missoula 1975.
Unnik W.C. van, 'The "Gospel of Truth" and the New Testament', in F.L. Cross (ed.), *The Jung Codex*, London 1955, 81-129.
--- 'The Origin of the Recently Discovered "Apocryphon Jacobi"', *VigChr* 10 (1956) 149-156.
--- 'The Newly Discovered "Epistle to Rheginos" on the Resurrection', *JEH* 15 (1964) 141-167.
Vielhauer P., *Ἀνάπαυσις*, in W. Eltester (ed.), *Apophoreta*, FS for E. Haenchen, *BZNW* 30, Berlin 1964, 281-299.
Walter N., 'Die Bearbeitung der Seligpreisungen durch Matthäus', *StEv* 4, *TU* 102, Berlin 1968, 246-268.
Werner A., 'Die Apokalypse des Petrus—Die dritte Schrift aus Nag-Hammadi-Codex VII', *ThLZ* 99 (1974) 575-584.
Wilmet M., *Concordance du nouveau Testament sahidique*, *CSCO* 124, 178, 183, Louvain 1950, 1957, 1958.
Wilson R. McL., 'The New Testament in the Gnostic Gospel of Mary', *NTS* 3 (1957) 236-243.
--- *The Gnostic Problem*, London 1958.
--- *The Gospel of Philip*, London 1962.
--- 'The New Testament in the Nag Hammadi Gospel of Philip', *NTS* 9 (1963) 291-294.
--- 'A Note on the Gospel of Truth (33.8-9)', *NTS* 9 (1963) 295-298.
--- Review of Schrage, *Verhältnis*, *VigChr* 20 (1966) 118-124.
--- *Gnosis and the New Testament*, Oxford 1968.
--- 'Old Testament Exegesis in the Gnostic Exegesis on the Soul', in M. Krause (ed.) *Essays on the Nag Hammadi Texts. In Honour of Pahor Labib*, *NHS* 6, Leiden 1975, 217-224.
--- 'The Gospel of the Egyptians', *StPatr* 14, *TU* 117, Berlin 1976, 243-250.
--- 'The *Trimorphic Protennoia*', in M. Krause (ed.), *Gnosis and Gnosticism*, *NHS* 8, Leiden 1977, 50-54.
--- Valentinianism and the *Gospel of Truth*', in B. Layton (ed.), *The Rediscovery of Gnosticism. I. The School of Valentinus*, Leiden 1980, 133-145.
--- 'Nag Hammadi and the New Testament', *NTS* 28 (1982) 289-302.
Wisse F., 'The Redeemer Figure in the Paraphrase of Shem', *NT* 12 (1970) 130-140.
--- 'The Nag Hammadi Library and the Heresiologists', *VigChr* 25 (1971) 205-223.
--- 'On Exegeting *The Exegesis on the Soul*', in J.-É. Ménard (ed.), *Les Textes de Nag Hammadi*, *NHS* 7, Leiden 1975, 68-81.
--- 'Gnosticism and Early Monasticism in Egypt', in B. Aland (ed.), *Gnosis* FS for H. Jonas, Göttingen 1978, 431-440.
--- 'Stalking those Elusive Sethians', in B. Layton (ed.), *The Rediscovery of Gnosticism II. Sethian Gnosticism*, Leiden 1981, 563-576.
Zandee J., "*The Teachings of Silvanus" and Clement of Alexandria: A New Document of Alexandrian Theology*, Leiden 1977.
Zeller D., *Die weisheitlichen Mahnsprüche bei den Synoptikern*, *FzB* 17, Würzburg 1977.

INDEX OF AUTHORS

INDEX OF AUTHORS

INDEX OF PASSAGES CITED

3. New Testament

INDEX OF PASSAGES CITED

INDEX OF PASSAGES CITED

INDEX OF PASSAGES CITED